Counseling and Psychotherapy With Religious Persons

A Rational Emotive Behavior Therapy Approach

The LEA Series in Personality and Clinical Psychology
Irving B. Weiner, Editor

Counseling and Psychotherapy With Religious Persons

A Rational Emotive Behavior Therapy Approach

Stevan Lars Nielsen
Brigham Young University

W. Brad Johnson
United States Naval Academy

Albert Ellis
Albert Ellis Institute

 LAWRENCE ERLBAUM ASSOCIATES, PUBLISHERS
2001   Mahwah, New Jersey   London

Lawrence Erlbaum Associates, Inc., Publishers
10 Industrial Avenue
Mahwah, NJ 07430

Cover design by Kathryn Houghtaling Lacey

Library of Congress Cataloging-in-Publication Data

Nielsen, Stevan L.
Counseling and psychotherapy with religious persons : A rational
emotive behavior therapy approach / Stevan L. Nielsen, W. Brad
Johnson, Albert Ellis.

p. cm.

Includes bibliographical references and index.
ISBN 0-8058-2878-8 (cloth : alk. paper)
ISBN 0-8058-3916-X (pbk. : alk. paper)
1. Rational—emotive psychotherapy. 2. Counseling—Religious
aspects. 3. Psychiatry and religion. I. Johnson, W. Brad. II.
Ellis Albert. III. Title

RC489.R3 N54   2001
616.89'14—dc21

2001018771
CIP

Books published by Lawrence Erlbaum Associates are printed on acid-
free paper, and their bindings are chosen for strength and durability.

Printed in the United States of America
10 9 8 7 6 5 4 3 2

Dedications

To Dianne, wife, friend, and colleague (SLN)

To Laura A. Johnson, for everything you are (WBJ)

To Janet L. Wolfe, whose support with this book, as with everything else, has been most valuable (AE)

Contents

Preface

Since the early 1990s, interest in psychotherapy for religious clients has increased. The number of books, chapters, and journal articles that have included the topics *psychotherapy* and *religion, religious belief, religiosity,* or *religious membership* in their titles and abstracts has gone from 86 published in the 1950s and 84 published in the 1960s, to 99 published in the 1970s, 145 published in the 1980s, and 330 published in the 1990s.

Among these 744 scholarly publications, just five controlled studies have examined how religion can be used in psychotherapy to treat religious clients. These five studies reported scientific tests of religion-oriented cognitive or cognitive-behavioral therapies (Johnson & Ridley, 1992; Johnson, Devries, Ridley, & Pettorini, 1994; Pecheur & Ewards, 1984; Propst, 1980; Propst, Ostrom, Watkins, & Mashburn, 1992). Two (Johnson & Ridley, 1992; Johnson, et al., 1994) focused on religion-oriented REBT. It makes perfect sense that cognitive and cognitive-behavioral therapies, and especially REBT, would be used in pioneering attempts to use religious belief material during psychotherapy.

Why? Because REBT is a belief oriented psychotherapy. REBT's famous A-B-C model proposes that it is not A, Adversities or other Activating events, but B, Beliefs about A, which yield C, self-defeating emotional and behavioral Consequences. It is wholly consistent with the

A-B-C model to assess, accommodate, and assimilate belief material from clients' religious belief systems during REBT.

This book describes how REBT can be used to treat religious clients. We first offer our rationale and explain why REBT, because of its belief-oriented theory of how we humans disturb ourselves, is so well-suited to treating religious clients. Since rational-emotive-behavioral theory is constructivist as well as cognitive, emotive, and behavioral, REBT can anticipate, accommodate, and assimilate religious diversity in its interventions. We show how the beliefs considered irrational in rational-emotive-behavioral theory can be distinguished from religious beliefs.

We then move from the general of rational-emotive-behavioral theory to the specifics of practicing REBT with religious clients. We describe assessment of religiosity, assessment of clients' belief patterns, and especially assessment of irrational beliefs; again, we show how rational and irrational beliefs can be separated from religious beliefs. We explicate the links between rational-emotive-behavioral assessment and REBT's interventions and provide demonstrations of how assessment and intervention occur during typical therapy sessions. We give particular attention to explaining and demonstrating REBT's most unique intervention, disputation, and showing how disputation can accommodate religious belief. We show how religious material can be integrated with rational-emotive-behavioral disputation during treatment of religious clients.

Finally, we discuss guilt and forgiveness, and explore the use of REBT with adherents of several major religious denominations. We are not attempting to present these specific treatments in exhaustive or definitive detail. We are attempting to demonstrate how general REBT methods can fit diverse kinds of religiosity. The varieties of religious experience, including the varieties of distress arising in combination with clients' different religious beliefs, is too broad a subject for any single book. But we hope to provide therapists with clues about how to deal with their religious clients' unique problems. For example, as we demonstrate how REBT was used to deal with a Mormon client's self-defeating, perfectionistic guilt, the reader may see how REBT might be used to deal with clients' depression, panic or anger about keeping kosher or fasting during Ramadan.

Examples from cases, including dialogue derived from transcripts, are presented throughout the book. The clients involved were kind enough to give permission for use of material from their cases. We thank these clients. Names and incidents from these cases have been altered to mask clients' identities.

In addition to clients, many others helped get this book going. It had its informal beginning some years ago when I (SLN) suggested to my friend and mentor, Allen Bergin, that it was again time for him to debate Albert Ellis about the role of religion in mental health and mental illness. Allen and Al had debated twice before, once in the pages of the *Journal of Consulting and Clinical Psychology* (Bergin, 1980; Ellis, 1980) and again at the annual convention of the American Psychological Association (comments later appeared in the *American Psychologist*: Bergin, 1991; Ellis, 1992). Allen declined, but suggested that if I wanted to see such a debate I could have a "most interesting and instructive experience by challenging Ellis to a debate" myself. A bit intimidating! But I took his suggestion.

As I considered what we might discuss, I decided I didn't really want to talk about how religiosity contributes to better or worse mental health. Rather, since I considered myself a practitioner of cognitive-behavior therapy (CBT), including REBT, I decided it would be interesting to discuss the merits and risks of integrating religious material, including scripture, with REBT. I suggested that we might discuss this subject at APA and Al quickly accepted my invitation. I think he liked the title I proposed, "Religion and RET: Don't throw out the therapeutic baby with the holy water." He warned me, however, that because he was probably the most notorious atheist in the APA, our discussion might not be accepted by the Division 36 program committee. (Division 36 is called Psychologists Interested in Religious Issues.)

Al was prophetic in his prediction. APA's division 36 convention program committee rejected the proposal. The program chair did not send a typical APA rejection form letter, however. He explained that after animated debate the program committee had rejected the proposal by a close vote. A majority of committee members doubted there was much new that another discussion or debate about religion and psychology with Albert Ellis could contribute to psychology.

I felt quite sad about this lost opportunity to become famous by debating Al Ellis, but, happily, the matter was not settled. About a month before the APA convention, the PIRI program committee invited us to have our discussion in the less formal setting of the Division 36 hospitality suite. Al agreed again and we had our discussion. I was delighted to find that while Al and I disagreed about the biggest of religious issues, whether there is a God, we agreed about many, many other issues, including the main point of this book: Religious beliefs are not so difficult to accommodate during

REBT and religious material can be mixed with REBT to the benefit of religious clients.

Peter Hill, then editor of the *Journal of Psychology and Christianity* (*JPC*), was present in the hospitality suite for our discussion. He knew at the time that the *JPC* editorial board had commissioned a special issue to focus on the uneasy relationship between REBT and Christianity. A guest editor for the special issue had already been selected, Paul Watson. Professor Hill subsequently suggested to Professor Watson that elements from the hospitality suite discussion might make an interesting addition to the *JPC* special issue. Professor Watson contacted Al and I and encouraged us to prepare and submit papers. Happily, "Rational Emotive Behavior Therapy and religion: Don't throw the therapeutic baby out with the holy water" and Al's response were included in the special edition (Ellis, 1994; Nielsen, 1994).

During the editorial process Professor Watson asked if we had other suggestions for the special edition. I proposed that an informal discussion about REBT, religion, mental health, and treatment of mental illness might be interesting for *JPC*'s readers. Professor Watson agreed and Al and I set aside three hours at the following year's APA convention for a private discussion. Professor Hill and Brad Johnson, whose review of previous debates between Al and religionists also appeared in the special issue (Johnson, 1994), joined us for this discussion. The discussion was transcribed and appears in the *JPC* special issue (Nielsen & Ellis, 1994). It was during this discussion that Al, Brad and I first worked together. It was here that I learned of Brad's innovative research examining the incorporation of Christian beliefs with REBT. This book was an outgrowth of that meeting.

So, blame for this book should go not just to the authors, but also to Allen Bergin for declining another debate with Al Ellis and encouraging me to do the debating myself, to both the reluctant and the willing members of the PIRI program committee, whose initial rejection and subsequent modified acceptance turned my idea for a grand debate into a more intimate affair where Al and I could meet on a more personal level, to Peter Hill and Paul Watson, who helped get Al, Brad and I together as a working trio. These events and people helped plant and water the seeds which became this book. Susan Milmoe at Lawrence Erlbaum deserves special thanks as an enthusiastic, but patient editor. Actually, she was really only patient with me (SLN), since Al and Brad are highly efficient writers with whom she did not need to use her patience. Al and Brad undoubtedly allowed Susan to build up her reserves of patience for use with me and others like me whose writing plods along slowly.

Note please, that two of us, Johnson and Nielsen, are Christians–though we come from very different faith backgrounds–and that Ellis is a probabilistic atheist. (A probabilistic atheist because he does not *insist* that there is no God, but rather considers the likelihood that there is a God or Gods or some other higher, lower, or otherwise supernatural existence so remote that altering his life style against that particular chance is unreasonable.) Note that this book about treating religious clients was written by two religious psychologists and one irreligious psychologist and that we disagree about many facets of the role of religion in life. Indeed, we three disagree about many of the most basic, spiritual elements of religion. Nonetheless, it was quite *easy* for us to work together on this project. It was easy because rational-emotive-behavioral theory and REBT worked for us throughout this project. We were easily able to get around most of the problems that beset the world of religious diversity since we did not make any demands of one another about religious belief. Finally, we were able to work well together because we are in strong agreement about the focus and proposition of this book, which is that accommodation and integration of religious material with REBT can help religious clients.

—*Stevan Lars Nielsen, January, 2001*

REFERENCES

Bergin, A. E. (1980). Psychotherapy and religious values. *Journal of Consulting and Clinical Psychology, 48,* 95–105.

Bergin, A. E. (1991). Values and religious issues in psychotherapy and mental health. *American Psychologist, 46,* 394–403.

Ellis, A. (1980). Psychotherapy and atheistic values: A response to A. E. Bergin's 'Psychotherapy and religious values.' *Journal of Consulting and Clinical Psychology, 48,* 635–639.

Ellis, A. (1992). Do I really hold that religiousness is irrational and equivalent to emotional disturbance? *American Psychologist, 47,* 428–429.

Ellis, A. (1994). My response to "Don't throw the therapeutic baby out with the holy water": Helpful and hurtful elements of religion. *Journal of Psychology and Christianity, 13,* 323–326.

Johnson, W.B., & Ridley, C.R. (1992). Brief Christian and non-Chritian rational-emotive therapy with depressed Christian clients: An exploratory study. *Counseling and Values, 36,* 220–229.

Johnson, W.B. (1994). Albert Ellis and the "religionists": A history of the dialogue. *Journal of Psychology and Christianity, 13,* 301–311.

Johnson, W.B., Devries, R., Ridley, C.R., & Pettorini, D. (1994). The comparative efficacy of Christian and secular rational emotive therapy with Christian clients. *Journal of Psychology and Theology, 22,* 130–140.

Nielsen, S. L. (1994). Rational Emotive Behavior Therapy and religion: Don't throw the therapeutic baby out with the holy water. *Journal of Psychology and Christianity, 13,* 312–322.

Nielsen, S. L., & Ellis, A. (1994). A discussion with Albert Ellis: Reason, emotion, and religion. *Journal of Psychology and Christianity, 13,* 327–341.

Pecheur, D., & Edwards, K.J. (1984). A comparison of secular and religious versions of cognitive therapy with depressed Christian college students. *Journal of Psychology and Theology, 12,* 45–54.

Propst, L.R. (1980). The comparative efficacy of religious and nonreligious imagery for the treatment of mild depression in religious individuals. *Cognitive Therapy and Research, 4,* 167–178.

Propst, L.R., Ostrom, R., Watkins, P., Dean, T, & Mashburn, D. (1992). Comparative efficacy of religious and nonreligious cognitive-behavioral therapy for the treatment of clinical depression in religious individuals. *Journal of Consulting and Clinical Psychology, 60,* 94–103.

I

REBT and the Religious Client

1

Elegant Psychotherapy for Religious Clients

This book proposes that rational emotive behavior therapy (REBT) is uniquely and exceptionally well suited to treating the problems and concerns of religious clients. It offers a theoretical framework, practical recommendations, and examples from practice for accommodating clients' religious beliefs. It discusses why interventions derived from the theory of REBT are seldom at odds with clients' religious traditions and can, therefore, usually accommodate client religious beliefs even when client and therapist have very different religious orientations—even when a devoutly religious client, for example, is treated by an nonreligious, atheistic therapist. Moreover, because rational emotive interventions focus so specifically on beliefs, REBT is particularly well suited to integrating clients' religious beliefs in its interventions. The book further proposes that integrating religious material with rational emotive interventions can render them particularly personal, forceful, vivid, and deep for religious clients.

Neither accommodating clients' religious beliefs during therapy nor integrating their religious beliefs in rational emotive interventions are at all foreign to the preferred practice of REBT. Because REBT is essentially a constructivist psychotherapy, it is both accommodative and integrative of client values and beliefs, including religious beliefs. As is described in

3

greater detail later, REBT's emphasis on finding core beliefs allows for a simplicity and elegance of focus that is neutral with respect to most particulars in a client's situation, including the particulars of a client's religious beliefs.

Although REBT can and usually does approach most problems from a neutral, constructivist perspective, its fundamental principles are quite sympathetic with most religious beliefs and "may actually be closer to the Judeo-Christian position than . . . most other systems of psychotherapy" (DiGiuseppe, Robin, & Dryden, 1990, p. 362). A number of rational emotive behavior therapists (REBTers) have noted profound similarity between the premises of REBT and Christian theology (Beaman, 1978; Beit-Hallahmi, 1980; Carter, 1986; W. B. Johnson, 1992; Jones, 1989; Lawrence, 1987; Lawrence & Huber, 1982; Nielsen, 1994; Warnock, 1989; Young, 1984). Attempting to build on this congruence, several REBTers have developed and articulated their own Christian-oriented versions of REBT (Backus, 1985; Hauck, 1972; W. B. Johnson, 1993; Nielsen, W. B. Johnson, & Ridley, 2000; Powell, 1976; Robb, 1988; Stoop, 1982; Thurman, 1989). In addition to this pioneering work, five realizations regarding the potential elegance of REBT as a treatment approach for religious clients inspired and prompted this book.

First, because most people are religious, most psychotherapy clients will be religious. This means that most people either belong to and participate actively in a church or temple or adhere informally to a religious tradition, believing in a deity or some other religious, mystical, supernatural, or spiritual principle or reality. Thus, the majority of clients are likely to maintain some kind of religious faith or commitment. And their religious beliefs may figure prominently in both their views of difficulties and in their hopes for possible solutions to their problems.

Second, clients' religious beliefs may provide essential structure to their organizing schemata. Psychotherapies that accommodate or, better still, integrate clients' religious beliefs in interventions are more likely to be congruent with their organizing schemata, and therefore are more likely to facilitate therapy.

Third, congruent with most religious traditions, and unique among most contemporary psychotherapeutic models, REBT focuses on beliefs and belief change. Organized religions typically instill beliefs specific to organized doctrine, strengthen these beliefs, or attempt to correct beliefs that conflict with dogma. Rational emotive theories about the fundamental importance of understanding the effects of beliefs, REBT's fundamental goal of changing irrational beliefs, and many rational emotive techniques for changing belief are likely to seem straightforward and perhaps even familiar to religious clients.

Fourth, despite wide variation in doctrine, the basic undergirding religious tenets, doctrines, stories, and traditions in major religions will very often support fundamental elements in the theory of REBT. Fundamental tenets of the world's major religious traditions seldom interfere substantially with rational emotive theory or goals for reducing self-defeating upset.

Fifth, because REBT's core assumptions and fundamental goals are likely to be at least somewhat similar to the core tenets in most religious systems, fundamental elements of client religious traditions can be used during REBT's belief-oriented interventions. This may help move the therapy along. Integrating religious material from a client's religious tradition with rational emotive interventions can increase an intervention's effectiveness by rendering it more vivid, more forceful, broader, and deeper. The following pages elaborate on each of these areas of congruence and explain why using REBT with religious clients makes good (and rational) sense.

FIRST, YOUR CLIENTS ARE LIKELY TO BE RELIGIOUS

Religious believers are in the majority. According to *Britannica Book of the Year* (Barrett & T. M. Johnson, 1998), in 1997 nearly 4.9 billion of the world's 5.9 billion people were adherents of, or believers in, some religion or religious tradition. By comparison, less than a billion people consider themselves nonreligious or atheist. Nearly 2 billion people considered themselves Christian, just more than 1 billion of these were Roman Catholic. About 1.1 billion people were Muslim, about 746 million were Hindu, and another 353 million were Buddhist.

As the population of the world increases, it is estimated that the proportion of those who consider themselves to be religious will increase slightly relative to those who consider themselves to be nonreligious or atheist (Duke & Johnson, 1990, cited in Palmer & Keller, 1990). The fall of communist governments, many of which were officially–often dogmatically–atheistic, may further contribute to a trend of increasing the proportion of religious to nonreligious individuals. The vast majority of Americans acknowledge some belief in God, and a full one third avow firm religious commitment (Gallup, 1989).

In stark contrast to the likelihood that clients will be religious, recent surveys suggest that psychotherapists are typically nonreligious. Compared to the general population, psychologists are particularly unlikely to report religious belief or participation in church-related activities (Ragan, Malony, & Beit-Hallahmi, 1980; Shafranske & Malony, 1990). Bergin and Jensen (1990) found that only 25% of those from a large sample of psychotherapists who responded to survey questions about their religious belief viewed religious concerns as important for inclusion in the content of therapy sessions. Interestingly, nearly one fourth of these same psychotherapists also admitted to having had negative experiences with religion that may have contributed to antireligious sentiments.

Antireligious sentiments could lead psychotherapists to discount or disparage client religious beliefs. Psychotherapists may assume that religious beliefs and practice cause psychopathology. No such link is supported by research. Rather, a growing body of research reveals a positive relation between religious commitment and physical health; summaries of studies examining a link between mental illness and religion find that religion is either a neutral factor or there may be a positive relation between mental health and religious commitment (Bergin, 1980, 1983, 1991; Bergin, Masters, & Richards, 1987; Bergin, Stinchfield, Gaskin, Masters, & Sullivan, 1988; Donahue, 1985; Gartner, Larson, & Allen, 1991).

Religious clients often report concerns that their faith will be discounted by mental health professionals (Rayburn, 1985; Worthington, 1986). Clients who adhere to Christian beliefs frequently express concern about nonreligious professionals and are inclined to prefer mental health practitioners they believe will have similar religious beliefs (Dougherty & Worthington, 1982; Worthington & Gascoyne, 1985). Concerns about such a "religiosity gap" (Genia, 1994) are not unreasonable if comparatively few religious psychotherapists are available for the majority of clients who acknowledge a belief in God or if many therapists do convey hostility for religion. Two sets of findings are relevant to such a religiosity gap: First, clients' values, attitudes, and beliefs appear to change during successful psychotherapy, usually in the direction of therapists' values (Beutler, 1972). Second, therapist understanding and sensitivity to client values, including sensitivity to client religious beliefs, appear to be critical indicators of successful outcome; religious values appear, therefore, to be important "matching variables" in therapy relationships (Kelly & Strupp, 1992).

Concerns about this kind of religiosity gap and about past neglect of religious concerns by psychotherapists have prompted renewed interest in client religious beliefs (APA, 1992; Giglio, 1993; Hawkins & Bullock, 1995). Professional mental health organizations are advocating careful examination of the religious values and religious concerns of psychotherapy clients. Exploration of religious issues is increasingly seen both as an appropriate part of comprehensive treatment and an important component of informed consent, development of the therapy contract, and formulation of the treatment plan (Hawkins & Bullock, 1995; Richards & Bergin, 1997).

SECOND, RELIGION MAY BE INTEGRAL TO YOUR CLIENT'S SCHEMATA

Consider Sam's presentation at intake: Sam, a 23-year-old university student, indicated on his intake questionnaire that he wanted help with study skills. Sam was actually performing quite well at the university, earning A's in nearly all his courses. Nonetheless, he felt quite guilty about a C he had earned in a calculus class. Early in his first session he told me (SLN), reading from the Scriptures he carried with him in his backpack "You know, the Lord told Joseph Smith, 'Wherefore, verily I say unto you that all things unto me are spiritual'" (Doctrine & Covenants 29: 34). He said that he felt that by getting a C in calculus he was letting the Lord down. His life was so infused with religion that earning an average grade, in what for many students is a very difficult class, was a sin for him!

Sam's view of calculus was extreme, but it is not atypical for religious individuals to view their life as consecrated to God. Membership in an organized religion or adherence to a belief tradition may color or contribute to client distress or difficulty (Bergin, 1980). Clients who have rejected earlier religious training or beliefs and now consider themselves nonreligious or atheist may bring what could be called spiritual concerns–antispiritual concerns, really–to therapy, because they may define themselves through their rejection of religion (Lovinger, 1984). Client religiosity, especially if a client belongs to a specific organized religion, will often offer clues for understanding the client and tailoring treatment for maximal effect. For example, orthodox Christian clients are likely to value prayer, meditation, biblical teaching, and application of belief-congruent techniques (Gass, 1984), any of which could prove important to understanding a religious client's life, or could become important elements in the therapy.

THIRD, REBT IS FUNDAMENTALLY FOCUSED
ON BELIEF CHANGE

REBT and organized religions overlap in focusing on the importance of belief. This is epitomized in REBT's famous A-B-C model of emotion and behavior. The A-B-C model stipulates that it is not an Activating event (an A), such as adversity, by itself, that causes distress, but Adversity (A) plus a Belief (B) about A that leads to C, a distressing, self-defeating Consequent emotion or behavior. Rational emotive theory holds that in the broad array of clients' thoughts, it is core irrational beliefs about potential or actual adversities that cause client distress (Ellis & Dryden, 1997). Thus, $A \times B = C$. Furthermore, REBT holds that therapeutic change will occur most quickly and changes will be most pervasive when core irrational beliefs are accurately detected, actively disputed, and replaced with alternative rational core beliefs.

Importantly, supernaturalism and mysticism in religious beliefs do not provide prima facie evidence of irrationality in REBT. Although many would consider a belief irrational if it were arbitrary, internally inconsistent, illogical, antiempirical, or otherwise unscientific, rational emotive theory holds that two additional components of beliefs are more important to understanding and treating distress. These additional elements are fundamental to REBT's definition of irrationality: First, if a belief creates self-defeating upset, then it is irrational. Second, beliefs are likely to be irrational if they include an absolute evaluation, usually a demand that people and conditions absolutely must be better than they actually are (DiGiuseppe, et al., 1990).

An REBT therapist might disagree with a client's religious belief tradition (just as they might disagree with a client's political affiliation, dislike a client's favorite art or music, or abhor a client's taste in food). However, REBT's criteria for irrationality will not usually conflict directly with the fundamental religious tenets that form the foundation for the client's religious faith. Rather, REBT's criteria for evaluating beliefs focus on clients' evaluations of their world, certainly including their evaluative beliefs about their religious world. Although an REBT therapist may disagree with the verity of the client's religious worldview–indeed, the therapist may consider the religious view inconsistent, illogical, impractical, and decidedly unscientific–this kind of irrationality (from the therapist's point of view) is probably not relevant to the client's self-defeating emotion. The theory of REBT holds that what likely will be relevant to the client's self-defeating upset are *absolutistic evaluative* beliefs about the religious and nonreligious world.

Furthermore, because religions address and attempt to change beliefs that are incongruent with doctrine or scripture or that are based on a distortion of doctrine or Scripture, REBT's goals of understanding and replacing a client's core irrational belief (IB) with an alternative rational belief (RB) will seem familiar to the religious client. More importantly, when an REBTer understands a client's religious beliefs well enough to integrate these beliefs into the current session's belief-oriented therapeutic interventions, integration of the client's religious beliefs in REBT interventions is likely to speed the therapy.

REBT is, and always has been, a multimodal, integrative therapeutic approach. An REBTer will happily use interventions from a wide range of therapeutic techniques, including many cognitive, emotionally evocative, and behavior modifying or conditioning techniques (Ellis, 1994b, 1996b, 1998, 1999, 2000b). Modification of beliefs is, however, REBT's unique focus; it is the theoretically integrative glue that binds interventions together according to the theory of REBT. Whatever technique is used, the essential purpose for applying each cognitive, emotive, and behavioral technique is to help clients understand and modify their beliefs. It is this overarching goal that makes REBT more than an eclectic bundling of cognitive, emotive, and behavioral techniques (Dryden, 1995; Ellis, 1994b, 1996b, 1999, 2000b; Walen, DiGiuseppe, & Dryden, 1992).

The definition of belief in *Webster's Unabridged Dictionary* is quite relevant here. According to Webster's, belief is

> 1: a state or habit of mind in which trust, confidence, or reliance is placed in some person or thing: *faith.* 2a: something believed; specifically: a statement or body of statements held by the advocates of any class of views; 2b: trust in religion: persuasion of the validity of religious ideas . . . a statement of religious doctrines believed: *creed* . . . (Gove, 1981, p. 200, italics added)

As the word "belief" is most often used in American English, then, it is synonymous with "faith," a word closely identified with religious experience. Furthermore, belief is also very often used as synonymous with religious faith. Thus, as *Webster's* describes the use of the word "belief," both everyday and religious uses can refer to similar processes of mind.

The B in the A-B-C model is more important than might be suggested by the helpful positioning of the letter B in a mnemonic. To be sure, the A-B-C model does provide clients and therapists with a helpful, easily remembered way to understand and work at changing problems. The A-B-C model is catchy and easily remembered. When taught that the A-B-C model depicts both the likely genesis of their distress and the likely solution to their problems, clients are usually quick to grasp, accept, remember, and begin to use the A-B-C model to work at changing.

As is noted later, and as is evident from offerings in the catalogue of REBT materials available from the Albert Ellis Institute, REBTers are delighted to use catchy slogans on posters, T-shirts, buttons, pencils, and other materials to help their clients remember how to change (e.g., "Do! Don't Stew!" "I will not *should* on myself today!" etc.). A different sequence of letters might spell out a more easily remembered mnemonic—perhaps a catchier, more memorable phrase. If B is removed from the A-B-C model, or, more accurately, if the importance of understanding and changing beliefs is minimized during therapy, then REBT is not being practiced—REBT would lose its most distinctive and fundamental element.

From its beginnings, the goal of REBT was to attend to and change clients' core, life-guiding, evaluative philosophies. Call these schemata, constructs, perceptual matrices, or, as in the theory of REBT, core beliefs. This goal was based on the philosophical notion that people's view of the world creates their distress, summarized succinctly by the first-century Stoic philosopher, Epictetus: "People are disturbed not by things, but by the views they take of them" (trans. 1890). More importantly, Epictetus also held that individuals' upsetting views can be modified to render them less upset and less upset-*able*.

The theory of REBT holds that whereas a good many cognitive, emotive, and behavioral techniques may help clients, these techniques are maximally effective when they integrate important thinking, feeling, and behaving elements that interactively affect each other. They then may be called an organizing construct or schema, but calling it a core belief system is equally descriptive (Ellis, 1994b, 1996b). From its inception, REBT's "approach to psychotherapy [has been] to zero in, as quickly as possible, on the client's basic philosophy of life, to get them to see exactly what this is and how it is inevitably self-defeating" (Ellis, 1973b, p. 13). But it does so in forceful, dramatic ways rather than purely cognitive ones (Ellis, 1999, 2000).

Belief, a basic religious philosophy, is likely to be a defining issue for religious clients, just as a coherent belief structure (doctrines, tenets, etc.) is a defining element of religion itself (King, 1987b; McClenden & James, 1975; Whitehead, 1957). Religious doctrines or tenets will usually form the basis for a religious client's philosophy of life. Religious clients will usually understand that beliefs exert a pervasive, multifaceted influence in their life. Most religious clients simultaneously understand a belief to be a tenet or creed, a rule for living, and a feeling. Many religious clients will consider faith (belief) to be linked with works (behaviors). Religious clients are also likely to view belief as a process akin to what psychotherapists call cognition.

Because a religious client is likely to live in a world oriented toward or focused on faith and belief, when taught the A-B-C model, the notion of the importance of beliefs will be familiar. Furthermore, the therapist will probably be able to use the religious writings of the belief tradition to which the client adheres to buttress the A-B-C model. The REBT therapist might remind the Christian client that Paul wrote in his general letter to the Hebrew Christians (in the New Testament), that "without faith it is impossible to please God: for he that cometh to God must believe that he is, and that he is a rewarder of them that diligently seek him" (Hebrews 11: 6, King James Version). A Muslim could be reminded that Mohammad wrote, "Those who believe [what Mohammed revealed], and those who are Jews, Christian, Sabeans or whoever believes in Allah and the Day of Judgment, they shall have their reward and there is no fear nor grief for them" (Koran 5: 69).

Note that scripture would not be cited by an REBTer to encourage clients to believe in God, Allah, or any other particular religious tradition or to encourage them to move from one belief tradition to another. Seeking to support or reduce the client's convictions about a particular religious tradition, whether the client's religious beliefs are shared or disagreed with by the therapist, raises distinct ethical concerns. If pressed by a client to discuss the verity of religion, brief discussions of the theological merits of particular religious doctrines are relatively harmless so long as they are distinguished from psychotherapy. If clients seek answers to theological or ecclesiastical questions or if they seek help to change a religious belief, then the request would probably be dealt with through reference to their own authoritative ecclesiastical resources or through referral to a variety of religious missionary organizations.

Epictetus described belief as a cognitive process. To paraphrase Epictetus, people's beliefs "color" their perception of events to so great a degree that these beliefs can create or relieve disturbance. If beliefs are processes that can alter perception, then they are also phenomenological personality processes. This view of belief is consistent with currently popular constructivist (cf Mahoney, 1991, 1995) and schema theories in psychotherapy. REBTers want to teach clients to understand and use this phenomenological aspect of belief to reduce their distress. Almost any available cognitive, behavioral, or emotive technique, including REBT's own uniquely forceful and vivid techniques (Dryden, 1990; Ellis, 1999, 2000b), would then be gladly used to deepen or make more pervasive the extent to which the client changes phenomenological beliefs.

We contend that this view of belief as a constructive process is paralleled in most religious traditions. While postmodernism has contributed to growing interest in constructivism, this is hardly a new psychological position (cf Bartlett, 1932; Kelly, 1955). This philosophical view was not new even in Epictetus' day! If traditional chronologies can be believed, Epictetus' philosophical position, voiced at some time during the first century C.E., would have seemed familiar and old to Buddhists. The Buddha is held to have said something quite similar as much as 600 years earlier. It is written that he said suffering could be relieved by following the Noble Eightfold Path, "namely: right view, right aspiration, right speech, right action, right livelihood, right effort, right mindfulness, right concentration" (Saccavibhanga Sutta: The Noble Eightfold Path, Majjhima Nikaya iii.251). Paralleling the REBT position, "right view" is sometimes translated as "self-helping belief" or "right belief," and "right aspiration" is sometimes translated as "healthy goal-seeking" or "right thought."

The Buddha is also recorded to have said, "All that we are is the result of what we have thought: it is founded on our thoughts and is made up of our thoughts" (Dhammapad 1.1). This Buddhist doctrine might be called an identity function: We are what we believe. Our self or our ego is based on what we believe about our self. This further parallels REBT theory that a person's view of self is pervasively powerful in determining emotional distress or comfort.

If, as tradition holds, Solomon wrote the Hebrew Proverbs, then Solomon anticipated the Buddha's view by as much as 300 years when he wrote about man that, "as he thinketh in his heart, so is he" (Proverbs 23: 7, King James Version)—*another* identity function. The Buddhist view would have seemed familiar to Hebrews who had heard, listened to, and believed the Proverbs.

Solomon's view accords with the Bhagavad Gita and likely would have seemed familiar to Hindus: "The faith of every man . . . accords with his nature. Man is made up of faith; as is his faith, so is he" (Bhagavad Gita 17.3)—yet another identity function! Tradition holds that the Buddha was an Indian prince, so he may well have been quite familiar with the Gita when he spoke of right views, right thoughts, and right beliefs.

Perhaps you can understand the contention that REBT and religion hold similar constructivist views that thought processes accompany and influence individuals' emotions and actions. This congruence is very helpful during therapy, for even if religious clients are not immediately familiar with those components of their scriptures that support the importance of belief as a phenomenological process, an REBTer familiar with clients' belief traditions can use scripture (which clients likely already accept or believe) to remind or teach clients of this principle. Therapists might familiarize themselves with a range of relevant religious references. It is strongly recommended that they do so, especially where it is possible to anticipate the religious traditions that will be more frequent among their clients. In the pages that follow, some references are provided and other sources are suggested.

Robb (1993) proposed that justification for beliefs based on the supernatural will likely have roughly the same practical effects as the nonsupernatural system employed in most REBT. For the religious client, the religiously based—and perhaps supernaturally justified—belief system may prove more salient than a nonreligious or even religion neutral presentation. Here is an example of how I (SLN) taught Esther, a religious client, about the relevance of beliefs to psychological and emotional distress using the client's own religiously grounded beliefs:

SLN: If I've understood correctly, you feel anxious [*this is C, the consequent emotion, the self-defeating upset*]. When you go to Church, especially when you have to teach Sunday School, you feel anxious [*Teaching Sunday School is A, the Activating event*]. Have I understood?

Esther: Yes.

SLN: You'd like to be able to teach without getting so anxious [*The client wants C to change in a particular way*]

Esther: Yes.

SLN: Well, I'm going to assume that if you teach Sunday School you have some strong religious convictions.

Esther: Oh, yes.

SLN: I would guess then that you believe in the Bible.

Esther: The word of God. Yes.

SLN: Someone pointed this out to me in the Bible and I wonder what you think of it, "As a man thinketh in his heart, so is he." It's in Proverbs. What do you think that means?

Esther: I've read it, but I'm not sure I know.

SLN: Well, I'm not completely sure I know what it means either. But what if it means that your beliefs go a long, long way toward determining how you view yourself and how you feel? Would that make sense? If you believe something about yourself or if you believe something about a certain situation, then that may control how you end up feeling?

Esther: That makes sense.

SLN: Okay. Does this make sense? To paraphrase Proverbs, if *you* think in *your* heart that you *have to, have to, have to* be *absolutely* expert when you teach [*this is an attempt to assess the client's beliefs by giving voice to what the therapist infers to be the core irrational belief*], the belief that you *have to* know is liable to make you feel anxious, especially if you are a little unsure about how to teach something or if you discover that you don't have an answer to a question asked by someone in your class.

Esther: That makes sense, too.

SLN: Now in my view it is your believing that you *have to* know that makes you anxious. How strong a belief is "have to"?

Esther: Pretty strong.

SLN: And is that what you "think in your heart" when you are about to teach your Sunday School class? That you *have to* be an expert?

Esther: Yes. But *don't I have to be* an expert to teach?

The verse from Proverbs was used to establish in the client's mind the connection between belief and self-defeating emotional or behavioral consequences. This is what REBTers call *establishing the B-C connection,* or teaching the client that it is not the activating event, but that event plus the irrational belief about the activating event that is upsetting. The therapist in this excerpt has presented the B-C connection and, by tone of voice and implication, has also begun to D, or Dispute, the client's demand that she *has to be* expert. The therapist believes this may be a main cause of anxiety. The client is also beginning to feel the emotional significance of this belief and sense that the therapist may not agree when she says, "*Don't I have to be* an expert?"

This verse from Proverbs might also have been used to introduce the B-C connection to an observant Jew. Similarly, the verses noted from the Bhagavad Gita or from the sayings of the Bhudda might have been used to introduce a Hindu or Buddhist, respectively, to the A-B-C model.

Understanding the effect of beliefs—the B-C connection—is a fundamental step in helping clients understand and change the source of their self-defeating distress. REBTers attempt from the first session on to teach clients the A-B-C model, emphasizing the role of irrational beliefs in causing self-defeating emotions and behaviors.

It might, of course, go less smoothly in therapy than was the case in the excerpt presented earlier. If the client had disagreed with the therapist at some point during the dialogue, then, like other artisans practicing a skilled craft, the REBTer would look for alternative ways to get to the therapeutic goal of teaching the B-C connection. Ultimately, it might not work to use a verse from the Scriptures with a specific religious client. Nonetheless, use of the Scriptures to augment teaching the B-C connection would remain in the REBTer's armamentarium.

FOURTH, THERE IS FUNDAMENTAL CONGRUENCE BETWEEN CORE REBT TENETS AND RELIGIOUS BELIEFS

There are, to be sure, important differences—sometimes divisive differences—in the fundamental tenets, doctrines, or customs of different denominations or religious traditions. And consider that religious wars rage and there are other violent conflicts that blend culture, ethnicity, and religious belief. These wars focus on elements of religious difference. This is especially ironic given that the cardinal tenets of the religions, to which the warring parties subscribe usually explicitly proscribe violence.

There is, however, good news to be found even in the face of such divisiveness. These same acrimoniously divided religious positions are likely to be discussable under REBT's therapeutic system, which stresses that people are entitled to their own radically diverse desires, goals, and values, but merely recommends they not hold them too absolutistically or so rigidly that they defeat themselves and other humans. There appears to be ample room in the tenets, doctrines, and creeds of major religious traditions to absorb the fundamental focus of REBT, which is changing irrational beliefs. For example, Lawrence (1987) noted that "while there are many differences in religious dogma among various [Judeo-Christian] denominations, a balanced biblical position will never support irrational or dysfunctional conclusions" (p. 15).

Although different religious traditions may strongly disagree about God, creation, sex, gender, sin, salvation, holy days, diet, dress, and so forth, most major religious traditions will support the following REBT therapy goals: acceptance of human worth as a constant, acceptance of uncontrollable situations, and acceptance of life's inevitable discomforts.

REBT holds that human rating, demanding, catastrophizing, and low frustration tolerance (LFT) are strongly implicated in almost all self-defeating upset. When a client is distressed by some self-defeating emotion or behavior ("C," the Consequent emotion or behavior), you will usually, with just a bit of psychotherapeutic exploration, find an irrational Belief that fits one of these four categories. Whatever else may be true of your client's situation, whatever their complex and adverse psychosocial situation or biological state, they will almost always also have learned, created, and cultivated irrational beliefs that elevate their upsets about adversity to self-defeating levels. More to the point, it is likely that they will be cultivating one, two, three, or all four of these irrational beliefs while they are sitting in your office during the session.

After detecting clients' irrational belief, or IB, the REBTer attempts to demonstrate or teach clients the IB-C connection, the link between their particular irrational beliefs and their self-defeating emotions and behaviors. The REBTer then works to D, Dispute, the clients' IB's. More importantly, the therapist also attempts to teach clients to Dispute their own IB's. Finally, it is the goal of REBT to help clients E, Establish, a lasting Effective rational philosophy of life. Disputations and an Effective rational philosophy of life could be seen as providing antidotes to irrational beliefs. A client who works to dispute an upsetting irrational belief will likely experience fairly fast relief from a self-defeating emotion. Moreover, clients who adopt a consistent rational philosophy of life will eventually become emotionally robust and less upsettable.

Religious traditions are rich in life-guiding philosophies. Many of these life-guiding philosophies can contribute useful rational antidotes to irrational beliefs. Scriptures, sagas, and parables will usually include material that may intimate, suggest, or directly dispute human rating, demanding, and catastrophizing with acceptance of uncontrollable, imperfect humans (including oneself) and events. Religious clients may have a head start on establishing Effective rational philosophies of life if they can discover how to adapt the religious philosophies they already believe to developing new philosophies for living. Consider the following examples:

Human Rating

If, after failing to accomplish a goal (A, the Activating event), one rationally tells oneself (B, Believes), "I failed to accomplish my goal, this is a bad outcome," then one will likely feel sad (C, the Consequent healthy negative emotion). This emotion, although unpleasant, could helpfully motivate one to approach the goal more effectively in the future. If, however, one resorts to irrational beliefs involving human rating at B, then same adverse Activating event or adversity will likely yield, at C, an unhealthy self-defeating emotion such as depression: "I have failed at this important goal, what a *failure I* am!" As is discussed further in later chapters, this IB is very common during depression.

Depression linked with failing to accomplish a goal might be radically reduced and changed to the healthy emotion of sadness by adopting the belief, "Yes, I failed to accomplish my goal, and that is lousy, for it was a very important goal. But because I fail at something, even at this very important thing, that *does not* generalize to *all* of me. That doesn't make *me* a failure. I am just a human being who failed to do something!"

Religion and Human Rating

Disputation of human rating is often easily facilitated through use of supporting material from the client's religious background. Scriptures usually represent core beliefs and life-guiding philosophies held strongly by religious clients. The New Testament, for example, contains many passages that maintain that all are equally worthwhile and that all are sinners. The therapist might remind a Christian client that Paul wrote," all have sinned, and come short of the glory of God" (Romans, 3: 23, King James Version). The therapist might then ask, "Now what would that mean about the Apostle Paul (since he wrote it)? Me? You? If we all sin 'and come short of the glory of God,' why not dislike sins and try to change them, but accept us all as fallible human beings or, if you will, sinners?"

Demanding

Anger usually arises because of some rigid demand. For example, on hearing that one's child has misbehaved badly (the Activating event), a parent might believe and tell herself, "I told him a hundred times not to do this. I can't believe this. He knew better. It is just *unacceptable* for a son of mine to do such a thing!" With this kind of belief the client might well feel intense anger.

If the client wanted help to feel less angry, then the REBTer might begin by disputing the idea that it is unacceptable for a human being to make a mistake: "How does it follow, considering all the millions of sons alive on the planet, including the millions who have been taught how to behave—how does it follow that your son must not be one of the many who ignores that training and misbehaves?"

Notice that even if the client were to agree there is indeed no absolutistic rule saying her son must remember and obey parental teaching or that her son among all sons must behave well, it would not necessarily remove all distress. It is not the REBTer's goal to convince the client that an undesirable situation is good or even just neutral. Rather, the goal is to help the client believe that people have little rational choice but to accept that which cannot be changed. This would be especially true of things that have already happened. It is quite sensible to feel irritated or sad about a family members' misbehavior, but it is irrational and needlessly angering to demand that a family member not do what has already been done. The goal of the disputation would be to reduce the distress from a self-defeating level, in this case anger, to a self-helping level of emotion. In this case, a self-helping level of upset might be the healthy negative feeling of irritation or frustration.

Religion and Demands

Consider how a client's religious belief system might be used in the same situation. Again, the client is asking for help to deal with anger about a child's misbehavior. If the REBTer knows the client is committed to a Jewish, Christian, or Moslem tradition, then the therapist might use the creation story to formulate a disputation. It might go something like this: "As I remember, God told Adam and Eve how to behave while they were in the Garden of Eden. Is that the way you remember it? But even after they were told by God how to behave, they still misbehaved! I don't think I'm making this up, that's what scripture tells us. Right? Now, if Adam and Eve didn't obey, even after God, Himself, gave them specific instructions, how does it follow that *your* son *should* have listened to you?"

If the story of Adam and Eve has meaning for the client, as it does for many (but not all) Jews, Christians, or Moslems, then this use of the creation story for disputation of rigid demanding might help the client be more accepting. A disputation like this is enhanced by the emotional value of a metaphor meaningful to the client (DiGiuseppe, 1991). This metaphor, by an implied analogy, compares the client's relationship with a son or daughter to God's relationship with Adam and Eve. Because this metaphor accesses the client's emotions about the creation story, the disputation is emotionally enhanced. Emotional enhancement is one example of what the theory of REBT refers to as forcefulness. The metaphorical use of the story of Adam and Eve would contribute enhanced emotional meaning and forcefulness to the disputing in proportion to the depth of the client's belief in God, God's creative work, and God's relationship with Adam and Eve.

Notice that the REBT therapist in the situation described could be an atheist and still use this particular disputation maneuver. There is great variability in how the creation story is viewed among those who consider themselves religious. In some religious communities, Adam and Eve are believed to be real, specific individuals—literally, our first mother and father. In other religious communities, the story of Adam and Eve is considered symbolic of the general human relationship with deity, without accepting that there were two first humans named Adam and Eve. A religious therapist using REBT could come from a religious community with either view and use this kind of metaphorical disputation. Likewise, a therapist who did not believe in God, but knew of the client's belief in God, could adapt the client's beliefs about Adam and Eve to this kind of disputation.

Catastrophizing

Concern is a somewhat unpleasant, but helpful, emotion. Concern turns to panic, an unpleasant *and* self-defeating emotion, when individuals catastrophize about an adversity. Catastrophizing and awfulizing are REBT terms for believing (irrationally) that a situation is worse than it should be (i.e., terrible, awful, horrible), too bad to be stood emotionally. Consider, for example, a client who is anxiously contemplating the possibility of unemployment: "I don't know what I'll do if the business closes. I couldn't stand it!"

Disputing this belief could begin with the belief that the client could not stand being unemployed. The therapist might begin with a statement like this, "It sounds as if you would then have two problems. One, you would face all the hassles of losing your job. Two, you would suffer from 'I-can't-stand-it-itis!'" Calling the client's irrational belief "I-can't-stand-it-itis" is an attempt to humorously dispute the irrational belief. The humor associated with the disputing increases the forcefulness of the disputation. The REBTer might continue with something like this, "Losing your income would be quite a headache, what with having to look for another job, perhaps one where you earn less. Lousy! But telling yourself you couldn't stand losing your job makes you feel panicky now, even before you know for sure what is going to happen! If you tell yourself you couldn't stand it, does that help you do the job you now have? Does it help you plan for the future?" Again, it would not be the REBTer's goal to persuade the client that losing a job is good or even neutral. REBT holds that not getting, or in this case not keeping what one wants is undesirable. The goal is to help the client view the problem as an undesirable human event, not as a totally bad or worse than bad event.

Religion and Catastrophizing

If the client were a Sikh, disputation of the client's I-couldn't-stand-it-itis might include reference to excerpts from the Adi Granth, canonized Sikh writings, "I thought I alone had sorrow; Sorrow is spread all over the whole world. From my roof-top I saw every home engulfed in sorrow's flames" (Adi Granth, Shalok, Farid, p. 1382). The REBTer might then ask, "What do you think the Guru is saying about suffering here? Does it sound as if he believes humans can escape suffering? How is this verse different from what you are telling yourself about your potential difficulty? What might you tell yourself about the troubles you face compared with the troubles that others face?"

Religious scripture will almost always help an individual who believes in the scriptures to place difficulties in a broader, religiously philosophical context. It is a common human event to become unemployed. Often, perhaps usually, it is an unfortunate event. Calling it an event that cannot be stood puts the event in the most extreme context imaginable. The extremeness of one's awfulizing belief is likely to create an extreme and dysfunctional emotional reaction. Because religious clients likely already invest scripture with great emotional significance, and give a higher emotive investment to scriptural material, this emotional context may aid greatly in changing the meaning of the client's adversity from the horrorizing the client is adding to it. The religious context then tends to deawfulize it.

Low Frustration Tolerance

Low frustration tolerance (LFT) is a self-defeating mixture of demanding and catastrophizing beliefs about life difficulties. LFT is closely linked with procrastination and avoidance, probably the primary component of poor compliance with treatment regimens in medicine and psychotherapy, and a main reason humans fail to follow through with their best intentions for completing rewarding tasks. LFT is so ubiquitous, so automatic, and so close to fallible human nature that it is often difficult for beginning REBTers to see it. Simply stated, LFT is epitomized by the "too" in "too hard." For example, when asked about neglected homework assignments, clients will often report–and will almost always be thinking!–"The home-work was *too* hard."

If a client says, "It was too hard," then it is quite instructive to ask them to define the "too" in "too hard." How was the homework too hard? It is, of course, empirically possible for a task to be too hard. Some tasks are physically impossible for humans. For example, going without oxygen for more than a few minutes is too hard. But the "too hard" of LFT really means "harder than I wanted," "harder than it should have been," or "harder than I cared to put up with."

Consider a mundane task most individuals probably really do want to get accomplished eventually, but that they we are prone to put off in self-defeating ways, such as balancing the checking account after a long period of neglect. When LFT is operating, an A like balancing the check-book activates Beliefs something like: "It shouldn't be so hard to balance my checkbook," or "I just can't take that much tedium today," or "I need a break from this right now," or "I bet Bill Gates [or Tiger Woods or Martha Stewart or Queen Elizabeth or some other prominent person] doesn't have to balance his or her checkbook–so neither should I!" These beliefs result in avoidance and inaction, at least until some other influence (e.g., over-draft notices) exert more insistent pressure.

LFT is disputed by helping clients identify their demands for and their awfulizing about uncomfortable, frustrating circumstances and by showing them, in a variety of ways, that their LFT is irrational, antiempirical, and, most importantly, self-defeating, because it prevents one from accomplish-ing tasks by making the tasks seem more unpleasant and onerous than they really are. I (SLN) often point out to my male clients who are sports fans that their favorite athletes are likely to put in far more than 40 hours of training, practice, and competition per week during the athletic season, and often put in as much as 40 hours of training and practice during the off season. For example:

> *SLN:* I remember watching some years ago as Steve Young ran a "victory lap" around the football field after the San Francisco 49ers beat the Green Bay Packers to win the NFC championship. He seemed to be enjoying himself quite a lot. I bet he enjoys his multi-million dollar pay checks, also. Tell me, do you think he enjoys all the hours of weight lifting and running he does? The hours of memorizing plays? Each of the daily meetings with coaches? Living out of suit cases while he travels? Being thronged by autograph seekers everywhere he goes?

> *Client:* Maybe some of it, but not all of it, no.

> *SLN:* Did he enjoy getting tackled when he was playing in cold cities like Cleveland or Green Bay during the Winter months? Did he enjoy being spit on or having things thrown at him by fans in rival cities?

> *Client:* No.

> *SLN:* What do you think he told himself about how hard or uncomfortable or boring or irritating or physically dangerous these activities were? Why didn't he quit as soon as he was rich, despite boring workouts, boring practices, boring travel, often painful injuries, and insulting, profane fans?

> *Client:* Probably because he thought it was worth it.

> *SLN:* Couldn't you tell yourself something like that? "This is boring and I don't like boring stuff, but in the long run it is likely to be worth it." Would it feel any different when you are faced with your check book [or term papers or cleaning the kitchen, etc.] if you told yourself that?

Religion and LFT

Religious scripture is filled with admonitions to tolerate difficulty with patience. This may help religious clients understand and dispute their

LFT. I (SLN) have found a particular verse from Latter-day Saint scripture helpful in dealing with my devout Mormon clients' LFT about tedium and boredom. The verse comes from the 64th section of the Book of Doctrine and Covenants (the D & C). The D & C contains 140 brief sections that Mormons believe were revealed to Joseph Smith and other of their latter-day prophets. I have used the verse many times in a manner something like this:

SLN: Why would the Lord bother to give us commandments?

Client: So we'll know what He wants from us.

SLN: Is it obvious to us *before* he tells us?

Client: Maybe sometimes, but not usually.

SLN: So why would He have said this: "Wherefore, be not weary in well-doing, for ye are laying the foundation of a great work. And out of small things proceedeth that which is great" (D & C 64: 33)? What would this say about our tendency to get weary, that we easily get weary or that we almost never have any trouble with getting weary?

Client: He would have said that because we are prone to getting weary.

SLN: When the Lord mentions small things do you think it means we get physically tired from doing small things or that we humans get psychologically weary from doing small things? Could this kind of weariness be like boredom?

Client: "Small things" would suggest that details can make you feel weary or bored.

SLN: Sure. Now you said that you *need* breaks from studying. You're telling yourself that you need a break from weariness What if you began to tell yourself that the small stuff *is,* indeed, *tedious,* but that it can pay off with big stuff if you just keep at it and don't let your boredom and weariness stop you? What if you began telling yourself, "If I keep at this small stuff it will pay off with bigger rewards eventually?"

Short scripture-based dialogues like this one have helped many of my devout LDS clients understand how their LFT has led them to avoid and procrastinate tasks they themselves consider important, helped them accept that the weariness and procrastination it causes are pretty common, and provided alternative, religiously rational, motivational self-statements (e.g., "out of small things proceedeth that which is great") that have helped them counter their LFT and avoid future procrastination.

FIFTH, ELEMENTS OF RELIGIOUS TRADITION AND PRACTICE ARE CONGRUENT WITH REBT THEORY AND PRACTICE

Religious activities are myriad in their variety, yet distinct categories of religious activity can be identified, among them: Most organized religions or religious traditions actively teach and preach. They actively encourage religious study. Adherents of most organized religions use icons or icon-like objects to remind them of important beliefs. To the end of encouraging specific beliefs, religious traditions use worshipful language, sometimes renaming people or ideas in faith-specific terms. Religious adherents often practice recitation or memorization of specific creeds. Religious worship includes music, including setting doctrines, beliefs, Scripture, and holy sagas to music in the form of hymns. Religious denominations encourage acts of faith in the form of sacraments, pilgrimages, or religious duties. Similarly and strikingly, REBT's array of therapeutic techniques parallel a broad range religious activities.

Teaching

Most religions overtly work to teach correct belief (Moran, 1987). In reacting against the indirectness of psychoanalysis, REBT has been, from its inception, an open, direct, educational approach to psychotherapy. Ideally, clients in REBT are actively taught about REBT's A-B-C model of self-defeating emotions and behaviors from their first session on. Typically, it is the REBTer's goal to "zero in" (Ellis, 1973a, 1999) on the client's core irrational beliefs in the first few sessions; teach the client about these IBs; identify the connection between IBs and self-defeating emotions and behaviors ("Cs"); teach the client how to D, Dispute their IBs; and E, establish an Effective rational belief system during the first session. Thereafter, REBTers work continually to teach clarity of thought.

REBT's direct emphasis on teaching probably leads to many similarities between its preferred practices and the practices of many organized religions. When trying to teach, especially when trying to teach philosophies for living, there are likely common educational modes toward which humans tend to gravitate.

To the extent that an organized religion directly, overtly teaches traditions, tenets, doctrines, dogmas, creeds, rituals, and so forth—as most organized religions do overtly teach—REBT's direct teaching will likely seem comfortable to religious individuals seeking psychotherapeutic help. A highly indirect, subtle, slow-to-give-a-direct-answer therapeutic approach may well seem foreign to religious clients familiar with and comfortable with direct teaching.

Religious scripture supports teaching as a religious enterprise, for example:

From the *Rig Veda* (Hindu): "One not knowing a land asks for one who knows it, he goes forward instructed by the knowing one. Such, indeed, is the blessing of instruction, one finds a path that leads him straight onward" (Rig Veda 10.32.7).

From the *New Testament* (Christian): Jesus said, "You call me teacher and Lord, and rightly so, for that is what I am" (John 13: 13, Revised Standard Version).

From the *Doctrine and Covenants* (Mormon-Christian): "Teach ye diligently and my grace shall attend you, that you may be instructed more perfectly in theory, in principle, in doctrine, in the law of the gospel, in all things that pertain unto the kingdom of God, that are expedient for you to understand; of things both in heaven and in the earth, and under the earth; things which have been, things which are, things which must shortly come to pass; things which are at home; things which are abroad . . ." (Doctrine and Covenants 88: 78, 79).

Since 1965, the Albert Ellis Institute (formerly the Institute for Rational-Emotive Therapy) has actively and energetically offered lectures, workshops, and public demonstrations that present the theories and techniques of REBT to the general public and interested mental health professionals (Ellis, 1994b, 1996b). Like many organized religions, the institute developed an educational curriculum based on its principles and ran a school for children that, in addition to a regular, general curriculum, taught rational emotive principles and philosophies for living. A rational emotive curriculum plan is available for elementary and secondary grades (Vernon, 1989a; 1989b).

More than 150,000 members of the general public have participated in these educational programs. For more than 35 years, the institute has offered its famous weekly Problems of Daily Living workshop, during which volunteer participants sit with an REBT therapist "on stage" and work through problems using REBT while members of an audience of 100 to 200 watch and ask questions. The Friday night workshop is one of the institute's most popular programs.

The institute has recently added a training course in rational emotive pastoral counseling (S. Johnson, 2000). The course, for ministers and mental health professionals who counsel in religious settings, focuses on the principles and techniques explored here. Faculty members include ordained clergy who are REBTers.

Preaching

Most religions include sermonizing and often religionists use forceful preaching to change or strengthen beliefs (Moran, 1987; Speight, 1987; Watt, 1987). REBT therapists likewise directly and forcefully dispute their clients' irrational, upsetting beliefs. REBT therapists also teach and encourage their clients to forcefully dispute their own irrational beliefs. When clients learn to do this, they become free to work at changing their beliefs between sessions (Ellis, 1994b, 1996b, 2000b). REBT holds that a range of techniques may be useful in helping clients change. This certainly includes the use of history taking, reflective listening, and Socratic questioning (part of many psychotherapies). However, whereas some psychotherapeutic approaches abjure directness (emphasizing a diplomatic approach), it is not unusual for an REBT therapist to provide a client with straightforward, didactic minilectures about the principles of REBT (Ellis & Dryden, 1997; Walen, et al., 1992).

Reading and Study

Most religions encourage or even require reading or recitation of commentaries, sagas, canonized scriptures, sutras, treatises, tracts, upanishads, vedas, and so forth (King, 1987b). Religious individuals may even structure their lives around the reading, recitation, pondering, or memorization of such scriptural works. REBT therapists likewise strongly encourage— but do not require—clients to read and study material from among more than 200 different self-help works. Many self-help books, pamphlets, essays, video- or audiotapes, comic books, and coloring books are available from the Albert Ellis Institute's catalogue (Ellis, 1998, 1999). Clients will usually begin therapy with a packet of reading materials, including pamphlets presenting the basic principles and practices of REBT. Just as study of Scripture helps religious clients keep their thoughts focused on religious beliefs, the theory of REBT holds that reading and studying REBT material helps clients in REBT remember and practice or anticipate the therapist's interventions.

Icons

Many religions encourage or even require the use or worship of religious pictures, symbols, jewelry, statuary, symbols, artwork, and so forth (Cândea, 1987). Religious adherents may use iconlike materials to establish shrines in their homes, offices, or vehicles. For example, statues of Jesus or the Holy Virgin are commonly seen on the dashboards of automobiles owned by devout Roman Catholics. Observant Jews attach a mezuzah to the doorframe of their home. The mezuzah is inscribed with the word *Shaddai,* and it contains a parchment on which is written the *shema.* The mezuzah is a metal tube, sometimes ornately decorated, *Shaddai* is a Hebrew name for God, and the *shema* is an excerpt from the Torah encouraging one to keep devotion to God always in one's heart. The *shema* includes the words:

> Hear, O Israel: The Lord our God is one Lord: And thou shalt love the Lord thy God with all thine heart, and with all thy soul, and with all thy might. And these words, which I command thee this day, shall be in thine heart: And thou shalt teach them diligently unto thy children, and shalt talk of them when thou sittest in thine house, and when thou walkest by the way, and when thou liest down, and when thou risest up. And thou shalt bind them for a sign upon thine hand, and they shall be as frontlets between thine eyes. *And thou shalt write them upon the posts of thy house, and on thy gates.* (Deuteronomy 6: 4–9, King James Version, italics added)

The flag of Saudi Arabia is itself an icon, consisting of these words in Arabic: "There is no god but God; Muhammad is the messenger of God." This is written in Arabic script, over a saber, and on a plain green field. This profession of faith, the *shamada,* is the first of the Five Pillars of Islam.

Although REBT avoids sacredizing anything, it does encourage clients to frequently remind themselves of important insights and lessons learned during sessions. Clients are encouraged to listen to recordings of their psychotherapy sessions (Ellis, 1996b). Additionally, the Albert Ellis Institute offers a wide range of reminders available to clients, including games, nicknacks, T-shirts, posters, and pencils, which humorously remind of REBT philosophical points such as, "Do, Don't Stew," "Don't Should On Me," and so forth.

Rituals and Sacraments

Ritual, sacred acts may be defined as conscious and voluntary, repetitious and stylized symbolic bodily actions entered into for sacred reasons (Zuesse, 1987). They are fundamental to most religions (Beit-Hallahmi, 1989). Sacraments are, by definition, sacred activities, and, as already noted, REBT avoids making its principles or techniques sacred. However, although not sacredized, some REBT techniques have been used and tested over many years so as to become highly, almost ritually, familiar.

From its beginning, REBT therapists have given homework assignments. These between-session activities are designed to reinforce and deepen the belief changing principles presented during the session. REBT continues to encourage active therapeutic work, including a range of in-session and between-session homework and behavior change activities. These may include tape recording and reviewing the clients' attempts to dispute their own irrational beliefs, role reversals during sessions, attempting to teach family members or significant others what has been learned during sessions, and so forth. Many of these techniques, are presented in the following chapters, including methods for accommodating and assimilating clients' religious beliefs during these activities.

A particularly unique REBT innovation is the famous shame-attacking homework assignment: Clients are encouraged to engage in harmless tasks that, formerly they would have experienced as shameful. Shame-attacking exercises might include singing out loud in public or calling out stops on subway trains or elevators. These homework assignments help clients overcome their self-defeating, shame-inducing beliefs (Ellis, 1994b, 1996b, 1999, 2000b).

Creeds and Articles of Faith

Many religions imbue specific statements, including prayers, chants, meditations, or affirmations of faith with particular significance. Religions frequently encourage or even require recitation or repetition of these special statements, treating the speaking of certain words or phrases with special, sacred significance, as in prayer (Moran, 1987; Speight, 1987). Judaism's *shema* and Islam's *shemada* (mentioned earlier) are also examples of creeds, the recitation of which are sacred responsibilities for both Jews and Moslems. Counting recitation of prayers using rosary beads is a means for marking passage of such sacred acts.

Again remember that REBT does not sacredize anything, including its own formulations about rational and irrational beliefs. However, REBT holds that some beliefs or ideas are risky, whereas other ideas are likely to counter and relieve self-defeating upset. Rational ideas are likely safer, more efficient beliefs (Ellis, 1994b) that are likely to help the client if they are internalized. REBT encourages clients to work to internalize rational beliefs.

REBT was neither the first psychotherapy to encourage self-talk, nor the only current psychotherapeutic approach to encourage and study self-talk (cf. Meichenbaum, 1977). But REBT was probably the first and most influential approach among modern cognitive behavioral therapies to encouraging self-statements (cf. Mahoney, 1974). As is discussed in detail in later chapters, REBT is probably the psychotherapy that attempts to be most careful and exact in its use of self-talk. REBTers attempt to identify and develop the most efficient and philosophically elegant—*fine tuned*— ideas for clients to repeat to themselves (cf. Ellis, 1994b, 1996b, 1999, 2000b; Walen et al., 1992).

Just as religious creeds are often spoken with care and exactness, self-talk in REBT is approached with an eye toward philosophical elegance and semantic precision. In the case of religious creeds, care and exactness are usually based on a desire for maintaining doctrinal correctness and sometimes are based on a desire to retain the sacredness of the words spoken. In REBT, semantic precision is sought for philosophical elegance and to achieve greater therapeutic efficiency. It is the contention here that philosophically elegant self-talk will yield more efficient therapeutic outcome and reduce the client's future disturbability.

Naming

Many organized religions imbue names and the process of naming with great religious significance. For some religions and religious traditions, certain words or names are sacred. Important figures from religious history had their names changed for holy reasons. For example, Jesus gave Simon, the son of Jonas, the new name of Peter. Many Christians believe this renaming was a sacred play on words used as a sign for Peter's duties to come, his subsequent leadership of the Christian church. Jesus said, "And I say also unto thee, That thou art Peter, and upon this rock I will build my church; and the gates of hell shall not prevail against it" (Matthew 16: 18, King James Version). The Greek word for rock or stone is *petrus*, hence Peter could be seen as the foundation stone on which the Christian church was built.

It is written in Genesis that Jacob, the son of Isaac and the grandson of Abraham, wrestled with an angel. Afterward the angel told him, "Thy name shall be called no more Jacob, but Israel: for as a prince hast thou power with God and with men, and hast prevailed" (Genesis 32: 28, King James version). Israel, or Yisra'el, in Hebrew can be interpreted as "God prevails." Thereafter, the descendants of Jacob became the nation of Israel—the nation through or for which God prevails. The name *Israel* therefore takes on religious and psychological significance. It might be speculated that it could become an identity function for an entire nation. Many other examples of this kind of religious renaming could be given.

From its beginnings, REBT has used humorous renaming of concepts in order to elucidate and emphasize the upsetting effects of irrational beliefs and the upset relieving effects of rational beliefs. For example, clients can develop an easily remembered way to accept themselves by adopting the self-rating scheme of seeing themselves as no more or less than fallible human beings (FHBs). And they can easily remember to work to develop unconditional self-acceptance (USA). These simple acronyms can become shorthand expressions for new ways of thinking and feeling better.

At least two words coined in REBT are famous and immediately recognizable to many therapists if not unforgettable to clients: It is difficult to be as concise or as memorable when describing the human tendency to demand the impossible than to call it "musturbation," the process of rigidly demanding that the world, others in the world, or people themselves MUST be different than they are. REBT's term for global, internalized, negative attributions is equally concise, and probably even more memorable: "shithood," which explains, in one word, the reducing of a person's essence, or "personhood," to the lowest possible value. Of course, some religious individuals may find the term *shithood* offensive, whereas others find it helpfully humorous. The issue of profanity in work with religious clients is discussed later in this book. Renaming of REBT concepts, especially renaming its concepts in a humorous form, provides the client with a concise means for remembering the ridiculous irrationality of an irrational idea.

Music

Most religions include music in worship (Ellingson, 1987). Many religions set important beliefs to music in the form of hymns, conduct their rituals to music, or consider music and hymn singing a form of prayer. Religious leaders urge personal hymn singing as a defense against temptation. Presumably, beliefs are rendered more emotive and more memorable through the combination of meter, melody, rhythm, and rhyme that turns words into a hymn (Wulff, 1991).

In a similar manner, many REBTers (Ellis, 1977b, 1987b, 2000b; Nielsen et al., 2000) help their clients attack their upsetting beliefs by singing them satiric, humorous, rational emotive songs. Clients in REBT might be encouraged to sing rational emotive songs to themselves and to others (Ellis, 1987b), particularly if they are having trouble changing their beliefs (Ellis, 1985). Of course, having clients attempt to sing such songs outside the session can also serve as one of the shame-attacking exercises already mentioned.

RELIGION INTEGRATING REBT: A SYNERGISTIC MIX

The rationale for integrating religiosity in treatment is really quite simple. As Propst (1982) noted, "Therapeutic expectations are made more powerful if the active ingredients of a psychotherapy are translated into the language and belief structures of the patient" (p. 85). Couching cognitive behavioral interventions in religiously meaningful terms will likely render interventions more easily understandable for religious believers. Integrating interventions by defining them in religious terms may make them more vivid for the client. The beliefs and commitment of religious clients can thus be functionally utilized to reduce distress and strengthen treatment gains.

Following is an example of how religious material might augment REBT during the most important phase of therapy, disputation of irrational beliefs. Disputation is the meat and potatoes of REBT (no offense intended to Jainists, Hindus, Buddhists, Adventists, or other vegetarians;

choose another idiom if you prefer). An excerpt is presented from a therapy session using religious material to strengthen disputation of a religious client's self-tormenting irrational practice of relentlessly rating himself according to his most subtle acts, his thoughts.

Tom (not his real name), a depressed, compulsive, perfectionistic student had been meeting with one of us (SLN) in psychotherapy. Tom was a former missionary who had been evacuated from his mission field after suffering a serious depressive episode. His depression could not be effectively treated in the country where he labored, so he returned home. He complained in this session—it would have been about his ninth session—that he struggled with his beliefs and desires. He was especially troubled that he flip-flopped between sometimes wanting to go to heaven, and sometimes not wanting to work hard enough to get there:

SLN: So you go back and forth between saying it's worth it and it's not worth it.

Tom: And then I guess I question my beliefs because, I think that, "We're taught it's worth it."

SLN: So, you're saying to yourself, "Here I am questioning my beliefs. Here I am vacillating about what I've been taught." Right?

Tom: Well, it's just confusing to me, because I believe one thing, yet there's—I don't know—just a conflict in what to believe.

SLN: Right. So what are you telling yourself about having these conflicting ideas? That's what seems key to me.

Tom: Um, well, I just think that maybe I don't believe what I say I believe.

SLN: Right, and if you don't believe what you say you believe . . .? What are you telling yourself about that?

Tom: Well, that kind of makes me a liar, I guess.

At this point I was confident that Tom's depression was strongly linked with perfectionistic self-rating. He was intensely scrutinizing his motives. This is probably a dubious process anyway, especially for a person with perfectionistic ideas. Motives are unstable, ephemeral, internal states. The very act of focusing attention on one's internal states may itself change the internal state so that it cannot be grasped. If the internal state is judged bad, as Tom did judge his internal state, then this may create anxiety. If this creates more strongly focused attention, as it apparently did for Tom, then more strongly focused attention may alter the internal state even more. Because Tom considered purity of motive important, his inability to grasp his motives may have created more anxiety, creating more scrutiny, creating more anxiety, less ability to grasp his motives clearly, more scrutiny, more anxiety, and so on. My hypothesis was that Tom believed that if his motives fluctuated, then that made him a lower class of human being, or "a liar."

SLN: I think *that* is the important issue that we need to talk about right now.

Tom: Okay.

SLN: You just defined yourself.

Tom: Yeah.

SLN: "A," the activating event, is you vacillating between what you believe at time 1 and what you believe at time 2, and then at time 3 you might believe something else; you bounce between believing these different things. Sometimes you believe strongly, "Yes it's worth it to go to Heaven, yes it's worth it for me to work hard at not getting angry." And then at time 2 you say to yourself, "Well I'm not sure it's worth it. I believe Heaven's there, but I'm not sure it's worth it, so I'm not going to give a hang about whether I get angry, I'm just going to sort of let go." [*The Activating event was noticing this way of thinking.*] Then, you just told me that you "B," Believe, "If I don't stick with it . . . if I believe one thing at one time, and I believe another thing at another time, that makes me . . ." What?

Tom: Well, probably a better word would be a hypocrite.

Perhaps a hypocrite is a slightly higher class of human being than a liar. Although, as becomes clear, a hypocrite is still an inadequate human being.

SLN: So, you have overgeneralized and defined you, all of you, as a hypocrite. I'm going to guess that you disrespect hypocrites.

Tom: Yeah.

Because Tom was highly devout in his religious beliefs, I decided to draw a metaphor between his vacillating motivations and the vacillating motives of a famous, sainted biblical figure. I drew an analogy between Tom and someone in the Bible in hopes that the biblical metaphor would be a forceful disputation:

SLN: Okay, let me give you an example of another famous hypocrite, then.

Tom: Okay.

SLN: I'm going to paraphrase a little, but you could, I think, find everything I'm paraphrasing in the New Testament in the Gospels, "Before the evening's over, Peter, you're going to deny me 3 times."

"No Lord, I'm not going to do that! I won't do that! No!"

"Before the night's over, before the cock crows 3 times, you'll deny me 3 times."

And what did Peter do?

Tom: He denied Him.

SLN: He denied Christ, right? Didn't that make Peter a hypocrite?

Tom: It didn't make him a hypocrite, it made . . . I mean, depending on what definition you use.

Defining a person is often just another way to rate the person. Tom was overgeneralizing by labeling himself a hypocrite. So, by drawing an analogy between his vacillating faith and St. Peter's vacillating faith, I was putting pressure on his self-rating. Unless he was willing to similarly overgeneralize to Peter, a figure he revered, he had to accept that he was being unfair to himself. He resisted this, as I both expected and hoped he would:

SLN: I agree completely! It doesn't make him a hypocrite unless you define him as a hypocrite! Peter denying the Christ, even though he protested that he wouldn't, that proves he's . . . what? [*long pause, Tom didn't answer.*] You know, That's an interesting story for several reasons, because in at least one of the versions several people said to him, "Now weren't you with Jesus Christ?" Remember that?

Tom: Uh-huh.

SLN: And in one version a young woman said to him, "You know, you speak like a Galilean. You've got a Galilean accent. I know you were with that Jesus fellow." And do you remember what it says in the scripture? Peter swore *and* he cursed (cf Matthew 27: 74 & Mark 15: 71). So what would that mean? That he cursed?

Tom: I don't know.

I saw that a possible solution would be for Tom to label Peter a fallible human being who behaved hypocritically in this instance and then apply the same rules to himself—He, Tom, is just a fallible human being, like Peter. I focused on another of Peter's misbehaviors, use of profanity, because I had noted during previous sessions that Tom was very proper in his use of language. He did not laugh, for example, when I had earlier used the term "manurehood" to emphasize how he down-rated himself at times. I guessed from his earlier reactions that he would be quite conservative about the use of profanity:

SLN: Swearing *and* cursing sound to me like he used profanity. That's what it means to curse, doesn't it?

Tom: Oh, maybe.

Tom seemed resistant to the idea that Peter would have used profanity. Doesn't it seem that way to you? This seemed, to me, to support my hypothesis:

SLN: If it says he swore *and* cursed, does that mean he said, "Rats!"? Is that cursing?

Tom: No.

SLN: No. So what does it prove about the chief apostle, Peter, that he used profane language and denied the Christ?

Tom: That he was fallible.

SLN: What does it mean about Tom . . . if Tom gets confused about his goals?

Tom: It just means that I'm fallible.

SLN: Yeah. But can you believe it?

Tom: That's a good question. That's really interesting, the point you bring up. Because I don't think that Peter is a liar or a hypocrite, but if I were to do that, boy, I would really give myself Heck [*sic*]!

Bingo! Tom seems to be having an emotional insight here about how unfair he is being with himself. Also note that this is probably the furthest extent of Tom's ability to use profanity:

SLN: But you don't think of yourself in the way you think of Peter.

Tom: No

SLN: So what's the difference?

Tom: There really isn't any.

SLN: Well, I'm glad to here you say that, but what can we do to help you believe it?

Tom: I don't know, just . . .

SLN: What if you read that story? It's reproduced in all four of the Gospels, isn't it?

Tom: I don't know.

SLN: Yeah, it's in all four of the Gospels, and in at least one of them it mentions that Peter swore and cursed. How about if you, as a homework assignment, read about Peter denying Christ?

Tom: Okay.

SLN: Because if he denied Christ, what was happening in his head with his beliefs?

Tom: He was vacillating.

SLN: He was vacillating, right? So how about if you read that story?

Tom: Okay.

SLN: And what could you puzzle about as you read that story? "Here I am reading about this guy whose beliefs vacillate and . . . "?

Tom: What does that make him?

SLN: Right! Now if my beliefs vacillate, what would I say that makes me?

Tom: Right.

Nielsen: And up to now the answer has been . . . ?

Tom: Now . . . hypocrite.

SLN: "I would think it makes me a hypocrite!" Well, if it makes you a hypocrite, what does it make Peter?

Tom: A hypocrite.

SLN: If it makes you a hypocrite, it makes Peter a hypocrite. How do you feel, being in the same company as Peter?

Tom: Oh, I don't know, I can't look at Peter and think he's a hypocrite.

SLN: So you refuse to put him in that company, who else could you refuse to overgeneralize and refuse to call a hypocrite?

Tom: Myself.

I went on to push Tom to formulate a concise, elegant statement about both him and about Peter, specifically, that they were both fallible human beings (FHBs). This was my attempt to move beyond the metaphorical disputation of comparing Tom with Peter, and have Tom create his own Effective rational, and, in this case, religiously grounded philosophy of life. At this writing, Tom is making slow progress in therapy. As you can tell from this excerpt, Tom has a strong propensity to examine and question everything he does, so the focus has been on helping him act rather than perfectionistically analyze his every move–to do, not stew!

OUR GOALS

This book aims to demonstrate that there is reason to be quite optimistic about the benefits of practicing REBT with religious clients. To be sure, there are complexities and problems to be anticipated. To begin with, we three authors disagree among ourselves about religion—sometimes to a strong degree. Nonetheless, we all view REBT as a highly religion-neutral psychotherapy and we believe it can be highly efficacious with most religious persons.

We acknowledge, from the beginning, that the psychological complexity inherent in human religious experience is beyond our ability to represent or anticipate in any one book. It is also impossible to fully anticipate how human religiosity will play itself out in the therapy consulting room. As already noted, you must do your own trail-blazing and map-making with your religious clients. We acknowledge that our knowledge of world religions is limited. Although we attempt to give specific examples from well-known religious traditions, we are aware that we may have a distorted view of religious traditions to which we do not adhere and that we will neglect other important traditions altogether. Such are the limitations of fallible human beings and their limited abilities. The examples selected are based on our insufficient experience. If these examples match the religious traditions present among your clientele, then we have guessed well and right. If the examples we offer neglect some or most of your clients, then we hope you will let us know so we can correct ourselves.

For those that live in the United States and Canada, and probably for many countries in Europe, increasing religious diversity is a fact. For example, by most estimates there will soon be more Moslems than Episcopalians or Presbyterians in the United States. Islam and the Church of Jesus Christ of Latter-day Saints (the Mormons) are probably the fastest growing religions in the United States It is not uncommon to encounter Asian religions even in smaller communities. If psychotherapists practice in a major metropolitan area, as most do, then it becomes increasingly likely that they will have among them clients with unfamiliar religious traditions. We encourage you to become familiar with this very important element of diversity.

Finally, we are not wearing ecumenical-colored glasses: There are many important, meaningful differences in religious beliefs. We do not contend that all religious traditions will equally aid the REBT practitioner, or that REBT will be accepted by all adherents of all religions. We do not wish to suggest that REBTers have to adopt any particular stance toward religion except to accept that religion is a ubiquitous and basic human activity that is charged with highly emotion laden, emotion inducing, and behavior modifying beliefs. We only urge you to pay attention to your clients' religious beliefs.

In the beginning of his monumental work, *The History of the Decline and Fall of the Roman Empire*, Gibbon (1776/1946, p. 22) wrote, "in Rome, all religions 'were considered by the people as equally true; by the philosophers as equally false; and by the magistrate as equally useful'" (quoted in Lovinger, 1984, p. 24). Gibbon described a pragmatic attitude toward religion, perhaps implying that religious belief helped keep the people's behavior under control and was therefore useful to the magistrate. Even if you firmly reject a religious worldview, we nonetheless encourage you to adopt at least a pragmatic attitude toward your clients' religious beliefs. Whatever they believe, you, as their therapist, had better attend closely to their beliefs and attempt to understand the implications of their beliefs. If your clients are religious (and they probably will be religious), there may well be elements in their religious traditions that you can use to help them feel less upset now and become less upset-able in the future.

2

Rational Emotive Behavior
Therapy (REBT) Today

Rational emotive behavior therapy (REBT) has undergone many important changes since I (AE) first began to practice it in January 1955. This chapter summarizes some of its main aspects and shows how, unlike many other modern therapies, it is unusually constructivist and postmodern but at the same time is often highly active-directive. It also shows that in spite of my own negative attitudes toward some aspects of religion, I now see that religious beliefs (even those I consider absolutistic) can sometimes lead to emotionally healthy behavior (Ellis, 2000a).

REBT AND CONSTRUCTIVISM
AND POSTMODERNISM

Although I (AE) originally was a constructivist, I was also a modernist and a logical positivist. However, I changed in 1976 to a partially postmodernist position. REBT now takes the following constructivist and postmodern views:

1. Perhaps some kind of indubitable objective reality or thing in itself exists, but we only seem to apprehend or know it through our fallible,

personal-social, different and changing, human perceptions. We do not
have any absolute certainty about what reality is or what it will be—in
spite of our often being strongly convinced that we do.

2. Our views of what is good or bad, what is right and wrong, what is
    moral and immoral are, as Kelly (1955) pointed out, largely personal-
    social *constructions*. Kelly held that the identification of universal
    truths is an impossible task and all ethical beliefs have a constructionist
    nature (Raskin, 1995). I agree.

3. Although human personality has some important innate elements, it
    also largely arises from relational and social influences and is less indi-
    vidualistic than it commonly is thought to be.

4. People are importantly influenced or conditioned by their cultural rear-
    ing. Their behaviors are amazingly multicultural and there is no conclu-
    sive evidence that their diverse cultures are right or wrong, better or
    worse (Ivey & Rigazio-DiGilio, 1991; Sampson, 1989).

5. Either/or concepts of goodness and badness often exist and are rigidly
    held, but they tend to be inaccurate, limited, and prejudiced. More
    open-minded apperceptions of human and nonhuman reality tend to
    show that things and processes exist on a both/and and an and/also
    basis. Thus, almost every human act or condition has its advantages and
    disadvantages. Even helpful acts have their bad aspects. Giving people
    money, approval, or therapy may encourage them to be weaker, more
    dependent, and less self-helping. Berating may encourage them to
    become stronger, less dependent, and more self-helping. Because
    monolithic, either/or solutions to problems have their limitations, we
    had better consider the range of alternate, and/also solutions and test
    them out to see how well—and badly—they work.

6. Unfortunately, or fortunately, all the solutions we strive to achieve for
    our problems depend on our choosing goals and purposes from which
    to work. Such goals and purposes are just about always arguable, never
    absolute. Even the near-universal human goal of survival is not univer-
    sal, for some of us stress individual and others stress group or social
    survival. And at least a few people choose suicide; and a few think that
    the annihilation of the whole human race—and perhaps of the entire
    universe—is preferable. So we can arrive here at a consensus but not
    any absolute agreement of what goals and purposes are better and
    worse.

These postmodernist views have recently been promulgated by a host
of writers (Bartley, 1984; Clark, 1992; Derrida, 1976; Feyerband, 1975;

Gergen, 1995; Hoshmand & Polkinghorne, 1992; Popper, 1985; Simms, 1994). They have also been applied to the field of mental health counseling and psychotherapy by a number of other writers (Ellis, 1994b, 1996a, 1996b, 1996c; Gergen, 1991; Ginter, 1989; Guterman, 1994, 1996a, 1996b, 1996c; Ivey & Goncalves, 1988; Ivey & Rigazio-DiGilio, 1991; Kelly, 1955; Mahoney, 1991; R.A. Neimeyer & Mahoney, 1995). Postmodernism is an important, and growing, aspect of today's psychotherapy.

Rational emotive behavior therapy (REBT), along with other cognitive-behavioral therapies (e.g., those of Beck, 1976; Maultsby, 1984; Meichenbaum, 1977), have been criticized as being rationalist and sensationalist by a number of critics (Guidano, 1991; Guterman, 1994, 1996b; Mahoney, 1991; R.A. Neimeyer & Mahoney, 1995). I have refuted this charge and tried to show that REBT is quite constructivist, and in some ways is actually more so than many of the other constructionist therapies (Ellis, 1991, 1994b, 1996a, 1996b, 1996c, 1997, 2000b). It is particularly constructivist for several reasons.

First, Kelly (1955), Guidano (1991), Mahoney (1991), and other constructivist therapists show that disturbed people generate deep cognitive structures and had better be helped to adopt alternative models of the self and the world so that their deep structures can work in a more flexible and adaptive manner. REBT more specifically holds that the rigid, absolutistic musts and necessities by which people usually upset themselves are not merely learned from their parents and culture but are also created by their own constructivist, and partly biological, tendencies.

Therefore, REBT holds that both clients and their therapists had better work hard, preferably in a highly active-directive and persistent manner, to help bring about profound philosophic, highly emotive, and strongly behavioral changes. Discovering and disputing their automatic self-defeating thoughts, as most cognitive-behavioral therapies do, is not enough. In addition, they had better be helped to see that they create core dysfunctional philosophies and they can constructively change them by thinking, by thinking about their thinking, and by thinking about thinking about their thinking (Dryden, 1995; Ellis, 1994b, 1996a, 1996c, 1999, 2000b; Ellis & Dryden, 1997; Ellis, Gordon, Neenan, & Palmer, 1997).

Also, in dealing with people's basic problems about self-worth, REBT agrees with the constructivist and existentialist position of Heidigger (1962), Tillich (1953), and Rogers (1961) that humans can define themselves as good or worthy just because they choose to do so. But it also shows them how to construct a philosophically unfalsifiable position of choosing life goals and purposes and then only rating and evaluating their thoughts, feelings, and actions as good when they fulfill and as bad when they fail to fulfill their chosen purposes. In this REBT solution to the problem of unconditional self-acceptance (USA), people can choose to view their self or essence as too complex and multifaceted to be given any global rating. It exists and can be enjoyed without the rigidities and dangers of either/or evaluation (Ellis, 1994b, 1996a, 1996c, 1999, 2000b).

Constructivists like Guidano (1991) and Hayek (1978) emphasize people's tacit observations and reactions to life problems, and REBT has always agreed that unconscious and tacit processes create both disturbance and problem solving (Ellis, 1962; Goleman, 1995). But REBT also particularly emphasizes and abets peoples' innate and acquired constructive abilities to design, plan, invent, and carry through better solutions to life's problems and to self-actualization. It shows clients how to make themselves aware of their unconscious constructivist self-defeating tendencies—and also how to use their conscious intentions and plans to lead a happier more constructivist life (Ellis, 1999; 2000b).

Mahoney (1991), Guidano (1991), R.A. Neimeyer and Mahoney (1995), and other constructivists often hold that because people are natural constructivists (with which I agree), active-directive cognitive-behavioral therapy may interfere with their natural ability to change. But this is like saying that because children (and adults) have natural abilities to problem solve and help themselves, their parents and teachers should give them little, if any, instruction! REBT takes a both/and instead of an either/or position here, holds that clients do have considerable natural ability to make themselves both disturbed and less disturbed, and teaches them how to help themselves minimize their disturbances. Moreover, although encouraging them to use their self-aiding tendencies, which obviously they are usually doing badly when they come to therapy, it tries to give them greater understanding and determination to collaborate with the therapist to help themselves more. It also stresses therapist and client efficiency in their choice and practice of the multitude of therapeutic techniques now available.

Constructionist approaches often put down science, especially rational science, and in some ways they make good points. Science has many advantages, but it is hardly sacrosanct. REBT holds, with postmodernists, that science has its limitations, especially because the objective truths that it often claims to reveal are at bottom person centered and include important subjective aspects.

Science, however, is important for psychotherapy. For if we can agree on what the main goals of counseling and therapy are, then scientifically oriented observation, case history, and experimentation may check our theory and show us how accurately our goals are achieved—not certainly, but at least approximately. So science has its usefulness; and REBT, along with other cognitive-behavioral therapies, uses science and rationality, as well as other criteria, to check its theories and to change them and its practices. Healthy constructivism includes rational scientific method while abjuring dogmatic scientism.

For the aforementioned reasons, and more that could be presented, REBT tries to be equally constructivist, and in some ways more constructivist, than many other therapies. Like reality therapy (Glasser, 2000), it is a *choice therapy* that gives people distinct agency, will, and decision in constructing and reconstructing their goals and values. Whether it actually succeeds in its constructivist leanings, only further study, including scientific and experimental study, will show.

The foregoing positions sound, to my prejudiced ears, like open-minded, flexible, and postmodern views. I favor them and try to follow them in my life and in my theory and practice of therapy—with some difficulty! For although I am willing to live with answers and rules that I realize are not final, utterly consistent, and indubitably correct, I would like to have some degree of probability that the ethics I choose for my life and my therapy relationships are reasonably correct and beneficial. Kelly (1955; Raskin, 1995) thought that although we cannot be certain about the goodness or rightness of our morals, we can still have probabilistic faith that they are workable. I tend to agree with him.

The trouble with postmodern ethics, as a number of critics have pointed out, is that they can easily be taken to relativist and even anarchic extremes (Fuchs & Ward, 1994; Haughness, 1993; Held, 1995). Humans seem to require fairly clear-cut social rules when they live and work together; and counselors and therapists especially had better adopt and follow fairly strict ethical standards. Active-directive therapists like myself are particularly vulnerable in this respect, because they tend to be more authoritative, more didactic, and more forceful than are passive, quiescent therapists. Therefore, they are often accused of being more authoritarian, self-centered, and harmful than passive therapists. I do not quite agree with this allegation and could write a book on the enormous harm that is often done by passive therapists, who often keep clients in needless pain and solidly block what they can do to change themselves. But let me fully admit that directive therapy has its distinct dangers and show how I, partly from taking a postmodernist outlook, ethically deal with these dangers.

AN ACTIVE DIRECTIVE APPROACH

Consider one of the very important problems of therapy, which has distinct ethical considerations, to see how I use postmodern views to handle it. As a therapist, shall I mainly be a fairly passive listener, hear all sides of my clients problems, explore with them the advantages of their doing this and not doing that, have faith in their own ability to make presumably good decisions for themselves, and patiently wait for them to do so? Or should I instead, more active-directively zero in on what I think are my clients' core disturbances, show them what they are specifically thinking, feeling, and doing to needlessly upset themselves, and directly challenge them and teach them how to think, feel, and behave more effectively?

A number of schools of therapy (i.e., classical psychoanalysis, Rogerian person centered, and cognitive-experiential therapy) largely favor the more passive approach and a number of other schools (i.e., behavior therapy, cognitive behavioral therapy, problem solving, and Gestalt therapy) largely favor the more active-directive approach. Which one is more ethical and which shall I use?

By using the special form of rational emotive behavior therapy (REBT), I favor active-directive methods. I consider these to be ethical and efficient for several reasons:

1. Most clients, especially those with severe personality disorders, are disturbed for both biological and environmental reasons. They are innately prone to anxiety, depression, and rage, and they also learn dysfunctional thoughts, feelings, and behaviors. They practice them so often that they have great difficulty changing even when they gain considerable insight into their origin and development. Therefore, they had better be taught how they are probably upsetting themselves and taught specific and general methods to change themselves (Ellis, 1994b, 1996c, 1999, 2000b; Ellis & Dryden, 1997; Ellis & Harper, 1996, 1997; Ellis & Maclaren, 1998).

2. Clients are usually in pain when they come to therapy and active-directive methods, as research has shown, tend to be more effective in a brief period of time than are more passive methods (Elkin, 1994; Hollon & Beck, 1994; Lyons & Woods, 1991; Silverman, McCarthy, & McGovern, 1992).

3. Therapy is often expensive and it seems ethical to help clients benefit from it as quickly as feasible, which is what active-directive methods tend to do (Ellis, 1996b).

4. There is some evidence that the active-directive methods of cognitive behavioral therapy may lead to a more lasting change than do some more passive techniques (Alford & Beck, 1997; Hollon & Beck, 1994; Weishar, 1993).

5. More passive therapists (i.e., classical analysts and Rogerian person-centered practitioners) have often appeared to be passive but actually sneak in more active methods, and may therefore not be as honest as more active therapists who fully acknowledge their directiveness.

6. In REBT terms, passive techniques, such as relating warmly to clients instead of focusing on their specific dysfunctioning, may help them feel better but not get better. They often enjoy being endlessly listened to rather than urged to change, and feel conditionally better because their therapist approves of them rather than be unconditionally self-accepting, whether or not their therapist likes them (Ellis, 1972, 1991, 1994b, 1996b, 1999, 2000b).

7. Actively showing clients how to function better often helps them achieve a sense of self-efficacy, which may not amount to unconditional self-acceptance (USA) but nonetheless may be quite therapeutic (Bandura, 1977).

8. Active therapy may push clients to do difficult beneficial tasks (e.g., in vivo desensitization) that are quite beneficial but that they would rarely do on their own. Clients often change more when they first make themselves uncomfortable and then later become comfortable with their new behaviors. Active-directive therapy is likely to encourage them, more than is passive therapy, to uncomfortably change (Ellis, 1994b, 1996b; Ellis & Dryden, 1997; Ellis & Maclaren, 1998).

For all these advantages of active-directive therapy, its possible disadvantages must also be acknowledged, including:

1. It may be too directive and interrupt clients' innate pro-active propensities to work on their own problems and to actualize themselves.

2. It may induce clients to use methods that the therapist strongly believes in but that have little efficacy or may even be iatrogenic.

3. It may encourage clients to try suggested methods too quickly without giving them proper thought and preparation.

4. It may lead clients to adopt goals and values that the therapist sells them on and therefore not really to fulfill *themselves*.

5. Directive therapists may go to authoritarian, one-sided, and even righteous extremes and may neglect important individual differences,

multicultural influences, and other aspects of individual and group diversity.

6. Active-directive therapy may put too much power and responsibility on the therapist, disrupt a potentially collaborative and cooperative client–therapist relationship, and detract from the humanistic aspects of counseling.

Even though much published evidence shows that active-directive therapy is often quite advantageous and effective, we can postmodernistically question whether at bottom, these results are really effective, good, deep, or lasting. Such results have multiple meanings, some of which directly contradict other meanings of the same term. Which of these meanings shall be accepted as true?

My personal solution to this issue is to take an and/also rather than an either/or approach. Thus, in accordance with REBT theory, I usually zero in quite quickly on my clients' basic or core philosophies—especially on their dysfunctional or irrational beliefs— show them how to differentiate these from their rational and functional preferences, and how to use several cognitive, emotive, and behavioral methods to dispute and act against these beliefs. But I also show them some important other sides of their dysfunctional thinking, feeling, and behaving. Consider the following:

1. Even their highly irrational ideas—their absolutistic shoulds, oughts, or musts—have advantages and virtues. "I must perform well or I am worthless!" produces anxiety and avoidance, but it is also motivating, energizing, and brings some good results.

2. Even questionable ideas (e.g., pollyannaish beliefs like, "Day by day in every way I'm getting better and better" or "No matter what I do kind Fate will take care of me") may jolt one out of a depressed state and help one function better.

3. Strong negative feelings can be good and bad, helpful and unhelpful. When you do poorly, your strong feelings of disappointment and regret may push you to do better next time. But your strong feelings of horror and self-hatred may harm you immensely. Yes, but even your unhealthy feelings of horror and self-hatred may sometimes help you give up compulsive smoking or drinking!

4. Rational ideas and behaviors are not always really rational, and certainly they are not always sensible and helpful. Rationally and empirically believing that the universe is senseless and uncaring will help some people be self-reliant and energized, and will help others to be

depressed and hopeless. Accurately believing that no one in the world really cares for you will motivate some people to work at being more social and others to withdraw socially.

CAUTIONS AND LIMITATIONS

In spite of the disadvantages of active-directive therapy, I strongly favor it over passive therapy. But to make reasonably sure that I do not take it to extremes, I try to keep in mind several safeguards. Here are some of my main, and I think postmodernistically oriented, cautions:

Awareness of My Technique's Limitations

I do therapy on the basis of my sincere and strong faith in REBT—in other words, my belief that it probably works well with most of my clients much of the time but that it also has its distinct limitations. I tentatively endorse and follow it, but I keep looking for its flaws and its shortcomings. I keep checking my own results, those of my colleagues and trainees, and those reported in the literature. I try to keep especially aware of its dangers and its inefficiencies. Thus, I keep looking for the limitations of my active-directiveness, pointing them out to my clients, and encouraging them to be more active-directive in their own right (Ellis, 1996a, 1996b).

Awareness of Clients' Different Reactions to My Techniques

I assume that REBT methods help most of my clients much of the time, but not all of them all of the time. Although I often see them as having disturbances stemming from similar dysfunctional or irrational beliefs, I also keep reminding myself that even clients with the same problems (e.g., severe states of depression) have vastly different biochemical reactions. temperaments, histories, family, and cultural influences, socioeconomic conditions, therapeutic experiences and so on. Moreover, they react differently to me and my personality and preferences. Although I still start out with what I think are the best REBT methods for each of them, which usually means the ones I have successfully used with somewhat similar clients in the past, I remain quite ready to vary my methods considerably with each individual client. I even consider, when REBT does not seem to be working, using poor or irrational methods that REBT theory and practice usually opposes (Ellis, 1996a, 1996b, 2000b). Thus, I use more active-directive methods with some clients and less so with others. With those for whom I am consistently directive, I sometimes deliberately make myself much less so in order to see whether we achieve worse or better results.

Experimenting With Various Techniques

Yates (1975) once said that each session of therapy had better be an experiment, and one that leads therapists to change their tactics as the results of that experiment are observed. I add: I had better observe and review each series of sessions, and the length of therapy as a whole, as an experiment. As I observe the good and bad results of my sessions with each individual client, I try to repeat successful REBT methods and modify unsuccessful ones. If my REBT methods do not appear to be working, then I experiment with some non-REBT, or even anti-REBT, methods. If these do not seem to be effective, then I refer the client to another REBT or non-REBT therapist. As usual, I keep experimenting with a number of active-directive methods, and with some more passive ones as well.

Using Multimodal Methods

From the start, REBT has always used a number of cognitive, emotive, and behavioral methods with most clients; and over the years it has added to them a number of additional methods that appear to be effective (Ellis, 1962, 1975, 1988, 1994b, 1996b, 2000b; Kwee & Ellis, 1997; Lazarus, 1989). All of these methods have their disadvantages and limitations, particularly with some clients some of the time. I, therefore, try to keep these limitations in mind and to have available for regular or occasional use literally scores of REBT techniques, as well as a number of non-REBT techniques. I thereby remain open-minded and alternative-seeking in my therapy. Most methods of REBT are active-directive. But some, like the Socratic method of discovering and questioning irrational beliefs, are more passive. When directiveness fails, more passive methods are borrowed from psychoanalytic, person-centered, and other therapies.

Using Therapeutic Creativity

I originally used or adopted several REBT methods from other theorists and therapists, believing them to be effective implementers of REBT theory, which tentatively but still strongly holds several major propositions. I soon found that I could better adapt many of these methods to REBT, and to therapy in general, by slightly or considerably modifying them. And I also devised new methods (e.g., REBT's shame-attacking exercises and its very forceful and vigorous disputing of clients' irrational Beliefs) that seem to add to and improve on my original ones (Bernard, 1993; Dryden, 1995; Ellis, 1988, 1994b, 1996a, 2000b; Walen et al., 1992). I—and hopefully other REBT practitioners—remain open to using our therapeutic creativity to adapt and devise new methods with special clients and with regular ones. In most cases, I have created new active-directive methods. But I also designed the more passive method of exploring clients early irrational beliefs, as well as the dysfunctional beliefs of others, to prime them indirectly to note and deal with their own self-defeating ideas. I have also for many years encouraged clients to teach REBT to their friends and relatives and thereby indirectly learn it better themselves (Ellis, 1996b, 1999, 2000b). I use a number of paradoxical methods with my clients, such as encouraging them to get at least three rejections a week, so that they indirectly see and believe that being rejected is not horrible or shameful.

Varying Relationship Methods

REBT theory holds that the majority of therapy clients can benefit from achieving unconditional self-acceptance (USA)—that is, fully accepting themselves as good or deserving persons whether or not they perform well and whether or not significant other people approve of them (Ellis, 1972, 1988, 2000b; Ellis & Harper, 1997; Hauck, 1991; Mills, 1994). Consequently, I try to give all my clients what Rogers (1961) called unconditional positive regard; and, I go beyond this and do my best to teach them how to give it to themselves. I recognize, however, that even USA has its limitations, because some people only change their self-defeating and antisocial behavior by damning themselves as well as their actions. I especially recognize that different methods of showing clients unconditional acceptance range from warmly loving or approving them to unemotionally accepting them with their revealed failings and hostilities. All these methods have their advantages and disadvantages; and all of them work well and poorly with different clients. So I vary the specific ways I relate to clients and cautiously observe the results of my interactions with them. Occasionally, I even go along with their self-damning when, oddly enough, it seems to help them. So I generally give clients unconditional acceptance and actively teach them how to give it to themselves, but in many different individual and specific ways, including indirect and passive ones.

Varying Interpersonal Methods

REBT, again on theoretical grounds, teaches clients the advantages of unconditional other acceptance (UOA), or the Christian philosophy of accepting the sinner but not the sin (Ellis, 1977a, 1994b, 1996b, 1999, 2000b). I do this with my clients because I believe their anger, rage, and fighting frequently is self-destructive and also ruins relationships with others. A good case can be made that rage and noncooperativeness seriously sabotages human survival and happiness, and the essence of psychotherapy, therefore, is helping people achieve both USA and UOA (Gergen, 1991; Sampson, 1989).

Nonetheless, clients' achieving unconditional self- and other acceptance may well have some drawbacks, such as helping people to justify their own and other people's immoral behavior and thereby encouraging it. So I try to remember that it is not exactly a panacea.

Moreover, therapists' ways of giving and teaching USA and UOA can easily be *interpreted* wrongly by their clients. Thus, when Rogers (1961) showed clients unconditional positive regard, they often wrongly concluded they were good persons because of his approval of them. But this is highly conditional self-acceptance! Similarly, if I accept my clients unconditionally when, say, they have stolen or cheated, they may wrongly conclude that I do not really think their behavior is evil, and may therefore excuse their doing it.

So although I do my best to give my clients unconditional acceptance and encourage them to give it to others, I closely watch their reception and interpretation of what I am doing. I solicit their feedback, watch their reactions with themselves, with me, and with others, and, once again, use a variety of relationship and interpersonal relating approaches to determine which ones actually seem to work. I actively give and teach self-acceptance and forgiveness of others. But I also actively watch and try to counter its potential dangers.

Once again, REBT has always actively used the therapeutic relationship to help clients become aware of their interpersonal cognitive, emotional, and behavioral interpersonal deficiencies. But I keep reminding myself that if my clients involve themselves too closely with me, that may increase their neurotic neediness and interfere with their outside relations with others. I also am skeptical of my assumption that the main ways my clients react to me—and they may be uniquely accepting people in their life—are the same ways that they react to others. So I often tone down their involvements with me, encourage their participation in one of my therapy groups, recommend suitable workshops, talks, and books, and teach them interpersonal skills specifically designed to help them in their outside life. I do not assume their relationships with me are clearly transferred from their feelings and prejudices about their early family members, although occasionally that is so. Rather, I assume that they often have an idiosyncratic and personal relationship with me and I watch closely to see if it is over- or underinvolved and how it can be constructively used despite its possible dangers. When my actively relating to my clients seems to be iatrogenic, I try to deliberately ameliorate it with a more passive kind of interaction with them.

Skepticism About the Infallibility of the Therapist and the Main Therapeutic Methods Employed

REBT encourages clients to have two almost contradictory beliefs: First, they are able to understand how they largely disturb themselves, how they can reduce their disturbances and increase their individual and social fulfillment, and how they can use several REBT cognitive, emotive, and behavioral methods to try to actively work at doing what they theoretically can do. REBT thus tries to help clients to have an active, strong feeling of self-efficacy about changing themselves.

Second, it keeps encouraging them realistically to see and accept their human fallibility and imperfection, to acknowledge that they now are, and in all probability will continue to be, highly error prone, inconsistent, unreasonable, inefficacious individuals: Always? Yes. To a high degree? Yes.

Can clients, then, have confidence in their ability to grow and change, have a sense of self-efficacy in this regard, and still acknowledge and accept their human fallibility? Why not? People are fallible at all sports, but they may also have real confidence that they can play one of them well, and then they may actually do so. They may be highly fallible students—but feel efficacious, say, at test-taking and usually get decent marks. So it is almost certain that they are generally fallible. But, at the same time, they are highly proficient in certain tasks, know they are proficient, and help themselves remain proficient by having a sense of self-efficacy about these tasks.

So I can safely active-directively show my clients that they are generally fallible, and even often fallible about changing themselves. Nonetheless, they can, if they are willing to work at changing themselves, have what I call achievement-confidence and what Bandura (1997) called self-efficacy. Believing that this is highly probable—not certain—means they can change, and often do.

Therapists, too, can feel confident that they are effective—in spite of their fully acknowledging their therapeutic (and general) fallibility. This is what happens as I do active-directive REBT. I am quite confident that I often significantly help my clients, and help them more than if I used another main form of therapy. But I also know full well that I am a fallible human—quite fallible. I recognize that with each client I can, and at times easily do, REBT inefficiently. Nonetheless, with this particular client, I may well have my prejudices, weaknesses, hostilities, low frustration tolerances, ignorances, rigidities, stupidities, and so on.

While seeing a client, I therefore often do several things: (a) acknowledge my prejudices and weaknesses; (b) accept myself unconditionally with them; (c) try to ameliorate and compensate for them; (d) decide whether, in spite of my failings, I still probably am able to effectively help this client; (e) if I decide that I am able, I push myself on with a good degree of confidence or self-efficacy; (f) do my best to use REBT (and possibly other) methods with each client; (g) sometimes discuss my weaknesses with clients, to see if they are willing to continue to see me; (h) if so, I proceed actively, and energetically with the therapy—mainly with a high degree of confidence but also with some doubts; (i) keep checking on my doubts and often changing my tactics with this (and other) clients and/or referring some to another therapist.

REBT AND RELIGIOUS CLIENTS TODAY

Although I once considered religiosity, particularly devout religiosity, antithetical to good mental health (Ellis, 1980a; 1983a, 1983c, 1986), I have often reexamined my thinking about religion (Ellis, 1992, 1994a) and have recently concluded that religious attitudes and beliefs (even those that are extreme and absolutistic) can at times produce healthy emotional outcomes (Ellis, 2000a).

A good deal of research has shown that people who view God as a warm, caring, and lovable friend, and who see their religion as supportive, are more likely to have positive outcomes than those who take a negative view of God and their religion (Batson, Schoenrade, & Ventis, 1993; Donahue, 1985; Gorsuch, 1988; Hood, Spilka, Hunsberger, & Gorsuch, 1996; Kirkpatrick, 1997; D.B. Larson & S. Larson, 1994; Pargament, 1977). In light of this and other research, I now hold that religious and nonreligious beliefs in themselves do not help people to be emotionally "healthy" or "unhealthy." Instead, their emotional health is significantly affected by the kind of religious and nonreligious beliefs they hold.

I still consider absolutism to be highly connected to disturbance and some research supports the notion that religious inflexibility and rigidity are associated with emotional problems (Hunsberger, Alisat, Pancer, & Pratt, 1996). However, it is clear that not all rigid religionists have emotional problems and some devoutly religious people are quite well adjusted. In fact, many people who call themselves religious (i.e., ministers, priests, and rabbis who practice REBT) are pretty open-minded and nonabsolutist. Still, many devoutly religious people who adhere to negative and punitive views of God and the universe may make themselves emotionally disturbed by these beliefs. Overall, I believe it is rigid, absolutistic and dogmatic thinking that leads to neurotic disturbance, rather than religion itself (Ellis, 2000a).

I simultaneously see that religiously committed clients do benefit from versions of REBT that intentionally accommodate their beliefs (W.B. Johnson, Devries, Ridley, Pettorini, & Peterson, 1994; W.B. Johnson & Ridley, 1992a). So I hold that REBT can be compatible with many forms of religion, even absolutistic and devout religiosity.

To make this point clear, I recently speculated about how some of the main principles of REBT are similar to some aspects of a religious worldview (Ellis, 2000a). Table 2.1, briefly describes one of the main philosophies of REBT, then states an absolutistic, but still healthy, religious viewpoint that repeats the REBT philosophy in God-oriented language.

As can be seen from reviewing the comparisons of some REBT philosophies and their God-oriented counterparts listed in Table 2.1, both these basic outlooks have much in common. According to my personal view, and I am still a thoroughgoing secularist, secular REBT has several advantages over religious-oriented REBT and may help those who use it to achieve a more elegant, lasting, and thoroughgoing solution to their emotional and behavioral problems. This is because I think that God-oriented approaches to therapy require strong beliefs in superhuman entities and all-encompassing laws of the universe that are unprovable and unfalsifiable. On the other hand, secular-oriented REBT makes few unfalsifiable assumptions about humans and the world. It is more closely related to

TABLE 2.1

A Comparison of Some REBT Philosophies

and Their God-Oriented Counterparts

REBT Philosophy	God-Oriented Philosophy

Self-Control and Change

Because I often make myself undisciplined and self-defeating by demanding that I absolutely must have immediate gratifications, I can give up my short-range "needs," look for the pleasure of today and tomorrow, and seek for life satisfactions in a disciplined way.	God gave me some degree of free will and the ability to think for myself and control myself and I can, with God's help, use this ability to discipline myself. God helps those who help themselves.

Unconditional Self-Acceptance (USA)

I can always choose to give myself unconditional self-acceptance (USA) and see myself as a "good person" just because I am alive and human— whether or not I act well and whether or not I am lovable. Better yet, I can choose to rate and evaluate only my thoughts, feelings, and behaviors but not give myself, my essence, or my total being a global rating. When I fulfill my personal and social goals and purposes, *that* is good; but, I will never globally rate myself as a *good* or *bad* person.	My God is merciful and will always accept me as a sinner while urging me to go and sin no more. Because God accepts sinners, though not their sins, I can accept myself no matter how badly I behave.

High Frustration Tolerance

Nothing is *terrible* or *awful*, only at worst highly inconvenient. I *can* stand serious frustrations and adversity, even though I never have to like them.	With God's help I can weather the worst stress. If I worship God and uncomplainingly accept life's tribulations, I will cope better with them.

TABLE 2.1
continued

REBT Philosophy	God-Oriented Philosophy
Unconditional Acceptance of Others (UAO)	
All humans are fallible, and therefore I can accept that people will make mistakes and do wrong acts. I can accept them with their mistakes and poor behaviors and refuse to denigrate them as persons.	My God and my religion tell me to love my enemies, to do good, and pray for them. Blessed are the merciful.
Achievement	
I prefer to perform well and win approval of significant others, but I never *have to* do so to prove that I am a worthwhile person.	Because I am one of God's children, I am a good person and don't have to accomplish anything to prove myself. Although rigorous adherence to the rules and sacraments of my religion and obedience to God are desirable, I will be a worthy person even if I don't have any notable accomplishments.
Needing Approval and Love	
It is highly preferable to be approved of and loved by significant people and to have good social skills, but if I am disapproved I can still fully accept myself and lead an enjoyable life.	What does it profit me if I gain the whole world and lose my soul? Because I love God and God unconditionally loves me, I do not need the love and approval of other people.
Accepting Responsibility	
It is hard to face and deal with life's difficulties and responsibilities, but ignoring them and copping out is, in the long run, much harder. Biting the bullet and facing the problems of life usually becomes easier and more rewarding if I work at it persistently and diligently.	God and my religion ask that I face life's difficulties and responsibilities, no matter how hard I may find it to do so. My soul will suffer if I am a sluggard, but will be abundantly gratified if I am diligent and responsible.

TABLE 2.1
continued

REBT Philosophy	God-Oriented Philosophy

Accepting Self-Direction

I prefer to have some caring and reliable people to depend on, but I do not *need* to be dependent and do not have to find someone stronger than I to rely on.

I have my own resources to help me take care of myself, but I also have God to rely on and to help me.

Ability to Benefit From and Change the Past

No matter how bad and handicapping my past was, I can change my early thoughts, feelings, and behaviors today. I don't have to keep repeating and reenacting my past.

When I am united to God, I live in a new world. The older order has gone and a new order has already begun for me.

Accepting Life's Dangers

Life has many possible dangers, discomforts, and ailments. But I never need to worry obsessively about them. Continual worry will not help me to solve dangerous problems, will often interfere with my solving them, and even contribute to my making them worse. I can make myself concerned and cautious without indulging in obsessive worrying if I give up my demands that my life be absolutely safe and secure at all times.

God is with me and will show me how to deal with the dangers, discomforts, and ailments that may plague me. I need not be anxious about anything if, with prayer and petition, and with thanksgiving, I present my problems to God. Faith in God will calm my anxieties.

Nonperfectionism

Doing things perfectly well might be advantageous, but I am far from being a perfect person. So I'd better try to do well but not think that I *have to* do perfectly well. No matter how desirable perfection may be, it is never *necessary*.

Only God is perfect. I am merely a human, not a god, and I can therefore try to do well but not demand that I do perfectly well.

TABLE 2.1
continued

REBT Philosophy	God-Oriented Philosophy
Accepting Disturbance	
My disturbed feelings, such as anxiety and depression, are quite uncomfortable, but they are not awful and do not make me a stupid person for indulging in them. If I see them as hassles rather than as horrors, then I can live with them more effectively and give myself a much better chance to minimize them.	God will accept me with my disturbed feelings, such as anxiety and depression, and help me to successfully uproot them. If I am really disturbed, God's will be done, and I can therefore handle my disturbance.

checkable observations of how humans operate, how they manage to live more happily, and what can be done to help them create less disturbance. Secular REBT is, therefore, a more pragmatic and more realistic way of living in a difficult world than is any form of God-oriented religiosity. It provides clients with direct rather than indirect choices in making and keeping themselves mentally, emotionally, and behaviorally healthy.

This, however, is only my hypothesis. Although we cannot very well empirically investigate human processes that are attributable to God and other supernatural entities, we can research what will tend to happen to people who devoutly believe and who disbelieve in absolutistic religious concepts. So by all means, as all three authors of this book have suggested, let us do a great deal more research into the outcome of using REBT with religious-minded and nonreligious-minded individuals.

The examples of religious philosophies in Table 2.1 are largely taken from Christian writings, but many are also espoused by Jewish and Islamic sources. For the most part, these philosophies would be supported by religious scripture. For example, the New Testament offers many verses that support a God-oriented philosophy of unconditional acceptance of others (e.g., "You shall love your neighbor as yourself," Matthew. 19:19).

In sum, I believe that anyone who holds to the sort of religious philosophies summarized in Table 2.1 can also be "rational," that is, having self-helping beliefs, feelings, and behaviors. In this sense, therefore, REBT and devout religiosity are hardly the same, but they can at least be compatible and many religious clients stand to benefit significantly from REBT as a treatment approach.

Postmodern philosophy, when not taken to relativist extremes, has a great deal to offer to the field of psychotherapy, particularly in the area of psychotherapy ethics. Rational emotive behavior therapy (REBT) is active-directive but is also unusually postmodernistic and constructivist in that it specializes in showing clients how their conscious and unconscious absolutistic philosophies lead to much of their dysfunctional feelings and behaviors, and what they can do to make themselves more open-minded and flexible in their intrapersonal and interpersonal relationships.

Active-directive therapies, however, may dangerously neglect some aspects of constructivist therapy, such as ignore less intrusive and more passive ways of collaboration between therapists and their clients. This chapter shows how I (AE), as an active-directive practitioner of REBT, address some of its potential dangers and use postmodernist ethics and safeguards to retain its efficiency and reduce its risks. In particular, it stresses therapists becoming aware of REBT's limitations and of clients' different reactions to its techniques; experimenting with various multimodal methods of REBT and non-REBT therapy; using therapeutic creativity; varying relationship and interpersonal approaches; and remaining highly skeptical about the therapist's and the therapeutic method's infallibility. These caveats and cautions will not make active-directive REBT, or any other form of therapy, entirely flexible and safe. But they may considerably help.

Finally, the constructive philosophies of REBT are similar to those of many religious clients, especially with regard to unconditional self-acceptance, high frustration tolerance, unconditional acceptance of others, the desire rather than the need for achievement and approval, and other mental health goals. Overall, REBT is compatible with some important religious views and can be used effectively with many clients who have absolutistic philosophies about God and religion.

II

Practicing REBT
With Religious Clients

3

*Rational Emotive Assessment
With Religious Clients*

REBT therapists conduct thorough assessments with religious clients for the purpose of determining whether to engage them in treatment, and if so, to determine what set of therapeutic strategies may be most efficacious. During the assessment, it behooves REBT practitioners to consider their ability to ethically offer services to religious clients. For example, the APA Ethics Code (1992) cautioned psychologists to function within their boundaries of competence, to respect human differences (including those based on religious faith), and to identify and respond appropriately to assessment situations with special populations, such as religious persons for whom traditional assessment measures and techniques may not be valid or useful. Similarly, the APA guidelines for providers of psychological services to diverse populations (APA, 1993) emphasized the significance of client religious commitment and spirituality in offering interpersonal and community support, influencing the form of expressions of distress and disturbance, and determining the client's probable response to treatment. These guidelines and those from related mental health fields underscore the tremendous importance of honoring client religious beliefs and tailoring assessment and intervention practices to accommodate faith commitments.

Assessment with the religiously committed client presents the REBT therapist with a dilemma, particularly if the therapist has little training in treatment of religious clients and is largely unaware of the beliefs and practices common to the religion endorsed by the specific client (Rowan, 1996). Although professional guidelines highly endorse obtaining training and supervision in order to competently treat religious persons, the reality is that the range of religious communities, not to mention the idiosyncratic experiences and expressions of religion, make "expertise" with most religious populations highly unlikely. Furthermore, very little literature exists regarding the unique clinical issues common to specific religious groups.

This chapter recommends a careful and religion-sensitive approach to assessment with REBT clients. It begins with a brief summary of traditional or general REBT assessment and then addresses more focal assessment of both the personal and clinical salience of a client's religious/ spiritual status. It concludes by highlighting the pragmatics and perils of assessing a client's religious beliefs.

ASSESSMENT IN THE GENERAL REBT
TREATMENT SEQUENCE

Although REBT is widely recognized as one of the most efficient approaches to psychotherapy currently available, excellent REBT therapists are careful to conduct detailed assessments of all clients. As an example, here is DiGiuseppe's (1991) description of the standard intake assessment process for all clients at the Albert Ellis Institute for REBT in New York City. Clients are asked to arrive early for their first appointment in order to complete the assessment materials:

> They are asked to complete a four-page biographical information form, the Millon Clinical Multiaxial Inventory II (Millon, 1987), the short form of the Beck Depression Inventory (Beck & Beck, 1972; Beck, Rial, & Rickels, 1974), the General Psychological Well Being Scale (DuPuy, 1984), the General Health Questionnaire (Goldberg, 1972), the Satisfaction with Life Scale (Diener, Emmons, Larsen, & Griffen, 1985), and the Attitudes and Beliefs Scale 2 (DiGiuseppe, Exner, Leaf, & Robin, 1988) . . . The scales are computer-scored on the premises and are usually available to the therapist by the second session. The brief version of the

Beck Depression Inventory, the General Psychological Well Being Scale, the General Health Questionnaire, and the Satisfaction with Life Scale are repeated every four weeks so that therapists and clients can review their progress. (pp. 152–153)

Although there is nothing particularly sacred about the assessment protocol used by the institute, it is wise to collect broad spectrum assessment data on all clients as a prelude to REBT. Such an assessment will typically include information on personality functioning, symptom distress, and relational patterns, as well as detailed biographical material. In addition, utilization of brief symptom-specific measures for depression, anxiety, or anger is recommended and their selection should be tailored to the client's primary presenting complaint. In selecting measures for use in assessment, parsimony is recommended. Hayes, Nelson, and Jarrett (1987) wisely reminded clinicians to consider the treatment utility of tools selected for clinical assessment. Avoiding redundancy and collection of irrelevant data is critical for maintaining rapport and enhancing the efficiency and effectiveness of the assessment process. For this reason, projective measures and more than one measure of personality and/or global symptom functioning are rarely administered.

Beyond general assessment of psychological functioning, the REBT therapist is interested in rapidly gaining an understanding of the client's essential beliefs (including those that are evaluative, demanding, and disturbance inducing). REBT therapists begin with the assumption that psychological disturbance is equivalent to the tendency of humans to make extreme, absolutistic evaluations of themselves or perceived events in their lives.

The next chapter outlines the suggested sequence for an REBT therapy session. Certain steps are particularly relevant to the process of assessment with religious clients: specifically, agreeing on a target problem for the session and assessing beliefs, especially irrational, evaluative beliefs (IBs). The remainder of this chapter considers ways the therapist may specifically augment the assessment process in order to address client religiousness. A strategy is presented for both preliminary and advanced assessment of religiousness in REBT clients (W. B. Johnson & Nielsen, 1998). As noted earlier, client religious commitment and belief may become evident and relevant at various stages in the treatment sequence. During the REBT assessment process, a two-step approach for assessing the salience of religiousness to treatment is recommended.

PRELIMINARY ASSESSMENT OF CLIENT
RELIGIOUSNESS

The effective REBT therapist is likely to routinely consider the salience of religiousness in the lives of clients. In fact, this may be the most important question to ask in the process of assessing client religiousness: "Is my client's religion salient and therefore possibly relevant to understanding and treating the presenting problem(s)?" Worthington (1988) emphasized that clients high in religious salience may be either pro- or antireligious. In contrast, a person low in religious salience is unlikely to even consider religion. Those high in religious salience are prone to evaluate their world on at least three important religious value dimensions, including the role of authority of human leaders, scripture or doctrine, and religious group norms. When a client for whom religious faith appears quite salient who is also pro-religious is living a life or engaging in behavior incongruent with religious beliefs, psychological distress and conflict may ensue (Shafranske & Malony, 1996). Further, beliefs that are highly idiosyncratic or at odds with the client's religious tradition may suggest potentially disturbed or disorganized thinking. Of course, it is important to avoid making assumptions about the client on the basis of religious affiliation alone. Compared to members of their faith or religious community, how committed are they?

After determining that the REBT clients' religious faith is a significant component of their self and/or community experience (what is referred to as *personally salient religion*), the clinician must then determine the extent to which religious factors are connected to the essential presenting problem(s). The question here might simply be: "To what extent is the client's religious involvement relevant to the current disturbance?" When religious beliefs and behaviors are clearly linked to the unique expression of pathology, this is described as *clinically salient religion.* A religious college student presenting in the midst of an existential "crisis of faith" following several courses that have challenged core religious assumptions, or the middle aged woman who remains in a physically destructive marriage secondary to a belief that God demands this of her, might both be considered clients for whom faith is clinically salient.

A final preliminary assessment question involves determination of the extent to which maximal treatment outcome is likely to hinge on overt work with client religious material. In other words, having determined that religion is salient and connected to this person's presenting disturbance, the REBT therapist then considers the extent to which achievement of treatment goals requires more concerted assessment of religiousness and, possibly, intentionally religious interventions. Can standard REBT protocols be implemented or does maximal therapeutic gain hinge on a focal assessment of the nature of religious belief and expression? If the latter is indicated, is the therapist competent to conduct such an assessment? When the REBT therapist determines that religion is clinically salient for the client and that treatment will be enhanced by more careful exploration of client religiousness, we recommend some assessment of the following dimensions of religiousness.

ADVANCED ASSESSMENT OF CLIENT RELIGIOUSNESS

Religious Orientation

Allport and Ross (1967) distinguished between the extrinsic and intrinsic religiousness:

> Extrinsic values are always instrumental and utilitarian. Persons with this orientation may find religion useful in a variety of ways—to provide security and solace, sociability and distraction, status and self-justification . . . Persons with this (intrinsic) orientation find their master motive in religion . . . having embraced a creed the individual endeavors to internalize it and follow it fully. (p. 434)

The Religious Orientation Scale (ROS; Allport & Ross, 1967) is a 20-item measure with intrinsic (9 items) and extrinsic (11 items) scales (Donahue, 1985). The ROS may assist the REBT therapist in determining those clients who tend to "use" their religion (extrinsic) versus those who tend to "live" their religion (intrinsic). In addition, high scores on both scales suggest an indiscriminately proreligious stance, and low scores on both scales suggest a nonreligious approach to life. At present, no instrument in the psychology of religion field has been better constructed or researched.

Spiritual Well-Being

Traditional measures of well-being or satisfaction with life have tended to focus exclusively on material and psychological well-being. For this reason, the spiritual well-being (SWB) scale was developed to incorporate the dimension of spiritual satisfaction or well-being (Bufford, Paloutzian, & Ellison, 1991). The SWB includes 20 items and two subscales. The first assesses religious well-being (tapping the vertical dimension of spirituality or the relationship between person and God). The second is titled existential well-being and evaluates the horizontal dimension of well-being, including a sense of life purpose and life satisfaction. This measure has shown strong psychometric properties and may be especially useful in evaluating the extent to which clients view themselves as satisfied and adjusted in relation to God and the human religious community.

Degree of Conflict

The REBT therapist might additionally benefit from considering the extent to which religious people find themselves in conflict with the following: (a) Data-supported empirical reality; (b) their short- and long-term goals; (c) inner peace or a sense of well-being; (d) the environment, including family, friends, and the religious community; and (e) a healthful process of self-integration (Grau, 1977). In other words, if the client's religiousness results in substantial conflict in these important dimensions, there may be valid reason to pragmatically reconsider or challenge obvious incongruence among specific religious beliefs and behaviors.

Shallowness and Inflexibility

To what extent is the client's religiousness based on dogmatic adherence to a limited or narrowly defined set of doctrines or religious precepts? To the extent that the client appears inflexible cognitively and dogmatic in black and white commitments to acceptable thought and behavior, religiousness may be more highly correlated with dysfunction and disturbance. Although Rokeach (1960) and others attempted to assess dogmatism, there is no known clinical assessment device for this purpose. Clients presenting with very fixed and inflexible belief systems might be described as closed-minded (Rokeach, 1960). The degree to which they are closed or foreclosed and rigid in rejection of alternative perspectives will likely correlate positively with other characteristics, such as high distinction between beliefs and disbeliefs, stark rejection of all disbeliefs, a threatening view of the world, an absolute and authoritarian view of authority, a role within the religious community defined in terms of submission to obedience, a set of criteria for acceptance or rejection of others defined in terms of extent of agreement versus disagreement with sectarian authorities (Meissner, 1996). Again, from a clinical perspective, the concern for assessment is the presentation of broadness versus narrowness in perspective and rigidity versus flexibility in belief style. Although certain religious communities and belief systems may also be inherently closed or rigid, this does not mean that mere membership in such a community is confirmation of healthy or less healthy religiousness. We have each seen rather healthy and cognitively open and flexible men and women who are adherents to very dogmatic and personally stifling religious communities. The REBT model requires a focus on the pragmatics and outcomes of religious beliefs for individual clients, regardless of their specific beliefs or affiliations.

Potential Markers of Pathology in Religious Behavior

Skilled REBT therapists recognize that religion is multidimensional and the range of ways to "be" religious is nearly infinite (Hood, Spilka, Hunsberger, & Gorsuch, 1996). Attempts to link specific kinds of religious belief or practice with psychopathology are quite dangerous for the clinician and certainly for the client. The REBT therapist is careful to work respectfully with the client's religiousness as it is presented. However, the experienced therapist will also recognize certain expressions of religiousness that at times suggest underlying disturbance. Although none of these potential markers of pathology always indicate client disturbance, the clinician would be well served to pay attention to them and engage in more careful assessment of these particular expressions when they are observed or reported by a client. The following list of potential markers of problem religiousness is drawn from the work of Hood et al. (1996), Lovinger (1984, 1996), and Pruyser (1971; 1977):

1. *Self-Oriented Display*: Do the clients go out of their way to exhibit or overtly demonstrate their religious fidelity and fervor? It is possible that such a focus on public demonstration is somewhat narcissistic in nature or perhaps primarily anxiety driven or rooted in a deep sense of competitiveness with the therapist or others in the client's life?

2. *Religion as Reward*: Does the client view religion as a constant aid in navigating the most ordinary events of life? Does this seem relatively adaptive for the client, or is it reflective of substantial interpersonal neediness and/or emptiness?

3. *Scrupulosity*: When the client presents with an intense fear of committing sin or other error, this can be reflective of an obsessive-compulsive adjustment or another anxiety state. If the client is obsessed with sin avoidance, is the avoidance behavior leading to social and occupational consequences and are their related beliefs (e.g., an angry and wrathful God or sin as an indicator of utter personal worthlessness) that might be idiosyncratic or not supported by the scripture and doctrine of their faith community?

4. *Relinquishing Responsibility*: Do clients appear to "use" their faith in an antisocial manner to avoid or reject appropriate responsibility? This, of course, is the old "The Devil made me do it" use of religion in a self-serving manner.

5. *Ecstatic Frenzy*: Do clients have episodes of intense, unregulated affective/spiritual expression that might be an indicator of psychotic decompensation? Is such behavior congruent and normative within the client's religious community? It is important to understand the social and occupational consequences of such expressions.

6. *Persistent Church Shopping*: When a client has made numerous changes in church affiliation and appears unable to find a satisfying or acceptable religious community, the clinician might consider the possibility of a tendency toward interpersonal conflict, vulnerability to rejection, impulsivity, and/or phobic avoidance.

7. *Passive-Aggression in Religious Practice*: Has the client been the recipient of or perpetrator of behavior that has been clearly harmful yet cloaked in religious language and context? For example, a client may have been expelled or ostracized from a religious community secondary to a life event (e.g., divorce) or persistent weakness (e.g., substance abuse), with resulting guilt and shame about perceived religious or spiritual inadequacy.

8. *The Bible as a Moment-to-Moment Guide to Truth*: At times, a client may relinquish responsibility as a dependent (vs. antisocial) maneuver. In this case, clients may surrender ordinary or healthy self-direction and attempt to use scripture or concrete behavioral prescriptions and prohibitions from their religious community to navigate the complex demands of various life situations. Again, the concern here would be abandonment of a reasonable level of responsibility, freedom, and self-direction.

9. *Possession*: In our experience, very few clients present with concern about being possessed by the devil, a demon, or another evil force. Syndromes that may mimic demon possession as commonly portrayed in

popular literature include neurological disorders, psychotic processes, dissociative states, and endocrine dysfunction, to name a few. The clinician should evaluate the extent to which belief in demon possession is compatible with the client's faith community and cultural background.

10. *Sudden Conversion*: Literature from the psychology of religion suggests that sudden forms of conversion are associated with higher levels of anxiety and poorer chronic adjustment. Such sudden conversions tend to be fleeting and not sustained and may be reflective of a client's neediness and vulnerability to suggestion and the promise of relief for chronic discomfort.

11. *Glossolalia*: When a client speaks in "tongues" or a religion-specific language that is believed to reflect the direct leading of the Holy Spirit or God, the clinician should again be alert to the extent to which such behavior is accepted or normative from within the client's religious community. For example, Pentecostal, revivalist, and charismatic groups are considerably more likely to endorse glossolalia as a desired form of religious expression.

12. *Mystical Experience*: Does the client report mystical spiritual encounters? If so, it is important to evaluate the extent to which these are situation and community congruent. Some religious communities expect members both to have and report such experiences to the group. If this is not the case, then the clinician might again have obvious concerns about delusional or other psychotic events. Extreme emotional reactions and disturbing hallucinatory behaviors are atypical of mystical experiences.

REBT ASSESSMENT OF RELIGIOUS BELIEFS

"Arrogant" Versus "Collaborative" Assessment

Raymond DiGiuseppe, director of professional education at the Albert Ellis Institute, cautioned REBT therapists to avoid what he described as a "narcissistic epistemology" in the process of assessing client beliefs. In essence, narcissistic epistemology, or an arrogant (Miller, 1988) approach to assessment involves assuming that we understand clients and their religiousness without first carefully testing hypotheses related to our conceptualization of the clients. Here the therapist implicitly states, "What I assume about the client and his or her religion must be true." When REBT therapists adopt such an arrogant approach, they may prescribe a set of beliefs that are defined as "healthy," "rational," or otherwise desirable in stark contrast to proscribed beliefs that are (on the basis of no convincing evidence) deemed "unhealthy," "stupid," or generally pathology inducing. Not only is such an arrogant approach counter to good clinical work and basic professional guidelines, it may also serve to alienate many, if not most, religious clients.

In contrast, an intentionally collaborative approach to understanding client religiousness and the manner in which religion is experienced, understood and expressed in the life of the individual client is recommended. Several authors recommend such an approach in the conduct of psychotherapy (Lovinger, 1984; Richards & Potts, 1995; Rowan, 1996) and in cognitive-behavioral psychotherapy, in particular (DiGiuseppe, 1991; McMinn & Lebold, 1989; Miller, 1988). The REBT therapist will be well served to develop both an understanding of and tolerance of client religious views. Miller (1988) noted that a collaborative approach "respects the integrity of the individual's belief system, and begins with exploration rather than renovation" (p. 45). A truly collaborative approach to assessment involves understanding individuals from within the frame of reference of their own religious experience as well as the specific church affiliation or denomination (Lovinger, 1984). We concur with Richards and Potts (1995) that effective assessment and intervention from within the client's religious worldview requires effective rapport building, explicit permission from the client to explore religious issues, and a collaborative attempt to understand the client's unique religious beliefs and doctrinal commitments.

Are Some Religious Beliefs Irrational?

For Freud, religious beliefs were regarded as clearly delusional. This, of course was because no evidence existed to confirm or disconfirm them. Similarly, Ellis (1971) once encouraged disputation of client beliefs with religious content on the basis that they were irrational and unverifiable. Of course, the fact that a specific belief is unverifiable in terms of current data collection procedures does not necessarily make it delusional. As Meissner (1996) noted, "The problem in evaluating religious belief systems is that not only is there no convincing evidence for them, but there is also no convincing evidence contradictory to them" (p. 249). Attempts to evaluate specific religious beliefs as pathologic or healthy is a very dangerous and ethically troublesome endeavor (W. B. Johnson & Nielsen, 1998). Regardless of the clinician's experience with religion, evaluating the extent to which specific religious beliefs are pathologic will inevitably rely on subjective criteria. It seems that nearly any sort of human belief, religious or not, may become a vehicle for the expression of disturbance and attempts to assess the truth or validity of specific beliefs will always be less helpful than attempts to understand the client's style or manner of belief and the impact of this style on social, relational, and occupational functioning.

In a similar vein, Meissner (1996) discussed the importance of differentiating assessment of pathology from assessment of "truth value" in clinical evaluations of client religious beliefs. In essence, the truth value question asks whether the assertions of the belief system are true. In work with religious clients, such questions are not only ethically inappropriate, but largely irrelevant to the work of good REBT. Instead, concurring with Meissner, the clinician should be focused on the question of pathology related to belief. To this end, clinicians should ask "Does the religious belief system as held by this individual client and expressed via his or her unique cognitive and personality structure, result in substantial disturbance?" As an example, consider the remarkably common religious belief in an afterlife. The New Testament (Matthew 25:31-46) makes clear reference to the widely accepted Christian belief in a final judgment day when humans will be assigned to either heaven or hell. But, questions surrounding the validity or truth value of this belief are not within the scope of good psychotherapy. Instead, the REBT therapist is highly concerned with the extent to which this specific belief is related or unrelated to the client's presenting problem(s). Are they disturbing themselves about their belief in a judgment day? Do they present with debilitating anxiety related to fear of failure and eternal damnation? Do they possess poor frustration tolerance regarding the many unknown details about the future and life after death? Do they believe that their human inadequacies make them deserving of eternal damnation (in spite of many scriptural messages to the contrary)? The question ultimately then is "how does this client's belief in an afterlife relate (or not) to adaptiveness or disturbance and, perhaps more important, what about their *style* of belief contributes to this?

The heart of the A-B-C model of disturbance is the notion that the core of psychological disturbance is the tendency of humans to make devout *absolutistic evaluations* of the perceived events in their lives. These evaluative ratings are nearly always demanding in nature and the demands are typically stated as dogmatic Musts, Shoulds, Ought To's, and Have To's. Because these dogmatic demands are rarely ever achieved to the satisfaction of the person making them, additional forms of disturbed thinking emerge, including global ratings of self and others, awfulizing, low frustration tolerance, and dichotomous or black and white thinking. When working with religious clients, the REBT therapist is interested in quickly discerning the religious client's primary irrational and absolutistic evaluations and demands.

In assessing religious clients, it is important to recognize that religious and nonreligious beliefs in themselves do not necessarily help people to become "healthy" or "unhealthy." There are millions of men and women with devout and orthodox religious beliefs who are simultaneously well adjusted psychologically. Instead, their emotional health is largely affected by the specific form of their beliefs (including the form of their religious beliefs) (Ellis, 2000a). In essence, it is largely dogmatism that leads to irrational thinking and emotional disturbance. Typically, the elegant therapeutic solution will be for clients to become more flexible and less dogmatic in their way of believing about themselves, others, and the world. Ellis (1994) noted, "More than particular religious beliefs, it is absolute, dogmatic devotion to beliefs which helps to create emotional disturbance" (p. 323).

There are two essential assessment tasks here. First, the REBT therapist considers the extent to which a client's religious beliefs are rigidly or dogmatically adhered to. Important questions include: "To what extent is the client cognitively closed and rigid?" "Is this rigidity reflective of the client's way of believing in general?" "To what extent does the client present with a philosophy of rigidly demanding with respect to their faith versus a philosophy of desiring?" The therapist is encouraged when clients are able to strongly *prefer* that they think and behave in a manner consistent with their faith without demanding that they superhumanly do so at all times. Similarly, a healthy philosophy of desiring versus demanding is evident when religious clients are able to believe in heaven and an afterlife and believe that they will go to heaven after death without also demanding this must occur in precisely the manner they believe. Religiously healthy people do not insist their own view of life after death be absolutely accurate, or that no one should dare to challenge this belief or hold a different perspective on the afterlife.

The second assessment task involves some evaluation of the content of the client's idiosyncratic religious belief(s). Of course this is a more challenging and potentially problematic endeavor. Nonetheless, we believe that even those REBT therapists with little personal religious background, or comparatively little formal training in treatment of religious clients, can perform ethically and with basic competence in this regard. In considering the content of the client's religious belief, therapists are not interested in affirming or disputing the truth value of the belief, but in considering the extent to which the clients' religious beliefs (and only those that appear directly related to clear emotional or behavioral disturbance) are congruent with other aspects of their identified religion. In other words, the question may become, "To what extent is the disturbing quality of the client's religious belief related to an incomplete or clearly idiosyncratic interpretation of scripture or doctrine?"

DiGiuseppe, et al. (1990) noted that "people do not become disturbed because of their belief in religion: rather, their disturbance is related to their tendency to selectively abstract certain elements of their religion to the exclusion of attending to others" (p. 358). In other words, some religious clients will present for assessment with a clear pattern of emotional disturbance linked to incomplete and distorted religious belief. Often, in the assessment process, the therapist will notice that the primary disturbing belief appears quite incongruent with other components of the person's larger religious affiliation. For example, a male client may present with profound depression (C), which the therapist quickly links to an episodic activating event, masturbation (A). The belief (B) that appears most linked to the client's depression is that masturbation is a sin punishable by eternity in hell. Although it would be quite inappropriate for the REBT therapist to challenge this client's global religious commitment or his desire to believe and behave in manner consistent with his religious belief in sin, it would be quite appropriate to consider whether this client is engaged in selective abstraction. First, if the client is from a Judeo-Christian faith tradition, then he may be entirely overlooking the fact that masturbation is merely one of an infinite number of sins in which human beings can engage. Why has this one become such a depression inducing activating event? What about grace and forgiveness? If Christian, is he overlooking the fact that Jesus has already died to forgive his sin of masturbation? Adam and Eve made it only a few days in the garden of Eden before sinning, so why must he be perfect and never masturbate? There also appears to be a great deal of disagreement among biblical scholars about whether masturbation is a sin. Certain Old Testament Scriptures that were thought to comment on masturbation are more probably referring to disobedience to God.

The point of this example is to highlight the fact that careful REBT assessment focuses on both the rigidity/flexibility in religious beliefs and on the extent to which the beliefs themselves appear incomplete, selectively abstracted, or highly idiosyncratic and incongruent with the larger doctrine of the client's articulated religious group. So, in the case at hand (a bit of REBT humor), the client's actual irrational belief may go something like "Because I have masturbated, I will absolutely suffer in hell for eternity. I am also utterly worthless as a result of this sin, for masturbation is one of the worst sins of all and cannot be forgiven. Also, because I cannot seem to stop masturbating, it means I am irreverent and intentionally disobedient and God must be very angry with me which is AWFUL . . ." The REBT therapist may then carefully begin disputing those qualities and components of the client's belief system that appear selectively abstracted, incongruent, or based on a philosophy of self-rating and demandingness. Of course, the preeminent challenge is to simultaneously convey respect for the client's faith and even to bolster aspects of the client's faith to his advantage when possible.

The following chapters discuss the REBT treatment sequence (Dryden, DiGiuseppe, & Neenan, 2000), including those components most important in the assessment phase with religious clients. Following a careful assessment, which considers client religiousness, the REBT therapist commences the disputational process–arguably the heart of REBT intervention. Subsequent chapters explore the range of REBT interventions in light of the problems and beliefs most frequently presented by religious clients.

4

*Rational Emotive Case
Conceptualization
and Session Planning:
An Overview*

Once the REBT therapist has completed an initial intake assessment, collected preliminary client data, and carefully considered the relevance of religious belief and practice to the primary complaint or target problem, the focus of treatment turns to assessing and evaluating focal client rational and irrational beliefs. This chapter highlights the rational emotive approach to case conceptualization and outlines a strategy for session planning with religious clients.

ASSESSING AND CHANGING ABSOLUTISTIC EVALUATIVE BELIEFS

The fundamental difference between rational emotive behavior therapy and other models of psychotherapy is REBT's focus on *evaluative beliefs* (Ellis, 1994b; Walen et al., 1992). Rational emotive theory holds that evaluative beliefs are most closely associated with our emotions, supplying the motive force behind thinking and emoting about ourselves and others, about our world, and about what happens in our world. Most purposive human thought, behavior, and emotion flows from evaluative beliefs, some of which are conscious, many unconscious.

Evaluative beliefs are our core cognitions about what we do and do not want; what we like and dislike; what we believe, whether good or bad; and what we prefer or reject. Evaluative beliefs are the Bs of interest in REBT's A-B-C model. Rational emotive theory holds that preferential evaluative beliefs lead to helpful, healthy emotions, whereas absolutistic and rigid evaluative beliefs lead to self-defeating emotions. Absolutistic evaluative beliefs are, therefore, the prime targets for change in REBT.

Preferences

Preferences are relativistic and therefore realistic evaluations. They are relativistic in that they are maintained or proposed relative to one's realistic sphere of influence. It is preferential, relativistic, and realistic to say that, "I like semi-sweet chocolate more than milk chocolate." However, to believe that, "semi-sweet chocolate is always better for everyone than milk chocolate" is unreasonably, absolutistically evaluative, because it elevates a matter of preference, relative to and referable only to one's own likes and dislikes, to an absolute, universal level.

Preferential beliefs yield helpful, although not necessarily always pleasant, emotional reactions. For example, suppose that a client is lamenting the loss of his intimate relationship. The client informs you that whereas his former girlfriend was highly devoted to athletics, he viewed exercise as a necessary evil. She liked to spend her free time mountain biking, running, lifting weights, playing softball, racquet ball, or basketball, watching sports at the arena or on television, and so on. He preferred to read, attend plays, opera, and the ballet, to play chess, and sometimes to watch movies on television. She ended the relationship because of conflict about how they would spend their time together.

If you ask, "What are you telling yourself about this relationship?" He could believe something like this, "I do so wish that our interests had been a better match!" or, "I do so wish that she had been more patient with my interests!" So far these are preferential evaluative beliefs that would fit in the A-B-C model, as depicted in Fig. 4.1.

Human experience cannot be free of discomfort or upset. When we do not get what we want, especially what we strongly or deeply want, we will experience strong emotions: quite sad or frustrated about the loss of a lover or about the prospect of giving up favored activities (chess and opera) for less favored activities (racquet ball and softball). This is quite reasonable and, potentially, helpful.

FIG. 4.1 The A-B-C model.

Activating event or Adversity		Belief		Consequent emotion
Lost love	+	"I do *so* wish our interests had matched up better!"	→	sadness
		or		
Lost love	+	"I do *so* wish that she had been more patient with my interests!"	→	frustration

Helpful Versus Self-Defeating Upset

Sadness at finding that a person's likes or habits do not match the likes or habits of a desired partner could motivate that individual to attempt to expand likes and change habits to better match a lover's likes and habits. Alternatively, feeling frustrated about a failed relationship, the individual might resolve to search for partners who enjoy similar hobbies.

However, when anger, shame, discouragement, desperation, or depression result from a similar loss, they are likely to create trouble. Anger may lead to poorly thought out, impulsive outbursts. Shame would probably motivate an individual to hide or avoid others. Discouragement usually demotivates and retards behavior. Desperation leads to frantic, unplanned activity. Depression can yield a toxic amalgam of the worst of all these self-defeating emotions and behaviors. Rational emotive theory proposes that these self-defeating emotions naively arise because of absolutistic evaluative beliefs.

THE PSYCHODYNAMICS OF ABSOLUTISTIC EVALUATIONS

Humans are, of course, capable of much thought in a matter of moments, including many complex, sometimes contradictory, evaluative beliefs. Furthermore, cognitions are dynamically interactive; they play off and modify one another. The practice of REBT requires discerning among evaluative beliefs as they become evident during the session. Rational emotive theory can rightly be called a psychodynamic therapy because it focuses on the dynamics of cognitive activity. Evaluative beliefs are the most dynamic of psychic contents. REBT is, however, psychodynamic with a small "P." It deemphasizes most of the developmental constructs and associated rules for therapy generated and *venerated* in psychoanalysis, self-psychology, object relations theory, and similar psychodynamic therapies. In REBT, the fundamental dynamic is the contrast between wants and demands. REBT's most important goal is helping clients get more of what they want, and less of what they do not want, usually by dropping their demands.

The dynamics of evaluative beliefs hypothesize that individuals are prone to create their self defeating emotions by going beyond their nice, moderate, relative, preferential evaluations (i.e., our wishes and wants) to absolutistic evaluations (i.e., catastrophizing, demanding, frustration intolerance, and human rating). People often reasonably dislike the circumstances in which they find themselves; they dislike discomfort, inconvenience, and their own foibles. But often, they also elevate these preferences to absolute levels by evaluating situations and themselves as utterly, absolutely (and, *therefore*, irrationally) *un*acceptable and "horrible."

The client whose girlfriend drops him because of sports might think any or all of the preferential *and* absolute beliefs shown in Fig. 4.2. The last four statements in Fig. 4.2 express evaluations that go beyond strong preference to absolutistic evaluation: catastrophizing, demanding, frustration intolerance, and human or self-rating, respectively.

When clients catastrophize an event's unpleasantness, in this case the potential future discomfort of a new relationship, they elevate it from undesirable to the absolute of unbearable, yielding anxiety or panic. Demanding evaluates an unwanted situation—the former girlfriend's preferences for recreation—from inconvenient to utterly unacceptable and "terrible." This creates a should that leads to anger.

Frustration intolerance takes an individual's reasonable evaluative belief that exerting extra physical effort might be unpleasant and elevates that evaluation to an absolute: "It would be *too* unpleasant!" The absoluteness of too yields discouragement. Tasks actually can be "too" difficult: For example, if they are physically impossible, as in lifting thousands of

FIG. 4.2   The consequences of preferential versus absolutistic beliefs.

Activating event or Adversity	+	Belief	→	Consequent emotion
One or more moderate, personal, relativistic, *preferential* evaluative beliefs:				
Lost love	+	"I do *so* wish our interests had matched up better!"	→	sadness
		or		
Lost love	+	"I do *so* wish that she had been more patient with my interests!"	→	frustration
Plus one or more *absolutistic* evaluative belief:				
Lost Love	+	I can't *stand* another rejection.	→	anxiety
Lost Love	+	She *should* have given in more.	→	anger
Lost Love	+	Sports are just *too* hard.	→	discouragement
Lost Love	+	I am such a *clumsy nerd.*	→	shame

pounds with unaided physical strength or throwing oneself from a tall building. Notice, however, that humans are still willing to try such things! During frustration intolerance, however, "too hard" means unacceptably hard because something is harder than is wanted and that it absolutely should not be that hard.

Human rating elevates reasonable evaluations of personal characteristics to unreasonable, absolute levels. It is reasonable to dislike one's own inability to master a task or to dislike hassles that arise because of one's inability. But, human rating evaluates the self as a wholly different kind of person, a clumsy nerd, almost a different, inferior species. An evaluation of a trait is exaggerated and overgeneralized until it becomes an evaluative label applied to the whole, essential person. Evaluating the self as inferior creates shame or depression. Evaluating others as inferior leads to anger or derision.

THE PROCESS OF REBT

Organizing the REBT Session

Irrational evaluative beliefs are usually evident early in therapy in clients' descriptions of their presenting problems from the beginning of the first psychotherapy session onward. Evaluative beliefs that accompany upsetness manifest themselves in how individuals explain themselves, in how they justify or excuse their actions, and in how they explicate their problems. Evaluative beliefs will become evident after clients answer just a few questions: Why are they seeking therapy? What sort of problem would they like to deal with in the current session? How is their situation? How are they? As soon as evaluative beliefs become evident—in the first session and in each session thereafter—intervention can begin.

The rational emotive goal of helping the client understand and change irrational, evaluative beliefs suggests a simple pattern, repeatable in each session with almost every client:

1. Search for the irrational evaluative beliefs related to this session's concerns.
2. Help the client see and understand the nature and effects of evaluative beliefs.
3. Help the client move from irrational, absolutistic, evaluative beliefs toward preferential, evaluative beliefs.

Furthermore, because evaluative beliefs are clients' abstractions about themselves and their lives, changing evaluative beliefs about a particular sessions' problems contributes to generalized change. Self-defeating emotions usually arise from one or more of the same four irrational beliefs, whatever the problems–even for quite different problems. As irrational evaluative beliefs are replaced with rational beliefs on a session by session basis, clients have the opportunity to apply new, preferential, rational beliefs to a broadening range of problems and situations, yielding new, helpful, generalizing philosophies for living, and deep emotional change.

Dryden et al., (2000) recommended a specific sequence of interventions in REBT sessions that can maximize opportunity to help clients change (see Table 4.1) evaluative beliefs.

Steps 1 through 5 help client and therapist organize the session around the client's self-defeating emotions and behaviors. Steps 6 through 8 help therapist and client identify the link between evaluative belief and dis-

TABLE 4.1.

Suggested Sequence for a Rational Emotive Behavior Therapy Session

1. Ask the client for a problem.
2. Define and agree on a target problem for the session.
3. Assess C, the Consequent emotion. Distinguish between helpful and self-defeating emotional distress.
4. Assess A, the Activating event relevant to this problem.
5. Identify and assess secondary emotional problems–symptom stress.
6. Teach or help the client understand the relationship between B, Belief, and C, the Consequent emotion–the B-C connection.
7. Assess Beliefs, especially irrational, evaluative Beliefs—IBs.
8. Teach the client the connection between IBs and self-defeating Consequent emotions—the IB-C connection.
9. Dispute the irrational Beliefs—IBs.
10. Deepen conviction in rational alternatives to IBs—rational Beliefs or RBs.
11. Help the client put RBs into practice—develop homework assignments.
12. Check previous homework assignments if the client was seen previously and homework was assigned.
13. Facilitate the client's working through or learning RBs in their daily life.

Note. Adapted from Dryden et al. (2000).

tress. Steps 9 through 13 focus on replacing absolutistic evaluations with relativistic preferences.

Goal Clarification. Steps 1 and 2 of the REBT treatment sequence (Dryden et al., 2000) require the therapist to rapidly and collaboratively establish a target problem to address in therapy. These steps are particularly helpful for focusing client thinking about the session and, subsequently, focusing the session. Simple questions like, "What do you want to work on?" have a remarkably clarifying effect during confusingly emotional, distressed sessions. Such questions elevate the clients' role in therapy by highlighting their responsibility for change and by emphasizing that goals for the session are primarily those of the client, not the therapist. The therapist is really helping clients negotiate with themselves about goals for the session, but also adding the benefit of therapeutic experience about how problems of different sorts change—easily or with difficulty—and preparing to accommodate the therapy to the clients' goals.

It is possible that the religious client's identified problem will be religious in nature (e.g., "I'm scared to death that what I've done is beyond God's forgiveness," or "I'm not sure I believe in God any more and no one seems to understand"). More often, however, the stated problem itself will not offer many clues regarding the client's personal religious framework or whether that framework is relevant to treatment. Therefore, a solid initial assessment considering religiousness to be among several potentially relevant client variables is highly recommended.

What Dinah Wanted.   During her first group, Dinah reported that in first grade a janitor had undressed and fondled her. Several other group members expressed shock and anger, another wondered how she could stand it. I (SLN) asked, "What would you like to work on in group today?" She responded that she had recently told her boyfriend about the incident and he had insisted she come to the counseling center. Group was her quickest option for being seen for therapy. I again asked what she wanted to work on. This time she replied that she did not know.

Did she feel upset? She said no. Her boyfriend seemed upset. What did she feel? She was concerned about her boyfriend's reaction. I suggested that perhaps her boyfriend should come to group. What was she telling herself about the incident? She really only thought about it when she heard a news story about sexual abuse, which was not often; she usually thought something like, "Hey, that happened to me, too." Because of her boyfriend's upset, Dinah wondered if she should feel upset. A spirited discussion ensued during which group members expressed many "shoulds" and "awfuls" about child molestation, including discussion of emotional "scars."

Dinah did not express any of these demands and did not catastrophize, however. Dinah stated that the janitor did something wrong and could have hurt her physically. She was grateful she hadn't been hurt. She believed the incident had not affected her sexuality. She did not think about it when she felt aroused, as she often did with her current boyfriend. Based on recent experience, she was confident she could "go all the way with him and enjoy it." She didn't believe she was "scarred."

In the following group session, Dinah announced that she had given considerable thought to the incident. She and her boyfriend had discussed it at length. She did not feel upset and she probably was not going to come back to group. She thought she felt a bit afraid for the safety of her future children, but that was not really an issue now. She did not believe she should feel upset and had told her boyfriend that he could go into counseling if he felt upset, in which case she might come to group again to bring him back. She did not bring him back to group—not this group.

By focusing on what Dinah wanted, I prevented the group from diverting her through their presumptions about what she needed. Some group members and some of my colleagues believed that the situation was handled badly, averring that Dinah should have been encouraged to remain in counseling.

Sensitive collaboration with the client around target problems and a plan for the session often provide therapists with their first overt opportunity to understand, assess, and accommodate client religious beliefs.

Emotional Change

In the third step of the REBT treatment sequence (Dryden et al., 2000), the therapist commences a careful assessment of the client's primary consequence or disturbance (C). This is generally an unhealthy negative emotion such as anger, anxiety, or depression. It is unlikely that the religious client will present emotional or behavioral consequences that are unusual compared to those of nonreligious clients. However, we have found that religious clients often develop secondary emotional disturbances about their primary disturbance.

Step 3, identifying the C, clarifies for the client reasonable expectations and goals for the session and for therapy generally. It is usually unlikely that therapists can intervene to change clients' actual life experiences, their A's. One exception is that therapists may actually intervene in how couples or families communicate; but responsibility for changing their communication still rests with clients. It is especially important, both for clients and therapists, to distinguish between the reasonable goal of improving clients' efficiency in practical problem solving and the unrealistic goal of creating a Utopia devoid of problems or dysphoria for clients. Rational emotive theory holds that the goal of REBT is helping clients intervene in their own lives more efficiently by removing their self-hindrances. This process is best approached with patience, while acknowledging the limitations of therapy to remove unfortunate adversities (A's) in the clients' lives and to make them totally unupsetable.

Even if REBT could remove from clients' emotional repertoire feelings of sadness, frustration, annoyance, concern, or other helpful, but unpleasant, emotions, this would probably interfere with subsequently accomplishing important goals and responding appropriately to life's reversals. Although REBT, as well as cognitive behavior therapy (CBT), have a proven track record for reducing self-defeating distress and problems, all successful techniques of therapy have limits that may slow or prevent client recovery.

Finding the Most Current A

Step 4, specifying the A, and Step 5, checking for secondary distress, help delineate the cues most closely associated with client distress and help show the therapist and client where to begin the intervention. An activating event may be an observable event or an inference or interpretation about reality. Once again, it is infrequent, in our experience, for a client to present with a uniquely religiously connected A (e.g., "I get extremely nervous each time I enter the confessional," or "Each time God fails to answer my prayer for a husband, I get more depressed"). However, religion-focused A's may be more common in some communities.

Step 5 in the REBT treatment sequence is exploration of the clients' reaction to his or her primary disturbance. The speed with which thoughts, emotions, and behavior interact often creates a kind of experiential fog that is difficult to navigate. Adverse activating events, A's, and emotional Consequences, C's, are usually the easiest elements in this fog of experience for clients to understand. Whereas activating events are often easy to appreciate, strong emotions are often more salient for clients than activating events. Clients frequently feel ashamed or embarrassed about their emotional reactions, especially if they cannot control outward manifestations of emotion such as weeping, trembling, blushing, or hyperventilating. Such secondary distress can be quite severe. If clients have strong, absolutistic beliefs about their emotions, secondary distress can become a kind of negatively synergistic maelstrom, an escalating avalanche of distress.

Beth's PTSD. Beth was a sophomore at Brigham Young University (BYU), the largest religiously affiliated university in the United States. Like most other students at BYU, she reported strong commitment to the tenets of the Church of Jesus Christ of Latter-day Saints, which owns and operates BYU. During the intake interview, Beth explained that the previous spring her mother had caught her former boyfriend, David, peeking at her window. David confessed that he had been doing this for several months. Beth was shocked and immediately broke off the relationship. It was now mid-November, about 7 months later.

Beth described a recent flashback experience during which she felt as if someone was peeking in at her dorm window. She had the experience after discovering that she had changed her clothes in her dorm room without pulling the blinds down. She reported that, since the incident, she was having vivid nightmares in which David was watching while she walked around in the nude.

When I (SLN) asked Beth what she was feeling, she said that she felt panicky. When I asked what she was telling herself about her flashback and nightmares, she said, "I'm a real basket case. I feel like I'm losing my mind!" Why? "I never saw David looking in my window. Only my mother saw that!" She realized that she had created an image to match what she thought his voyeurism looked like. It seemed likely that she could have been awfulizing about her symptoms. Awfulizing could create a sequence in which the initial activating event, the primary A of the flashback, led to anxiety, but then the anxiety became an additional A, another activating event that then led to a cascade of awfulizing about losing control, feeling more anxious, awfulizing about losing control, feeling more anxious, and so on. This, I hypothesized, was the cause of her panicky feelings. Beth was upset enough at that moment that she probably would have had difficulty focusing on the A-B-C model of emotion.

I suggested that Beth's flashback and nightmares were not very surprising because many people who have been through traumatic events have flashbacks and nightmares about the experience. I told her that soldiers, police, emergency personnel, accident victims, and, victims of sexual assault often report such symptoms. I told her that flashbacks and nightmares are part of what is called posttraumatic stress disorder (PTSD) and that it is common for women who have been the victims of voyeurism to experience such symptoms. Beth said, "Maybe I'm not nuts, then," and seemed to relax quite a bit.

Step 4 in the Dryden et al. (2000) sequence had not yet been accomplished. It was still not clear which Activating event (A) and which Consequent emotion (C) we would focus on during the remainder of the session. The entire session might have been given over to dealing with Beth's secondary distress about her PTSD symptoms.

In our experience, religious clients have a somewhat greater potential than nonreligious clients for developing such secondary emotional disturbances. For example, it is not uncommon for a religious client to feel intense shame about feeling angry at God, the church, or a devoutly religious parent. A religious client may also report depression about inability to overcome social anxiety in spite of exhortations in Scripture to be bold and trust in God.

Tom, whose difficulties were described in the first chapter, was having difficulty with secondary distress related to his unhealthily dogmatic religiosity. Remember that he was downing himself because of wavering commitment. What he called his wavering faith was probably indecisiveness arising because of generalized anxiety. Because of his anxious indecisiveness, he labeled himself a worthless hypocrite. Tom's calling himself worthless added the secondary disturbance of depression to his anxiety. Anxiety, indecisiveness, plus depression became a toxic mix that tended to worsen in a cyclical manner.

Showing Clients the Psychodynamics of Their Upset

REBT's unique goal is to help clients understand the interrelation between their beliefs and distress, especially the effects of their irrational beliefs (IBs), and then show them how to change their IBs. The next steps suggested by Dryden et al., (2000) are fundamental to helping clients and therapists see how clients are defeating themselves. The goal of step 6 is assessing the client's capacity to understand this fundamental feature of REBT, the relationship between beliefs and consequent emotions. Assessment of client beliefs is also easier if the client understands what the therapist is looking for. The kinds of questions, explanations, and confrontations that arise during REBT are better tolerated if the client understands how beliefs cause distress.

At Step 7, client and therapist explore what and how the client believes. Clients have both rational and irrational beliefs (RBs and IBs) about their world, although they are unlikely to differentiate IBs from RBs with much clarity. Identifying irrational beliefs is often relatively easy for the REBTer, because IBs so often appear as sweeping, negative generalizations that clients make about themselves or others or as freely uttered *musts, shoulds, ought tos, have tos, awfuls, terribles,* and so forth. When clients come to see that IBs are quite different from RBs, Step 8 can be a fairly straightforward reprise of Step 6. When clients can see the effects of beliefs, especially when they can see the consequences of having irrational beliefs compared with the benefits of having rational beliefs about their problems, the benefits of changing irrational to rational beliefs will often seem an obvious next step.

Of course, clients differ in their ability to think about their experience. Some clients may have difficulty getting through the first few steps of the sequence. Even though Beth was experiencing strong secondary distress, she did exceptionally well during her first session. After addressing her secondary distress, we went back to Step 2, attempting again to define a target problem for the session. We were then quickly able to move on through all the steps suggested by Dryden et al. (2000):

SLN: Would you like to work on your panic?

Beth: I get upset whenever I think about David. Not as upset as when I saw the blinds up [while changing], but it's been months now and I still cry and cry; and I can't sleep very well. I want to get over this.

SLN: Sure. Tell me more about your upset.

Beth: Well, I told you about how upset I got when I saw that I changed my clothes in front of the window. But other times I just think about David and cry.

SLN: So what are you feeling when you're crying?

Beth: I don't know. Sad? Really, really sad? I just can't get over it.

We were back at Step 3, trying to separate out the emotions that would be our targets for the remainder of the session. Clients sometimes have impoverished or idiosyncratic emotional vocabularies. Beth was having trouble naming or clearly describing her distressing emotions. Rational emotive theory holds that emotions are not really separable from beliefs. Beliefs and emotions are intrinsically associated. The nature, quality, or identity of an emotion is often best understood by considering the whole of the experience, the ideas, feelings, and behaviors present for the client when they are distressed. Discovering beliefs associated with an emotional experience often identifies the emotion:

SLN: What have you been telling yourself about David and his voyeurism?

Beth: He seemed like such a nice boy! Why did he have to go and goof it all up? I miss him and I just wish he could have been . . . I wish he hadn't been so stupid!

SLN: Sure. If you lose someone you really liked, someone you wanted to be with, you'll feel sadness and grief. That makes sense. Don't we want people to feel sadness or grief when they lose someone they love? It also sounds like you feel angry or irritated at David.

Beth: A little angry, I guess. I almost wish Mom hadn't caught him. What made him do such a stupid thing?

SLN: Do you have an answer for your questions?

Beth: What?

SLN: Can you answer those questions? Why did he have to go and goof it up? What made him think of peeking at your window?

Beth: I don't know! [She seemed quite upset now.]

SLN: That really seems to upset you. Are you afraid of something here?

Beth: Well, maybe I did something.

SLN: Oh, you mean you did something to get him to look at you?

Beth: If I hadn't left the blinds up he wouldn't have been *able* to look!

SLN: No, I suppose not. And what are you telling yourself about leaving your blinds up? That you left them up on purpose?

Beth: Maybe I wanted him to look.

SLN: Did you?

Beth: I don't think so. I liked him, but I don't remember anything like that.

SLN: But it seems very important to you.

Beth: It is important whether I wanted him to look or not!

Beth was quite upset again. We still had not finished separating out Beth's emotions from one another, but she had given strong clues about the beliefs and emotions we could work on. She had voiced three qualitatively different beliefs which were probably associated with three different emotions. Her description of her secondary distress also provided clues about what she believed about her own emotions.

SLN: Look, you've done some very good work. You've described your reactions in a way that makes understanding them as straightforward as A-B-C. We've discovered some helpful reactions and some reactions that aren't so helpful: First, you called yourself a real basket case because you had that flashback and the nightmares. How did it make you feel to call yourself a basket case? How would it make you feel if someone else called you a basket case?

Beth: Not good.

SLN: Right. It's as simple as A-B-C: A, the Activating event was your reaction to seeing that the blind was up. Then B, you called yourself a basket case. And C, as a Consequence of calling yourself a basket case you felt lousy. Right?

Beth nodded. We had jumped directly to Step 8. It was easy to show her that name calling, which is a form of global human rating, was causing significant distress. Having seen the IB to C connection, we could also begin to investigate the connection between her rational beliefs and her helpful, but unpleasant, emotions.

SLN: Then we can see another A-B-C sequence: David did something that broke up your relationship. What he did and the end of your relationship are another A, another Activating event. Then you said you wish he hadn't done such a stupid thing to goof things up, because it was a nice relationship. So you B, believe you lost something good, something you really wanted. Because you lost something you really wanted, you feel quite sad. Feeling sad is C, a consequence of B, believing that you lost a nice relationship. So there we have the A-B-Cs of your sadness. If you B, believe you've lost something you really liked, the healthy emotion that would follow from that loss would be grief or sadness. Then we have another B: You believe that David did something stupid in sneaking around and peeking in on you at the window. It's both stupid and illegal. We have the same A, the breakup of your relationship, plus a different B, your belief that he did something foolish and unethical. The belief that he did something quite foolish, leads to C, the emotion of annoyance. You said you only felt a little bit angry.

Beth: Yeah, a bit.

SLN: So we have one activating event, one A, the breakup, and two different beliefs, two Bs, believing you lost something good and believing he acted stupid. The two different beliefs lead to two different emotions, sadness and annoyance. Both those emotions seem healthy to me, by the way. But you also said that you sometimes believe that you might have left the blinds up on purpose. Which upsets you the most, wishing that the relationship hadn't ended, believing that he did something stupid, or believing that you might have left the blinds up on purpose because you wanted him to watch you undress?

Beth: That I may have done it on purpose!

SLN: Because if you *had*?

Beth: I wouldn't be a very nice girl, would I?

SLN: This is *very* important. This is the most important set of A-B-Cs yet. You see you also believe that if you left your blinds up on purpose that would make you a bad person. Same A, same activating event, the break up, but a new B, belief, that all this may prove that you are a bad person. When people believe that something they have done makes them bad they usually feel anxious, depressed, ashamed, or some combination of all three. Is that what you're feeling?

Beth: Yeah, I think so. I feel really, really embarrassed around my parents since it happened. And I don't want anybody else to know. It was real hard for me to come in [to the counseling center] and talk to somebody.

SLN: Would you like to work on this feeling, how you feel when you think you might have left the blinds up on purpose?

Beth: I don't think I did, but I still feel upset. [She nodded.]

This was Step 3, although we had also accomplished Steps 6, 7, and 8. We had now differentiated shame from sadness and irritation. We had also decided on our target problem, so Step 2 was checked off for this session.

SLN: Right, because it seems like the embarrassment is making it hard for you to be around your parents. Did your parents suspect that you had done it on purpose?

Beth: I don't think so. They've been real nice to me. But I still feel real uncomfortable around them.

SLN: What are you telling yourself when you're around them.

Beth: I wonder what they're thinking about me.

SLN: See, we probably have the same belief causing the same kind of unhealthy emotion. If your *parents* think that you did something bad, then maybe you did. And if your parents think you're bad, then maybe you *are* bad.

Beth: It would be pretty bad if they thought I left the blinds up on purpose or if they thought we were having sex or something.

SLN: Yeah, *it* would be pretty bad–it *would* be a bad situation, but that wouldn't make *you* a bad person. You feel sad because you lost what you wanted. You feel irritated because your telling yourself that David did a stupid thing. But you feel embarrassed and ashamed because your telling yourself that maybe something about what David did or what you did or what your parents or other people might think about you would mean *you* are bad. Am I understanding what you believe about this?

Beth: I think so.

SLN: And telling yourself that you might be a bad person causes you to feel shame and embarrassment. That shame and embarrassment is really interfering with your life.

Beth: Yes.

So, we had a pretty clear understanding of Beth's beliefs. Beth was also probably coming to see the link between her global human rating and her most painful emotions. Steps 6, 7, and 8 seemed to have been accomplished, but this is really a guess or hypothesis about Beth's emotions. The best way for both therapist and client to check hypotheses about the client's irrational beliefs is to move on from A-B-C to *D*, Disputing the irrational beliefs.

Helping Clients Change Irrational Beliefs

Beth's invitation to work on her embarrassment set the stage for the intervention goal of changing her IBs through disputation. Steps 9 through 13 each focus on challenging and helping the client challenge what she believes:

SLN: It seems to me that the first thing we need to deal with is this notion that you could be a bad person. That's the belief, B in the

A-B-C sequence, that is causing the most trouble. As long as you believe that you're a bad person you're going to stay pretty upset. How can one rate or measure people?

Beth: By what they do and what they think.

SLN: And by what people think of them? In your case you're really worried about what your parents *might* be thinking about you.

Beth: Sure.

SLN: What if it's not really possible to rate people?

Beth: Isn't it?

SLN: Do you consider yourself to be religious? [Beth nodded.] What if the Lord doesn't rate people?

Beth: Doesn't he?

SLN: I bet you can finish this sentence, "Remember, the worth of souls is . . ."

Beth: ". . . great in the sight of God." [Doctrine and Covenants, 18: 10; Latter-day Saints believe the Doctrine and Covenants, or DC, to be Scripture revealed by God to Joseph Smith and other latter-day prophets.]

SLN: Do you believe that?

Beth: Yes.

SLN: About you? You're saying what to yourself about you? That the worth of *your* soul would be less because of something you might have done or because of something your parents might be thinking about you. Here [handing her the Scriptures], would you mind reading DC 18:10 & 11?

Beth: "Remember the worth of souls is great in the sight of God; for behold, the Lord your Redeemer suffered death in the flesh; wherefore he suffered the pain of all men, that all men might repent and come unto him."

SLN: What does he say about needing to repent? Which men need to repent?

Beth: *All* men.

SLN: Just *men*, or women, too?

Beth: No, women, too.

SLN: But what does he say about the worth of the souls of all these people who need to repent?

Beth: That it's great.

SLN: Just people who never sin, or people who sin?

Beth: No, people who sin, too.

SLN: Even *you*?

Beth: Yes, me, too.

SLN: So what could you begin to tell yourself about your worth?

Beth: That it's great in the sight of God.

SLN: Ah, but what if your parents *are* suspicious of what was going on between you and David. What if you *did* leave the blinds up on purpose? What if you *did* want David to look at you? You say you don't remember leaving the blinds up or wanting him to look at you, but what if you *did* want him to? Would your worth go down in the sight of God?

Beth: No.

SLN: Would it create hassles for you if your parents believed you left the blinds up on purpose? Might it not create problems if you changed your clothes with the blinds up every night?

Beth: Yes.

SLN: But would your worth go down?

Beth: Not according to what I just read.

SLN: I want to try a little experiment. Would you please read what I'm writing on this card, but read it in the way it's written. Do you mind? Read it as it's written, putting in emphasis where I did. [I wrote, "According to D & C 18:10, the worth of MY soul is GREAT in the sight of God even if I DID sin!" on the back of one of my business cards.]

Beth: According to D & C 18:10, the worth of MY soul is GREAT in the sight of God even if I DID sin!

SLN: How did that feel?

Beth: Pretty good.

We had accomplished Steps 9 and 10 in the sequence described by Dryden et al,. (2000). I believed that because Beth was a student at BYU she would both be familiar with and believe in her LDS scriptures. Her responses seemed to confirm my guess. She then discovered that she could feel better by strongly challenging her beliefs using Scripture as a foundation.

This was our first session, so there was no homework to check (Step 12). We did try to anticipate difficult times and work through how she might put this new, religiously derived, rational belief into practice, accomplishing Steps 11 and 13. We worked to deepen conviction in this new rational belief by discussing other sections of the scriptures that speak of the worth of sinners, including Luke chapter 15 in the New Testament. Luke 15 consists almost entirely of the parables of the Lost Sheep, the Lost Coin, and the Prodigal Son, all of which directly address the worth of sinners. The general strategy for the session was to challenge her global human rating. There was no good evidence that Beth had wanted to undress for David; no good evidence that she had left her blinds up a bit on purpose. It had not helped Beth to repeat this to herself, however. The crux of the matter was that even if she had done these things on purpose, which would have made trouble, it would not have made her trouble or proved her to be a bad person. I also tried to show Beth that her panic was perhaps linked to thinking that she would be a bad person if she lost her mind, because she called herself a basket case.

Beth left with the homework assignment to read the back of the business card several times a day and then read Luke chapter 15 every day (Step 11). She readily agreed to this. We finished the session with a plan to check the effects of these homework assignments and then discuss her nightmares and her relationship with her parents during our next session.

5

Disputation

Disputation, D in the A-B-C-D formula for change, is REBT's most unique intervention and usually the primary goal of each REBT session. Rational emotive disputation is a special form of cognitive restructuring consisting of challenging clients' absolutistic, irrational, evaluative beliefs, and replacing them with more moderate and rational evaluative beliefs. REBT is most successful when clients dispute their own irrational beliefs, especially when they can formulate their own rational alternative beliefs and rational philosophies for living.

DISPUTATION VERSUS OTHER
PSYCHOTHERAPEUTIC INTERVENTIONS

Rational emotive disputation is quite distinct from psychotherapies focusing primarily on support, reflection, and interpretation, because it focuses on active intervention designed to help clients alter their beliefs, as well as the dysfunctional thoughts, emotions, and behaviors associated with these beliefs. REBT introduced techniques for overtly modifying cognition to modern psychotherapy in 1955 (Ellis, 1958, 1975). Related forms of cognitive behavioral therapy followed REBT, such as cognitive therapy (Beck, 1976), cognitive behavior therapy (Mahoney, 1974), cognitive behavior modification (Meichenbaum,1977), and dialectical behavior therapy (Linehan, 1993). Many professionals have referred to these cognitive interventions as cognitive restructuring, sometimes with and sometimes without acknowledgment of REBT's pioneering formulations.

Disputation occurs through talk, to be sure, but it is more specific about its main goal, which is to change specific dysfunctional ideas. Rational emotive theory holds, however, that this kind of active disputing leads to deeper and broader change than comes with less focused talk therapy. Rational emotive disputation is deep and intensive because it deals with clients' core irrational beliefs about themselves and their world. It also sees these beliefs as having strong emotional and behavioral aspects (Ellis, 1962) and it therefore disputes them in experiential, emotive, behavioral, and ideational ways. It, therefore, integrates many cognitive, emotional, and behavioral interventions with its disputing and is one of the first truly multimodal therapies (Lazarus, 1968). Experiential, emotive, and behavioral modes of disputation are discussed in more detail in the next chapter to show that REBT always includes many kinds of active interventions. It is, consequently, one of the first integrative therapies. Clients may have difficulty engaging in its emotionally evocative and behavioral homework assignments. But this kind of integrated cognitive-emotive-behavioral approach is the goal of REBT. The best way to see that clients are convinced of and have integrated rational evaluative beliefs into their philosophies for living is to note that they act on their new, rational philosophies for living.

Disputation as Argument

Dispute and argue are synonyms, but rational emotive disputation is not an angry or contentiousness process. Rational emotive disputation is argumentative, but it is argument based on reasoning, argument that provides empirical and logical evidence for straighter thinking, argument that persuades with careful deliberation. During rational emotive disputation, client and REBTer carefully consider arguments for and against beliefs. Although not angry, rational emotive disputation is usually quite persistent, forceful, clear, and concise. It is preferably communicated with emotionally evocative language, often bluntly down to earth. But it is also done patiently, as best fits a client's response to the disputing process.

Therapists' disputations help them model their own self-confrontations, as they work to grapple with, drop, and reverse their own catastrophizing, demanding, frustration intolerance, and global human rating.

Disputation as Process

The goal of helping clients dispute their own irrational beliefs may be achieved early in treatment, even in the first session, depending on clients' ability to understand, experiment with, and adopt new principles for thinking and living. As noted in the previous chapter, progression toward clients' disputing their own irrational beliefs is usually straight-forward.

First, clients are induced to tell the therapist their goals for therapy. When clients have difficulty formulating therapeutic goals, they usually want to escape directly presenting problems, revealing emotional distress. Having set a goal for the session, rational emotive assessment reveals to both the therapist and client the link between clients' irrational beliefs and their emotional distress, that is, the B-C or Belief to Consequent emotion connection.

When clients see the link between their irrational beliefs and their disturbances, they almost always also see the benefits of replacing irrational beliefs with rational beliefs. Seeing the benefits of adopting rational beliefs, clients will want to replace irrational with rational beliefs. Wanting to adopt rational beliefs opens clients' thinking to the REBT teaching, coaching, consultation, experimentation, and homework that will help them work out their own new, personal, rational philosophies for living.

Of course, complications may arise that retard progress toward this goal. Such complications may arise for a range of reasons too broad to relate here. Quite often, the progress of disputation is hindered, as most therapy is hindered, by irrational beliefs about therapy, irrational beliefs about problems, and irrational beliefs about clients' *and* therapists' philosophies. Effective disputation usually involves patiently attempting to match the client's response to discussing these beliefs. The therapist's helpful disputation of the client's irrational beliefs can often begin in the first session.

Semantics and Depth

During disputation, REBTers attend carefully to client's explanations and descriptions of themselves and their problems, especially what they tell themselves about their problems. Because REBTers give careful attention to the words clients use as they relate their self-talk, describe their thoughts, and convey their beliefs, disputation and REBT itself are sometimes derided as mere semantics. Said this way, the word "semantics" is used to mean something like differences in words with trivial or no difference in meaning or, worse, "deliberate distortion or twisting of meanings" (Guralnik, 1982, p. 1293; this is the fourth definition for semantics and is described as a loose definition). Rational emotive disputation focuses on semantics in the technical sense of its first meaning: "concerned with the nature, structure, and, especially, the development and changes of the meanings of speech forms" (Guralnik, 1982, p. 1293). Ironically, given the sometimes notion that semantic differences are frequently trivial differences, the word "semantics" comes to English from the Greek σημαντιχός (semantikos), which means "significant" in the original (Gove, 1981, p. 2062). The source meaning of the word fits REBT's focus on semantics very nicely, because REBT focuses on significant differences in the meanings clients give their experience based on what they believe about their experience.

Rational emotive disputation actually focuses on living semantics; that is, it focuses on real-time meaning, or the meaning created by clients as they, during the session at hand, describe themselves and their lives, and as they explain what they are telling themselves about the issues arising during the session. Clients, after all—or, better said, before all—create the meaning in their lives. The meaning they create, as they seek to explain their problems, is focused during the REBT session, because it is then that the client's beliefs are most available for REBTer and client to explore, understand, and if necessary, dispute and change.

WHY DISPUTE? WHY WORDS?

Why focus on the specific words used when client's explain themselves? Why try to get them to change the words they use when they describe what they believe? It is useful because placing core, essential, irrational beliefs in the form of words gives the client more power to understand, manipulate, and change the irrational beliefs. Carefully crafted descriptions of irrational beliefs, especially words and phrases that accurately capture a client's deep beliefs, catch the essence of the client's beliefs. This more clearly defined essence then becomes more modifiable. If expressed accurately, then the explication of irrational beliefs in symbolic form as words and phrases makes them more fully available for therapeutic modification.

We can draw an analogy to music. Disputation is like showing clients the musical notation of their disturbing, self-defeating, irrational belief-melodies, helping them understand these upsetting belief-melodies through use of explicit notation, and then showing them, through use of notation mixed with practice in performing, how to change their self-defeating tunes into new, less disturbing, more helpful, more comforting, rational belief-melodies. Words used in this way work in much the same way that notes, musical staff and clefs, accent and articulation marks, repeat signs and symbols, ornaments, tempo terms (those Italian words that tell how fast to perform), and dynamic signs and symbols (abbreviations for those Italian words that tell how loudly to perform) explicate essential features of music that best facilitate working with and performing the music.

Of course, musical notation is not music. Similarly, the words and phrases used in rational emotive disputation are not actually beliefs. Although notation is not music, clear musical scores are invaluable tools, probably the best tools available for clarifying, changing, creating, and performing music. Similarly, although words are not beliefs, clearly understood, semantically precise words and phrases—used to describe and communicate about clients' beliefs as concisely as beliefs can be described—are the best tools available for clarifying and grappling with clients' essential beliefs.

Notation is not music and music clearly occurs without notation. People whistle or hum tunes without notation, jazz musicians play and improvise complex music by ear, and some cultures produce and reproduce their music completely without notation; furthermore, musical notation systems can vary widely between cultures. Nonetheless, notation can capture the essence of music sufficiently to allow reproduction. Beyond allowing performance, notation can enlarge and multiply music; music and musicianship expand and improve through use of notation, especially as notation contributes to music theory. Folk music can be captured, transmitted to new listeners, and mixed with other music through use of notation, for example. New music can be composed and communicated with notation. By understanding music theory, composers and arrangers can innovate and create new genres. Similarly, rational emotive theory holds that whereas the enterprise of changing self-defeating emotions and behavior can occur without careful use of words, therapy will proceed most effectively with use of clear notation comprised of words that describe beliefs clearly—with semantic precision sufficient to capture the essence of the client's beliefs.

To push the analogy a bit further: Musical notation—with notes, staffs, clefs, accent marks, dynamic markings, and so forth—is seldom enough to train a new musician up to expert status. Notation is usually most helpful when employed by a skilled pedagogue (e.g., a music teacher or coach) who assists struggling performers in their music reading and performance skills. Effective musical instruction usually includes assessment of and technical instruction in fingering, breath control, or some other performance technique; encouragement in performing in a variety of settings, often with different instruments; and reassurance and guidance while the learner attempts to perform solo, in duets, in trios, and in larger ensembles. The most effective musical instruction will organize instruction with some level of training in notation, from the simple beginning of note reading to more complex skills of recognizing key signatures, and so forth. Musical notation and music theory then become integrated with practice, performance, and understanding of music.

Similarly, clear explication of the words and phrases that capture the essence of rational and irrational beliefs may not be enough to change a client's thinking, and may work best when mixed with skilled instruction in skills for living. REBT is most effective when it includes modeling of new behaviors, guidance in imagery, and other consciousness raising exercises, evocation of such emotions as are associated with irrational and rational beliefs, and immersion in individual, couples, family, or group work.

Practicing and improving performance skills and enlarging one's understanding of music theory work synergistically to improve musicianship. Similarly, fleshing out the words and phrases that describe the essence of rational and irrational beliefs, along with training and practice in enlarged behavioral repertoires, new experiences and expanded or modulated emotional expressiveness will yield deeper conviction about rational philosophies for living, and freer, more enjoyable lifestyles.

HOW TO DISPUTE IRRATIONAL BELIEFS

Unlike many other systems of therapy, REBT does not hold that any specific form or quality of therapeutic relationship is necessary for change. This is quite straightforward: Many make deep, abiding, life-changing, emotional changes by reading self-help books, chief among which may be religious Scriptures such as the Bhagavad-Gita, the Old and New Testaments of the Bible, the Book of Mormon, the Koran, the Sutras of Buddhism, and so forth. Furthermore, religious devotees accomplish what they consider deep, abiding, life-altering emotional change leading to contentment through isolative monasticism (i.e., seeking to avoid relationships with people in favor of some kind of mystical relationship). Nonetheless, responding patiently, sensitively, flexibly, and with good humor to the client during the session at hand will probably best facilitate persuasive disputation of irrational beliefs.

Disputing a client's irrational beliefs during the session requires a transition from psychological theory and science to the art and craft of psychotherapy. Returning to the metaphor of music: Acoustical science, physiology, and medicine can help vocalists preserve their voices and better control the sounds they make when they sing. Music theory informs the style and goals of the singer. The singing itself, however, is the integrative product of an artistic craft.

Rational emotive theory holds that any communication that teaches or persuades a client to give up irrational beliefs and adopt rational beliefs may be effective disputation. It is unlikely that there is any best strategy or style. The process of disputation can be powerfully effective with some clients when it consists of simply telling a client that an alternative, rational belief will be less upsetting. With other clients, effective disputation may require experimenting with a broad range of approaches, including subtle ploys leading clients to discover ways to change their own thinking.

Disputation Strategies and Communication Styles

Cognitive science offers several important observations about argument that can guide the art of rational emotive disputation (cf. Chapman, 1993; VanEemeren, Grootendorst, & Kruiger, 1984): We humans appear to attempt to persuade one another by showing those who hold opposing positions that they really already believe in our position. This is done by demonstrating that tenets strongly held by our opponents are a better fit with alternative positions, a better fit with our position, than with the position held by the opponents. We show those with whom we argue that their acceptance of this or that fact argues for our premise and contradicts their premise.

For example, imagine trying to persuade someone to try escargot after they have said that eating snails seems disgusting: "Eat snails? Yuck!" At the same time, this person may enjoy calamari, hence, they have decided or accepted that squid is good to eat. Pointing out that snails and squid are both mollusks is an argument ploy that may help them change their view of what is and is not disgusting. After all, it could be argued that if a person finds one mollusk good to eat, then why wouldn't one find another mollusk just as tasty—perhaps, even tastier in that particular mollusk manner? So, by showing people who maintain that eating snails is disgusting that they have accepted that squishy, slimy mollusks can be tasty, calls their first premise into question and moves them closer to accepting the premise that escargot may also be tasty.

Changing beliefs may seem a daunting task, given the broadly varying range of opinions about infinite matters that people might hold. The rational emotive goal is much simpler, however, because the primary goal is only to help clients change one kind of belief: absolutistic evaluative beliefs. The irrational beliefs that the REBTer seeks to change are awfulizing, demanding, frustration intolerance, and global human rating; these are the primary causes for self-defeating emotions and behaviors.

Several rational emotive practitioners and theorists have suggested techniques for developing the flexible skills that yield effective rational emotive disputation (Beal, Kopec, & DiGiuseppe, 1996; Dryden et al., 2000; Kopec, Beal, & DiGiuseppe, 1994). Disputation is likely to go well if the REBTer is prepared with a range of strategies for persuading the client, delivered in a manner or style best suited to match the client's responses. The greater the repertoire of strategies and styles for delivering the disputation, the more flexible the response to the client's idiosyncratic irrationality, and the more likely that the therapist will be able to help the client see things differently.

Disputation strategies are steps along the way to persuading the client; strategies provide means to the end of persuasion. REBTers have identified at least five strategies that can help clients reject their irrational beliefs and adopt rational beliefs: *logical disputation, empirical* or *evidentiary disputation, pragmatic* or *functional disputation, heuristic disputation* or *disputation by means of cognitive dissonance*, and *disputation by inciting rational alternatives*. These strategies can then be communicated or delivered with at least five different styles: *didactically*, through *Socratic discussion*, by *therapist self-disclosure*, in *metaphor*, or with *humor*. The next sections discuss strategies first and then styles.

Five Disputation Strategies

Logical Disputation.   During logical disputation, the REBTer helps clients understand the unreasonable, arbitrary nature of their irrational beliefs. When clients see that their irrational beliefs do not follow logically from other logical premises or tenets that they freely accept, they are likely to begin doubting their irrational beliefs and begin accepting more logical beliefs.

Empirical Disputation.   During empirical or evidentiary disputation, the REBTer helps clients see that the facts of the world as clients accept the world do not support their irrational beliefs. Rather, the *good* evidence available supports rational beliefs. Scientific and empirical are the clearest or premiere examples of good evidence. Because science is both probabilistic and inherently skeptical, there is not and never really can be empirical or scientific foundations for absolutism. Not everyone adopts or accepts the skeptical, empirical approaches of science, however. Some clients may even have antiscientific attitudes. Other forms of evidence, such as the authoritative evidence of religious scriptures, may be quite persuasive for religious clients, some of whom may discount or reject scientific evidence.

Functional Disputation.   Functional or pragmatic disputation leads clients to see that irrational beliefs, in and of themselves, create a wide range of harmful consequences. In and of themselves, irrational beliefs cause self-defeating emotions and prompt self-defeating behaviors. The clients are led to see that many emotional and behavioral problems exist primarily because of irrational beliefs. Through pragmatic disputation, clients are led to see that as a function of adopting rational beliefs they will suffer less. It is, therefore, pragmatically better for the client to drop irrational beliefs and adopt the rational beliefs that are their antidotes.

Heuristic Disputation.   Heuristic disputation, or disputation by cognitive dissonance, proceeds by helping clients see that they have previously challenged and abandoned irrational beliefs in a range of situations and have benefited by doing so. Most clients will have ignored, discounted, or dropped some version of their current irrational beliefs in order to get through life. Their having done so can be used to help them drop the currently self-defeating irrational belief at hand. A client may, for example, commonly drive 57 or more miles per hour (MPH) in 55 MPH speed limit zones. He or she will have done this for reasons that seem quite sensible. For example, a client may have reasoned: "Speedometers are inaccurate, so 57 MPH is close enough to the limit," or "Everyone drives faster than the speed limit, so it's actually unsafe to drive slower than the surrounding traffic flow," or "It's just not that important." If such reasoning allowed a client to drop demands about driving, it could be adapted heuristically to help in dropping irrational demands about the problem at hand. Helping clients see that they have already adopted rational approaches to life in one or more areas can create cognitive dissonance about currently held irrational beliefs and increase the likelihood of adopting rational beliefs relevant to the current problem.

Disputation by Rational Alternative. Rational alternatives to clients' current irrational beliefs can be introduced to help clients experiment with the effects of dropping irrationality. When clients tell themselves rational alternatives to their irrational beliefs, they may feel differently about the issues they think are upsetting them; they may, almost immediately, feel relief. Rational alternatives can serve as antidotes to irrational beliefs, yielding experience with reducing distress or increasing desired emotions and behaviors.

These five strategies are not really mutually exclusive. Each may overlap with other modes of disputation. Each could also be delivered in at least five distinct styles. It is the job of the REBTer to determine which might be easier for the client to hear and accept.

Five Disputation Styles

Didactic Disputation. The didactic style is perhaps the simplest and most straightforward approach to disputation, consisting of directly telling, explaining, or instructing clients how their irrational beliefs cause self-defeating emotional consequences, why changing irrational beliefs would be a good idea, how to change those irrational beliefs, and how to exchange them for rational beliefs. Didacticism is often derided as crude or even counterproductive to good psychotherapy, but many clients listen quite appreciatively to, learn from, and then act on such didactic explanations. Many clients believe (and they are often quite correct!) that their therapist has expert knowledge about emotional problems that may be of great value in overcoming their problems.

Socratic Disputation. The Socratic style uses collaborative inquiry and questioning to enlist the client in a joint exploration and discovery process with the goal of understanding and then disputing irrational beliefs. This style allows the client both to discover the irrational belief and to formulate ways to drop the irrational belief. Questioning enlists the client's participation in the discovery process, which may allow the client to more fully "own" the process. Socratic collaboration offers many advantages. If clients are able to formulate disputations for themselves, then their disputations, expressed as they are in clients' own words, may be more familiar and meaningful. The meaningfulness and immediacy of disputations formulated in one's own words may render the disputation more vivid and persuasive.

Metaphorical Disputation. In using the metaphorical or analogical style, the therapist communicates disputations in the form of metaphors familiar and relevant to the client. The metaphorical style has the advantage of allowing clients to distance themselves somewhat from their actual situation and their current upset about it, while facing problem situations that, by analogy, are parallel to their problems. Considering an analogous situation allows the client distance, but still considers or clarifies the role of beliefs in causing upset similar to the client's. Seeing solutions in metaphor may loosen clients' conviction about irrational beliefs and persuade them toward rational beliefs.

Disputation by Therapist Self-Disclosure. With the self-disclosing style, therapists present themselves as a model of irrationality and rationality. A client may identify with the therapist and with the therapist's formerly irrational beliefs, with the therapist's reports of emotional upset caused by such beliefs, and most importantly, with the therapist's new, rational beliefs and with reports of the emotional benefits that came from adopting rational beliefs. Therapist self-disclosure is a special case of the metaphorical style; the therapist and the therapist's experience can serve as a metaphor for the client. The emotional connection the client may feel with the therapist emphasizes the importance of the self-disclosure and creates a vicarious source of learning. Therapist experience may provide an important source of evidence for rational beliefs, evidence against irrational beliefs, and a model for how the client may challenge irrational beliefs. Because therapists reveal their own previous irrationality and the distress arising from that irrationality and then describe the benefits of later adopting rational beliefs and philosophies for living, therapist self-disclosure presents a coping model. Extensive evidence from cognitive behavioral therapy suggests that clients learn better from coping models than from mastery models.

Humorous Disputation.   The humorous style consists of presenting disputations so that clients will find humor in their situation. If clients can laugh during disputation, then they are more likely to relax; humor can enliven therapy and ease distress about the hard work of change. A humorous presentation may also help clients come closer to realizing the unreasonableness of their irrational beliefs because clients may come closer to experiencing the absurdity of irrational beliefs. If clients laugh during therapists' disputations, then their laughter arises from a rational emotive-behavioral mixture: they understand absurdity in the argument, they feel humor, and they act on their understanding and feeling by laughing.

A humorous style may seem difficult to develop, because humor is, by its nature, spontaneous in the listener who experiences amusement. Humor is usually a bit of a surprise to the listener and may, therefore, seem to be out of one's control. It is not so spontaneous for the humorist, however. The same memorized joke can create humor with each retelling to audiences for whom it is fresh. Several approaches to presenting disputations are likely to create humor for most clients. These approaches, which can be planned and practiced, include exaggeration, use of irony, unexpected comparisons, and surprising juxtapositions. The most important skill to develop in attempting to use humor during disputation is to test potentially humorous interventions a bit at a time. Try the humor with a straight face and wait for a response. If the client begins to laugh, then try again with more of the same.

Which Disputations Work Best?

The brief definitions and explanations provided here are insufficient for communicating how to construct and deliver disputations. It is probably not possible to teach all that contributes to effective disputation, because honing disputation skills requires practice, experimentation, and more practice. Tables 5.1 through 5.4 present examples of how each strategy for disputing might be delivered. Each table presents each of the five strategies and five styles described as they might be used to dispute each of the four irrational beliefs that arise because of absolutistic evaluative thinking: *awfulizing*, *demanding*, *frustration intolerance*, and *global human rating*. Effective disputation is best formulated during sessions and delivered in a manner that is responsive to the client's reception of the intervention. The most effective disputations will be those that are eventually delivered by clients to themselves.

No one strategy, or style or combination of strategy and style, can work with every client. Disputation, like most interventions, is best guided by clinical judgments about what may work, tempered by what then seems to work with the client and problems at hand. A few general recommendations are possible, however.

The humorous style may be the most risky, although only slightly so—since distressed clients often feel confused about what is happening to them. Confused clients may have difficult understanding the ironies, exaggerations, or misdirections that create humor; client confusion could then yield further distress, including irritation. Self-effacing humor will almost always be safe to begin with. If the client can laugh at a therapist's self-effacing humor, then edging the humor closer to the client's situation will likely be safe.

The didactic style may carry extra risks for at least two reasons: First, the therapist runs the risk of losing contact with what the client really believes. This risk is simply avoided by asking for confirmation for your propositions. For example, "I'm guessing your downing yourself right now. Am I right?" or "I think you would feel better if you rated your actions but not yourself. What do you think?" Clients are usually willing to respond to such open invitations. Some clients have difficulty communicating that they disagree or dislike the therapist's approach, but whether and how such clients will respond to any particular style of therapy is difficult to determine or demonstrate in advance. Clients who have difficulty responding to an open invitation to report their discomfort or disagreement will probably have difficulty responding to any intervention style.

A second risk associated with the didactic approach to disputation arises from the popular influence of psychotherapy itself: Clients may have firm ideas about how psychotherapy should be practiced, especially if they are somewhat familiar with popular writings about psychotherapy, if they have taken introductory or undergraduate psychology classes, or if they are, themselves, trained to do other forms of psychotherapy. Clients may demand that their therapist should do psychotherapy in a specific way. Clients may believe that the only appropriate way to do psychotherapy is to gather an extensive developmental history, to have a certain kind of accurate empathy for the client's situation, or to establish a certain kind of Socratic dialogue with the client. A didactic approach may anger a client who believes, "Nothing else will do!" As with humor, experimenting with simple, brief, but directly delivered disputations can reveal how clients will respond to the didactic style.

The Socratic style, which encourages clients to discover both their own irrationality and their own solutions, is probably the most frequently used and most popular approach to talk therapy among cognitive and cognitive behavioral therapies. Mixing Socratic style with the rational alternative strategy (i.e., asking clients to develop their own rational emotive alternatives to their irrational thinking) is also probably the most efficient way to begin disputing: First, clients may actually generate their own persuasive disputation alternatives. Clients' own rational alternatives to irrational beliefs, constructed and phrased in their own words, may be more immediately salient and more persuasive than disputations formulated by even the most sensitive of therapists. Second, even if clients are unable to generate rational alternative beliefs, their inability to dispute provides useful information about their thinking, information about their general response to REBT, and information about their specific response to disputation.

A therapist may ask a client, "What might you tell yourself, instead?" Only occasionally are clients able at first to formulate effective rational alternatives to irrational beliefs. If clients respond, "I have no idea," then the response still provides important information about the degree to which clients understand or fail to understand their own irrationality, yielding the benefit of providing therapists with real-time assessment of the clients' thinking. This simple question repeated later, after training in disputing, reveals client progress in working toward greater rationality.

To reiterate, no single style, no single strategy, no specific combination of style and strategy will work with every client. Consider Deborah. During our first session, I (SLN) began to ask questions that were intended to help her, through Socratic exploration, understand the beliefs leading to her distress. About 20 minutes into the session, she said, "I freeze up when people ask me questions. My mind just seems to go blank sometimes. You seem to want me to *get* something, but I'm *not* getting it. If you want me to get something, you better just tell me."

Her frank statement was very valuable. She communicated that the Socratic style was not working for her. She made it clear that she was willing to tell what did and did not work. She made it clear that she wanted to be told what might help her situation and problems. I urged her to continue to complain if my style was not working for her.

Some who support the use of a Socratic style hold that didactic communications are immodest, directive, and almost inevitably doomed to create resistance in the client (cf. Overholser, 1995, 1999). Notwithstanding this view, Socratic questioning was quite frustrating for Deborah. A devout Socraticist might contend that Deborah's problems arose because of clumsy Socratic questioning. Nonetheless, I was the only therapist available to Deborah at that moment, and it turned out that she wanted direct statements, brief lectures, and directive homework assignments. Deborah's situation and her response to my disputations are discussed in more detail, later.

HOW TO DISPUTE THE BELIEFS
OF RELIGIOUS CLIENTS

When it comes to offering therapy to people who are religious,and particularly for people with clinically salient religious concerns (see chap. 3), professional practice guidelines and good clinical sense suggest that two primary problems may arise (Johnson, in press). These include ignoring religious concerns altogether and intentional disputation of the client's religious beliefs. Ignoring client religious concerns is likely to hinder both development of rapport and achievement of desired treatment outcomes. Similarly, overt attacks on religious belief and practice may thwart good therapy and may additionally be unethical (APA, 1992).

As an example of the latter case, consider applying some of the disputations, highlighted in Tables 5.1 through 5.4, to the religious belief and commitment of a young man who is depressed and anxious following an act (premarital sexual relations) that he considers a sin against God. In an effort to ultimately decrease the client's symptoms (Cs), an REBT therapist may offer the following disputations: "Where is the evidence that any God exists? Prove to me that any supernatural being gives a damn about you or ever will? In my view, believing your body is a 'temple' to any other being is both crazy and helping you to feel miserable. I guess you'll have to choose between being depressed or accepting the fact that sexual relations between consenting adults are normal and healthy—regardless of what your religion teaches!" In our view, these disputations are technically good, but each of them wrongly attempts to undermine or attack the content of the client's religiousness versus his style (evaluative, demanding) of being religious.

We have previously discussed assessment of different elements of clients' religiosity. When beginning the disputation process with religious clients, rational emotive theory holds that the two most important considerations are the role of religion in clients' Activating events and the role of religion in clients' evaluative Beliefs—religion in A's and religion in B's. Two approaches to disputing the irrational beliefs of religious clients follow from the distinction between Activating events and Beliefs: First, accommodating religious beliefs when they appear as Activating events; and second, integration of religious material with disputations, when religion appears in core irrational beliefs.

When REBT therapists *accommodate* religious beliefs, they treat religious elements of a client's concerns or presenting problems as equivalent with other Activating events. Although REBTers can and will attend to specifics of clients' presenting problems, these are less important than the evaluative and demanding nature of the client's beliefs.

In contrast, an REBTer may intentionally *integrate* religious beliefs of a client with disputations. Here the therapist assumes that elements of a religious client's belief tradition may serve as potential antidotes to their irrational beliefs. Specifically, elements of client's religious beliefs that are likely to counter absolutistic, evaluative beliefs about self and circumstance are used during disputation of Activating beliefs of all kinds. This is true whether or not Activating events are imbued with religious significance. The key to both rational emotive approaches for treating religious clients is rational emotive theory's goal of changing absolutistic, evaluative beliefs.

Accommodating Religious Belief

The disputations depicted in Tables 5.1 through 5.4 might be used with any combination of Activating events and irrational Beliefs, including Activating events strongly infused with clients' religious beliefs. The specifics of Activating events facing clients are less important than clients' evaluative Beliefs about Activating events. The focus in REBT is not so much on whether the Activating event really is as the client reports it to be, but rather whether the client's *evaluation* of the Activating event is absolutistic and therefore irrational.

Practicing REBT from an accommodative perspective, the therapist is careful to demonstrate respect for the client's religious beliefs and is

intentionally collaborative and humble in exploring and seeking to understand religious values, beliefs, and practices. Whatever the client's unique
views about God, the relationship of humans to God and the possibility or
reality of spiritual intervention and influence in life, the REBTer honors
and makes no attempt to change these beliefs. This stance was described
as *theistic realism* by Bergin (1980). Rather than address specific religious
belief, the accommodative therapist disputes the demanding and
unhealthy evaluative nature of the religious client's beliefs. So, the question becomes "How does this client's *style* of thinking about God and his
or her relationship to God make him or her distressed?"

Like all therapists, REBTers will, of course, have opinions about the
Activating events reported by clients. Therapists practicing REBT might
well tell themselves something like this about an Activating event, "I
don't believe this really happened the way it's being told," but this would
not be central to disputation. A therapist practicing REBT might offer
practical suggestions about Activating events, when the practical suggestions seem straightforward. Again, this would not be disputation, and
would not be the goal of REBT. They may or may not accept that the Activating event really is as the client reports it to be. However, regardless of
whether a therapist agrees with a client's religiosity, taste, or political
views, the therapist can still consider the extent to which the client is catastrophizing about the Activating event, making demands about the Activating event, intolerant of the frustrations associated with the Activating
event, or globally rating someone (self or other) because of the Activating
event. From an accommodation perspective, the focus is on Beliefs and
not Activating events (i.e., B's, not A's).

By analogy, an REBTer who belongs to a local political party would
not blend political opinions with disputations when treating a client whose
complaints focus on an event that occurred at a meeting of the local chapter of the opposing political party. Even if a therapist had passionate opinions about politics, the focus would remain on the client's irrational
evaluative beliefs about political intrigues, not the political intrigues
themselves. Given its focus on evaluative beliefs, REBT can accommodate Activating events of nearly all kinds, from practical day-to-day hassles to esoteric, existential angst; from highly realistic fears to delusions
such as might arise among seriously disturbed clients; from religious
issues considered sacred by the client to sexual matters a religious client
might consider profane.

The following thought experiment suggests why REBT can accommodate religious problems with relative ease. Imagine identical twins,

TABLE 5.1
Examples of Strategies and Styles for Disputing Awfulizing

			Disputation Strategies		
Disputation Styles	Logical	Empirical-Evidenciary	Functional	Heuristic/ Cognitive Dissonance	Rational Alternative
Didactic	It simply doesn't follow that because something is unwanted, unpleasant, quite sad, or painful, that it qualifies as "Awful," "Horrible," or "Terrible."	What you view as awful at this point in time may not be viewed as awful by someone else, or even by you later on. So there really is no standard by which we can label something AWFUL!	Call anything awful and you'll feel anxious about it. Call the anxiety awful and you'll feel more anxious, and awful. That builds panic!	No matter what you regard as Awful and catastrophic, there are at least 1,000 things much worse!	Because this thing I don't like could in fact be much more unpleasant, I had better stick with accurately calling it "bad" and not leap to falsely labeling it "catastrophic," or totally bad.
Socratic	I'm not sure I understand how this difficult event qualifies as truly Awful. Help me see how this is worse than 100% bad!	Where is it written that your circumstances constitute a catastrophe? If there were actually a Scale of Catastrophic Events, where on the scale would your situation fall?	Help me understand how labeling this as awful and horrible is helping you to cope with it more effectively?	I know you think your situation is awful (the worst imaginable), but so does the prisoner in a third-world prison who has just been gruesomely tortured for the 50th time. Who is right?	Rather than indoctrinating yourself with the belief that what you face is catastrophic and awful, I wonder what you could tell yourself to actually feel less distressed about it?

Metaphorical	A holiday snow storm brings delight to children and rage to airline passengers. The snow is the same, only the perspective is different.	Spending the night in a homeless shelter may be awful to one and comforting to another. There is no evidence that circumstances themselves are *awful*, only our assessment of them!	If a man volunteered to undergo what you are experiencing for the price of $10 million, how could he possibly endure this *Awful* thing that you cannot bear?	Assuming that some other human being somewhere once endured something like this, what might he or she have said *about* these events to make them seem more manageable?
Therapist Self-Disclosure	I used to think that several things in my life were *horrible* until I started watching the evening news. Now, I am convinced that most of what happens to me is at worst unpleasant!	Every time I think I've discovered something in my life which is *truly awful*, I find that I can imagine it being even worse. This seems to prove that it was not absolutely awful to begin with.	A colleague of mine was fired from his job, lost his marriage, and was imprisoned all in one week. I know realize that there is always a "worse" scenario and that the things I have to bear are indeed *bearable!*	When I am feeling anxious about an upcoming event, I ask "what's the worst that can happen?" So far, the "worst" thing I can imagine has never been fatal.
Humorous	I told my neighbor that the color he painted his house was "awful," yet he seems to like it. How is that possible?!	Please help me understand how your current discomfort rates as the most awful and unbearable circumstance in the history of mankind.	Perhaps we can market your new innovative technique for helping people cope effectively by telling themselves repeatedly: "This is Awful, Horrible and Terrible!"	Yes, this "sucks" big time. No, this does not "suck" more than some other possible bad things.

TABLE 5.2

Examples of Strategies and Styles for Disputing Demanding

Disputation Strategies

Disputation Styles	Logical	Empirical-Evidenciary	Functional	Heuristic/Cognitive Dissonance	Rational Alternative
Didactic	It makes no sense that because you would prefer something to be so, that it absolutely *Must* or *Should* be so. It simply makes no sense to demand what is not!	There is no good evidence that I, those around me, or the world in general *Should* be as I desire. Nowhere is it written that my demands must be met.	It is unlikely that dogmatic demands that life be different will help you to accept yourself, accept reality, or even change the things that might be changed!	You don't demand that everything in your life be precisely as you want it, so deciding these specific things *must* be perfect or different seems arbitrary and rather silly.	Rather than *demand* that life treat you as you desire, stick to *strongly preferring* that this be true and nondemandingly but diligently work to achieve those desires.
Socratic	How does it follow that because you would prefer something to be different, that it therefore *Must* be different?	I'm afraid I don't see any solid evidence to support the notion that you, other people, or the world *Must* or *Should* be any different than they are.	Help me understand exactly how demanding that life and reality be a certain way is helping you to feel better or create the changes you would prefer to make?	Do you sometimes wish you could sleep longer in the morning? [if the answer is yes:] What do you tell yourself to accept the reality that it is time to get up?	As an alternative to demanding that reality Must, Should, or Ought to be different, what might you tell yourself in order to feel less upset about your circumstances?

Style					
Metaphorical	An astronomer would love to see the entire universe using only his eyes. Would you agree that it would therefore make sense for the astronomer to *demand* that he have such visual powers?	I can stubbornly demand that I never get hit by a drunk driver. Unfortunately, there is absolutely no good evidence that this demand will at all alter the probability that I will get hit.	A terminally ill man insists that he *must* not die! Will making this demand prevent him from dying?	A 2-year-old tantrums when she doesn't get precisely what she believes she *must* have. How is her demanding belief making her disturbed?	Millions of people around the world have severe disabilities. What sorts of things might they tell themselves in order to cope well and live their lives with maximal enjoyment?
Therapist Self-Disclosure	I once believed that my wife should be exactly who I wanted her to be. Strangely, I've become happier now that I believe she *Should* be exactly who she *is*!	When I started running cross-country, I believed I HAD TO finish first in all my races, however, I never finished first. Clearly, I did not have to! I survived even without finishing first.	I used to demand that I not get anxious before a musical performance. Then, I realized this demand was helping me get more anxious! So I quit demanding, and surprisingly, I enjoyed the performances!	If Martin Luther King had demanded that others like him, I doubt you'd have heard of him. Using him as a model, I now try to just do the right thing and let others think what they want about me.	Instead of demanding that editors like and accept all my articles (which never happened!), I now say "I think this is good work and I hope it is accepted, but it doesn't have to!"
Humorous	"I demand, therefore I am." Of course, nondemanding people also "are" and they seem much happier too!	Roses should be red, violets should be blue, but where is the proof that shoulding helps you?	You know, you musturbate so often and so well, I can only conclude that musturbation is really helping you get what you want!?	Because you are so good at demanding, could you please demand that I receive $1 million by 5:00 p.m.? If you can do that, this session is over. I'm retiring!	The first law of the universe is that the universe should be exactly as I want it to be! (however, I recognize that the universe seems to ignore this law most of the time!)

TABLE 5.3
Examples of Strategies and Styles for Disputing Frustration Intolerance

			Disputation Strategies		
Disputation Styles	*Logical*	*Empirical-Evidenciary*	*Functional*	*Heuristic/Cognitive Dissonance*	*Rational Alternative*
Didactic	If you don't lose consciousness or die, you *will* stand it. Logically, you have no choice, but to stand it unless you choose to end your consciousness by killing yourself or by doping yourself up.	People have stood all kinds of lousy things: surgery without anesthetic during the Civil war, traumatic amputations, concentration camps, and so on. If they stood that, you can stand this.	If you want to not tolerate something, tell yourself you can't stand it. If you want to tolerate it, tell yourself you can stand it. Then, get on with your life!	Around the world every day, millions of people say "I *can't* stand this" and then somehow, many (probably most) go on to "*stand*" what they couldn't.	I suggest that you begin to tell yourself that if something doesn't cause you to lose consciousness or doesn't kill you, you'll *stand* it, you just won't *like* it.
Socratic	Help me understand why you couldn't stand it? What would you do instead?	Where is there any *good* evidence (scientific or legal or, even, practical evidence) that you couldn't stand it.	What does it do for you—and *to* you?!—to tell yourself over and over again that you couldn't stand it?	When POWs are being tortured or burn victims are undergoing painful skin grafts, I wonder what they tell themselves to stand it?	What could you tell yourself instead of telling yourself that you couldn't stand it?

Metaphorical	Climbers on Mt Everest know they can either choose to endure the intense cold, pain, and fatigue, or they can lay down and freeze to death. They simply tolerate in order to live!	Ironman athletes often think they can't possibly continue their grueling 10-hour races and yet the fact is they usually do finish. So, the evidence indicates we can tolerate more then we may believe.	Imagine identical twins undergoing a painful medical procedure. One says "I can't stand this!" and the other says "This is unpleasant but standable." Who will experience more distress?	If you were paid millions of dollars to tolerate the circumstances you now face, how would you manage to *stand* it then? What would you tell yourself to get by?	Young children sometimes have to undergo painful or nauseating cancer treatments. What might these children tell themselves in order to tolerate it?
Therapist Self-Disclosure	I used to tell myself I couldn't stand feeling anxious in social situations. Then, I realized I kept standing it over and over and so I decided the truth was that I just *really* disliked it!	I once believed I couldn't stand having a girl say "no" when I asked her out. The evidence is now in, however, Not only *can* I *stand* it, I can stand it over and over again!	When running long distance, I have found that telling myself how intolerable the run is helps me to feel more tired, uncomfortable, and cranky, nothing more.	As a child, I could never bring myself to pull out a loose tooth—knowing I couldn't stand the pain! Then, my father would pluck it out and I would celebrate my great pain endurance!	I certainly don't enjoy feeling anxious before speeches but I have leaned that I will survive even the most intense anxiety. I now tell myself speaking may be unpleasant at times, but never intolerable.
Humorous	How long have you been unable to stand this thing you *are* standing?	If this will actually be *unbearable* as you say, then I'm sure you can find evidence showing the mortality rate is 100%?	In the dentist's waiting room it helps me to say, "I can't stand needles, drills, the sounds of equipment, the smells, old magazines, tilting back in the chair, the bib, looking at his assistant, scheduling.	If terrorists took all your loved ones hostage and threatened to kill them unless you *stood* it, then could you? How?	Dog gone it! I can't stand that I keep standing all these things I can't stand!

TABLE 5.4

Examples of Strategies and Styles for Self-Rating

Disputation Strategies

Disputation Styles	Logical	Empirical-Evidenciary	Functional	Heuristic/Cognitive Dissonance	Rational Alternative
Didactic	It makes no sense to decide that because you make a mistake, you ARE a mistake. That is the worst (and most painful) kind of overgeneralization.	Look there's no good evidence that human worth changes. Science can only measure size or temperature, or some similar factor, not worth or goodness.	Look, if you rate yourself, everything you try will seem riskier. Not only will you face the risk of doing poorly, but you add the seeming risk of your value changing.	You don't rate yourself positively for everything you do that succeeds, so stop rating yourself negatively for the mistakes you make.	Instead of calling yourself a good or bad person, stick to telling yourself that you're just a fallible human being who does good and bad stuff.
Socratic	Explain to me the logic of generalizing from what a person *does* to what that person *is*? When do they *become* what they *do*? At 1%? At 51%? At 90%?	Where is there any *good* evidence that we can measure human-ness? Is there any scientific way to measure human worth? Any legal way? Any valid economic way?	What does it do for you—and *to* you?!—to constantly rate yourself?	You sometimes speed, right? [If the answer is yes:] What do you tell yourself about having driven too fast that allows you to continue to live with yourself?	What could you tell yourself instead?

Metaphorical	Big, aggressive dogs are good guards, but not good pets. Small, friendly dogs are good pets, but not good guards. They're neither good nor bad, just different, like people.	Gold used to cost $800 per ounce, now it's less than $300. But the nature of the metal hasn't changed. Popularity doesn't change the essential nature of people either.	Imagine identical twins of your gender. One self-rates, the other rates only his behavior or performance. They have your same problem. Who's more (or less) upset?	If *you* rode the bench for the last place team in the NBA for a whole year, how would you stand it? Could you say that same thing to yourself about just barely [getting by]?	Millions of Americans, some very bright, think their president is foolish, crooked, immoral, incompetent. What must he tell himself about their opinions? Could you tell yourself that?
Therapist Self-Disclosure	I used to believe that I had to do everything well in order to measure up. But I couldn't decide how to average push-ups, GPA, and height, so I decided I just was.	I've gained a pound a year since I got married. After 23 years it adds up. However, I stubbornly refuse to believe that my value has changed one half of a tenth of an ounce!	I used to feel panic before tests, and, if I did poorly, depressed after. If I did well, I was nastily arrogant. Either way, self-rating hurt me and hurt others! No more!	I used to worry about being a great golfer—I was never any good! But I told myself it just doesn't say anything about *me*. I moved on to believing that nothing else does either.	Before every game my coach used to say, "Let's go have some fun. Winning's more fun than losing, but either way, let's have fun." We won one game that year, but I still had fun!
Humorous	Look, Michael Jordan makes about 200 times more money in a year than the average American physician. He is, therefore, more valuable than 200 doctors, right?	So, I would like you to design and build a *human-o-meter*. You know, decide what it is that makes the needle go up and down and we'll start marketing it and get rich!	Are you passing the *BREATH* test? Make sure! Check every time: 21,400 breaths a day! *B*asic *R*ational *E*motive *A*dequacy *T*est for *H*umans	Uh-oh, I see a wrinkle in your shirt. You're an *FHB*! And also a wrinkle in your pants also—*FFHB!!* Not just a *F*allible *H*uman *Being*. Also a *F*allible *Flawed Human Being*!	You're a soldier in an epic, vital, historic, un*civil* war: *CSA* vs. *USA* Conditional Self-Acceptance vs. Unconditional Self-Acceptance

separated at birth, adopted, raised apart, and ignorant of the other's existence. One twin was raised in an atheist home, the other in a fundamentalist Christian home. Both twins have whole-heartedly adopted the beliefs of their parents. The twins, who live on opposite coasts of the country, have entered treatment for intense anxiety. Each is in treatment with a therapist who practices REBT. The therapists have very different views about religion. One has adopted atheist beliefs, and the other, in addition to working as a therapist, is quite religious and serves as an ordained lay minister in a Christian denomination. The REBTers know each other, but of course they do not know personal information about each other's clients and are unaware they are treating clients who are twins. The atheist REBTer is treating the fundamentalist Christian client, the religious REBTer is treating the atheist client.

Imagine that the twins have gotten themselves into nearly identical difficulties. Both twins work as accountants and both, through embezzlement and ill-advised financial misadventures, lost substantial sums of money belonging to the firms for which they worked. Both twins are suffering severe anxiety. The twin with atheistic beliefs is quite anxious about the possibility of arrest, conviction, and imprisonment. The twin with Christian beliefs is anxious about the prospect of going to Hell. The two therapists have led the twins to the following A-B-C analyses of their anxiety (see Fig. 5.1).

As is most often the case with anxiety, the anxiety-provoking event is only anticipated, and the Activating event has not yet happened. The anxiety is caused by awfulizing. Consider the following uses of hypothetical functional disputation and disputation by rational alternatives; Socratic disputation is attempted first and, when the client does not develop a rational alternative, the client is instructed in the use of rational alternative statements (this is not an actual transcript, but similar dialogues have taken place many times during REBT):

REBTer: So you see, telling yourself that you couldn't *STAND* to go to *X* is causing your anxiety.

Twin: Of course I'm telling myself that! I *couldn't* stand *X*!

REBTer: How can you know that? You haven't ever been in *X*, have you?

Twin: No, but every time I think about going to *X*, I feel *HORRIBLE*!

FIG. 5.1   A secular and religious A-B-C analysis.

The atheist twin:				
Activating				*Consequent*
event	+	*Belief*	→	*emotion*
Prospect of detection, arrest & going to prison	+	I couldn't *STAND* to go to prison!	→	anxiety
The religious twin:				
Activating				*Consequent*
event	+	*Belief*	→	*emotion*
Prospect of going to Hell	+	I couldn't *STAND* to go to Hell!	→	anxiety

REBTer: Right. But you're jumping to the wrong conclusion about X. You feel upset every time you think about *X*, but every time you think about going to *X*, you also tell yourself *firmly* and *insistently* that you couldn't *stand* it—and you *believe* it! You re-indoctrinate yourself every time you think about *X*; over and over and over again you tell yourself that you couldn't *stand X*. What could you say to yourself instead of saying, "I couldn't *STAND* to go to *X*?"

Twin: I don't know.

REBTer: How about this? You could, quite reasonably, tell yourself that going to *X* is the most unpleasant prospect you've ever faced, the most unpleasant experience you're ever likely to have. But then add that never having been in *X* you don't *know* what it would be like; unless *X* were to *destroy* you, you *would* stand *X*, you just wouldn't *like* it.

Twin: What good will that do?

REBTer: If you try to tell yourself that—*and say it stubbornly and forcefully!*—I'm betting that you will feel less anxious. When you tell yourself that you couldn't *STAND X* do you feel *less* anxious?

Twin: No, more anxious.

REBTer: What if you believed it would be lousy to be in *X*, but you would stand it unless it destroyed you?

Twin: I don't know.

REBTer: Try saying it.

Twin: But I don't believe it.

REBTer: Right, but try saying it as if you did believe it.

Twin: It would be lousy to be in *X*, but I would stand it unless it killed me.

REBTer: Pretty good, but now say it as if you really *believe* it. Like this, it would be *lousy* to be in *X*, but I *would* stand it unless it *destroyed* me.

Twin: Okay, it would be *lousy* to be in X, but I *would* stand it unless it destroyed me.

REBTer: Does that feel more or less anxious?

Twin: Less anxious, I guess.

Notice that the disputation would sound the same whether therapist or clients were religious or irreligious and whether *X* were prison or Hell. If a therapist is sensitive to the client's response to the session, then almost any Activating event could be dealt with, because the nature of the Activating event is secondary to REBT's primary therapeutic goal of disputing the irrational evaluative Beliefs causing the client's distress. The disputation strategies and styles presented in Tables 5.1 through 5.4 would work as well for Activating events rich in religious implications as they would for Activating events with nothing whatsoever to do with a client's religious beliefs.

Furthermore, notice that in the sequence presented, the therapist's opinions about the existence of God, Heaven, or Hell are irrelevant. It would amount to parlor talk, if the therapist were to attempt to dispute the risk of prison or damnation. Informed opinions about the probability that a felony or transgression would lead to prison or damnation in Hell would require expert opinions from an attorney or a priest, respectively. It is possible that a therapist who is an ordained minister could offer an expert opinion about Hell, but only if the therapist-minister were of the same religious denomination as the client and then only if the client was asking for a religious opinion. Disputation of irrational evaluative Beliefs, on the other hand, would be neutral with regard to religious realities and, therefore, accommodative of the client's religious beliefs and religious goals.

Integrating Religious Material With Disputation

In some cases, REBT practitioners may carefully move beyond mere accommodation of client religiousness to intentional utilization and integration of religious material in the REBT disputational process. This advanced or specialized approach to disputation poses both greater risk to the religious client and greater potential for effective and lasting change (Johnson, in press; Nielsen et al., 2000). When REBTers have some training and established competence treating explicitly religious clients, and when they are at least somewhat familiar with the client's particular religious faith, then disputation may be substantially enhanced by the integration of religious material.

Scriptures, biblical examples, and faith-based practices (e.g., scripture reading), because they are often well learned by religious clients, may carry particular authority and be maximally effective when employed as part of a disputation. Rather than threatening or diminishing a client's faith, integrative disputation may actually strengthen religious faith. In integrative disputation, clients are reintroduced to neglected components of their own faith (DiGiuseppe et al., 1990), problematic (inaccurate or incomplete) readings of Scripture are reinterpreted, and idiosyncratic religious beliefs (those clearly at odds with the client's stated religious denomination) may be questioned. As an example of this, Christian clients' belief that they "MUST be perfect" may be questioned in light of substantial biblical evidence that all human beings are imperfect and the scriptural statements that Christ gives grace freely to those who believe.

Tables 5.5 through 5.8 present religiously integrated versions of the five disputation strategies and five disputation styles presented in the previous tables. In each case, religious material from or inspired by the Bible is integrated with strategy and style to form a disputation likely to resonate with a Christian clients' religious beliefs. Prior to delivering any of these religiously oriented disputations, the REBTer should emphasize the compatibility of the REBT model with the client's own faith and religious scriptures (e.g., Proverbs 23: 7, "What a man thinks in his heart, so is he"). Clients may then be encouraged to frame their primary irrational beliefs (IBs) as beliefs that cannot be supported by evidence from their own religion (and usually they cannot). Further, these beliefs work at cross-purposes with God's desire that they be happy and productive in service to both Him and other people, or restated, "when you tell yourself untruths, the fruit in your life and emotions is rotten!"

The process of integrative disputation requires that REBTers persistently challenge the inconsistencies between the client's evaluative and demanding beliefs and the scriptural and doctrinal evidence from their own faith that appears to directly contradict the problematic belief. So a depressed Christian client may be asked "help me understand how getting depressed about your sin will help you to avoid that sin in the future or better serve God?", "How is it God's will for you to be depressed?", "Why are you choosing to be depressed about that sin and not all the others you commit daily?", and "So, what I hear you saying, is that 'all fall short of the glory of God' EXCEPT you?"

As in the case of accommodative work with religious clients, integration of religious components into the disputational process requires the REBTer to select both a disputational strategy and a disputational style while simultaneously giving thought to the client's unique religious commitments and values. Tables 5.5 through 5.8 offer examples of such disputations, but the skilled REBTer must consider when to utilize accommodative (Tables 5.1 through 5.4) versus integrative techniques. Consider once again the case of the young Christian client who has become anxious and depressed after having engaged in premarital sexual intercourse. The client views his act as an awful sin and his religious commitments would be considered clinically salient. In this case, the REBTer may use integrative disputations such as, "Where is it written that an act of sexual immorality means a Christian is 'lost'?"

Next, the therapist may offer biblical passages that clearly counter the IB that any sin is more awful than another or that a sin will render one rejected by God (e.g., 1 John 1: 19: "If we confess our sins, he is faithful and just and will forgive our sins and cleanse us from all unrighteousness"; Romans 8: 1: "There is therefore no condemnation for those who are in Christ Jesus").

If the client were to persist in the belief that His sin is worse than the sins of others, then the REBTer may again use scripture to counter this belief. "Well, I understand that you believe this kind of transgression is especially damnable and that you are somehow worse than others as a result, but the Bible says that all have sinned and fall short of the glory of God (Romans 3: 23). It seems God doesn't think any of us are special just because of the *way* we sin!" The following case example highlights several integrative disputations.

Religiously Integrated Disputation of Andrew's Low Frustration Tolerance. Andrew was an 18-year-old college freshman. He was referred to the college counseling center by a roommate after Andrew described a wish to die. During the intake session, Andrew appeared quite depressed and stared solemnly at the ground. A rather handsome and athletic young man, Andrew made little eye contact with the therapist and it was evident he had been crying recently. After some initial probing, Andrew finally described a break-up 3 days prior with his girlfriend of 5 years. The two had begun "going steady" in their freshman year of high school and had come to the same college together. Andrew and his girlfriend, Sarah, had been largely inseparable during high school and spent most of their leisure time together. They attended the same small church and their families were close friends. There was little doubt in anyone's mind that the two would marry, least of all Andrew's. During the first semester of college, Sarah began to spend more time with her new college dormmates and seemed to enjoy meeting and socializing with a range of male and female friends. Andrew became increasingly distressed and demanding of her time, which served merely to decrease Sarah's interest in spending time with him. Three days prior to the appointment, Sarah notified Andrew that the two were "no longer dating." This shocked Andrew, and precipitated 3 days of minimal sleep, intensely depressed affect, and eventually, thoughts of suicide. Andrew's clinic intake materials indicated he was quite devout in his Christian faith and very active in campus ministry activities:

WBJ: So it would be safe to say you feel very depressed right now.

Andrew: Yeah. You could say that.

WBJ: And not only depressed, but you also said you've considered killing yourself and that you haven't decided not to kill yourself.

Andrew: I don't think I would. I just started thinking about it . . . Like I don't think I can handle this. I'm sick of this whole thing. I've never felt this way before.

TABLE 5.5
Examples Integrating Religious Material with Disputation of Awfulizing

		Disputation Strategies			
Disputation Styles	**Theo-Logical**	**Religious Evidence**	**Religiously Functional**	**Religious Dissonance**	**Religious Alternative**
Didactic	Considering all the evil things God has seen men do and endure for thousands of years, it seems unlikely that this thing you face qualifies as truly *awful* (totally or 100% bad, and perhaps more than 100% bad).	I can assure you that nothing in Holy Scripture would support the idea that what you are facing is indeed *catastrophic*.	Telling yourself that this situation is awful will simply help you to feel miserable and forget that God's grace and presence have sustained people through even more unpleasant circumstances.	You may believe what you have done is awful, but God says "all have sinned and fallen short of the glory of God," so your sin doesn't appear to be any worse in God's eyes.	Proverbs says that as a person thinketh, so are they. If you tell yourself this is *awful*, it will *feel* that way. If you tell yourself this is unpleasant, it will *feel* that way.
Socratic	I'm having trouble understanding why this is truly *awful*. Did God send a special message indicating He was sending a true catastrophe your way?	I'm curious about the scriptures which say that this thing you are going through must be awful. I've heard of the Ten Commandments, but not the Ten Catastrophes!	Remind me how it is that rating your situation as *awful* is helping you to keep your focus on God and serve Him more effectively?	Job lost his wife, his children, and his property. He had painful boils covering his body. So how is it again that *your* situation is awful?	If God were standing here beside you right now (and He may be), what would He say about your situation? Could you say that as well?

Metaphorical	The death of Jesus on the cross was first viewed as catastrophic but we now see it as an important gift! What seems awful at first may not seem awful later.	Martyrs of the early church welcomed suffering if it brought God glory. Perhaps they would view what you call "terrible" as an opportunity or privelege!	When the Jews were enslaved in Egypt, some probably said "this is awful," and others said "The Lord will deliver us." Who do you imagine felt better?	If an earth-covering flood was not a catastrophe, but part of God's plan, how likely is it that this thing you face is a true catastrophe?	In the Lion's den, what might Daniel have said to himself [and to God] instead of "*this is awful!*"?
Therapist Self-Disclosure	I used to say that various things were *terrible* or *awful* until I realized that God may have designed them that way for His purposes.	Practically nothing is 100% bad and nothing is more than 100% bad. No matter what is wrong, I could be facing it without God. That would be worse!	When I tell myself something in my life is awful or *catastrophic*, I find it only helps me to become immobilized, angry, and distant from God.	When I start believing something is *awful*, I close my eyes and imagine walking through it without God. Suddenly, whatever it is seems less bad!	When anything seems awful to me, I imagine Christ putting a nail-pierced hand on my shoulder and smiling kindly and I realize nothing I face is especially *awful!*
Humorous	During the "awful" storm on the Sea of Galilee, Jesus slept peacefully while the disciples fretted. Might your own "catastrophe" make Jesus sleepy as well?	Yes, I'm certain the martyred saints of the church would agree your situation is the worst *any* Christian has *ever* faced. You win the Holy All-time Awful Award (HAAA!).	How exactly does your catastrophizing chant ("This is awful, this is awful!") help your spiritual walk and promote your faith in God?	If *this* is *awful*, then it could not be worse, so I guess that means this is worse than roasting in hell for eternity?	Lord, I know things could be worse, much worse, but how about no more "opportunities" for growth like this one for awhile?

TABLE 5.6

Examples Integrating Religious Material with Disputation of Demanding

Disputation Strategies

Disputation Styles	Theo-Logical	Religious Evidence	Religiously Functional	Religious Dissonance	Religious Alternative
Didactic	God never promises anywhere in the Bible that He will grant our every wish, so *demanding* that He do so seems rather crazy.	Scripture is full of examples of men and women NOT getting what they believe they *must* and *should* have!	Insisting that God obey *Your* commands and give you exactly what *you* want [which would make Him your servant, not God] seems unlikely to help you feel better *or* get what you want.	The Bible says life is hard [just ask Job!] and that suffering is part of life. Demanding that things *must* or *should* be as we want them to be doesn't fit with the Bible's message!	God loves me and wants my life to go well. Still, life is unpredictable and things will not always be as I would prefer.
Socratic	Help me understand how the sovereign God, Creator of the Universe, and Great I AM *should* or *must* ensure that the world be as *you* insist it should.	I wonder if you would show me the biblical passages that tell you that the world, your life, people you encounter, or you yourself will be precisely as you DEMAND?	Would Moses have been helped by dogmatically demanding that Pharaoh obey God immediately? Why not? How is demanding helping you?	In the hours before his crucifixion, I wonder why Jesus didn't *demand* that God save him?	Instead of stubbornly demanding that things be different than they are, what might God want to hear from you instead?

Metaphorical	God saw the good which would come from His son's death and Job's suffering, God sees things about our "unpreferred" circumstances that we cannot.	The scriptures tell us to humbly bring our troubles and requests to God. They do not say "*Demand* and it Shall Be Given!"	In the Whale's belly, Jonah might have screamed and kicked and demanded that he not be inside the whale. Would that have helped to change his circumstances?	The Bible says we should remove the log from our own eye before worrying about the speck in our brother's eye. Why demand that others be different when we ourselves have so much imperfection?	Al[...] the[...] will[...] in th[...] "Lor[...] thine[...] 26:39)
Therapist Self-Disclosure	I used to believe that I *should* be perfect (or close to it). Then I realized it made little sense to demand that I be someone *other* than the person God created!	As a child, I believed God *Had* to grant all my wishes. As an adult, I have learned that God does not respond to demands. He *musn't* do anything. He is God!	When I demand that I be different I become angry or anxious or depressed and less connected to God. Demanding has never helped me much!	One day I realized that if I'm not going to make demands about the big stuff (world peace, ending human suffering) why make demands about the everyday things?	Not being especially divine myself, I've decided to let God alone do all the commanding and demanding. I'm sticking to preferring and I seem to be much happier now.
Humorous	Hmm. If demanding works as well as you seem to think, then shouldn't all the souls in hell be able to demand their way up to heaven? Why should your demands work and theirs not?	Perhaps those scriptures proving that the world *must* or *should* be as you'd like it to be (*the Ten Demandments*) were lost in the Great Flood?	Does the Bible say "Demand and it shall be given?" Is there any instance of someone in the Bible shoulding or musturbating their way to happienss?	When we catch ourselves *demanding* that life treat us as we prefer, we might remember Jesus suffering on the cross. This might curtail our demanding!	When God advertises for an apprentice, I'll apply. Until then, I'll be better off not making God-like demands of myself, others, and the world.

TABLE 5.7
Examples Integrating Religious Material With Frustration Intolerence

Disputation Strategies

Disputation Styles	Theo-Logical	Religious Evidence	Religiously Functional	Religious Dissonance	Religious Alternative
Didactic	God created you, understands your capabilities, *and* has allowed you to end up in this circumstance. Therefore, God must believe that you CAN *stand* it!	God's people have stood all kinds of lousy things: slavery, torture, persecution, homelessness, and so on. If God helped them stand it, he will help you too.	Telling yourself you can't stand this is guaranteed to make you feel lousy. Telling yourself this is God's will and that He will sustain you will help you focus and endure.	You don't tell God He is wrong about most things, so it makes little sense to tell Him He is wrong about your ability to tolerate this circumstance!	God, grant me the serenity to gracefully accept (tolerate) the things I cannot change, and the courage to change the things I can.
Socratic	Help me understand exactly how it is that God could know every hair on your head and yet *not* know what you can and cannot stand!?	God says that "In this world, you will have tribulation" (suffering) [John 16:33]. So where exactly is it written that *You* will not?	Which will help you tolerate this better? (a) I can do nothing to tolerate this! or (b) I can do all things through Christ who strengthens me [Phil. 4:13]?	Explain to me how it is that Job suffered the loss of all he owned, his children, his family and his wealth and still managed to *stand it*, yet you can't stand this?	Instead of telling God He has goofed and you really can't stand this burden He has allowed you to carry, what could you say instead?

Metaphorical	Jesus promised that those who believed and followed Him would suffer the world's hatred and rejection [John 15:18-25]. How does it follow that *you* would not suffer?	The Apostle Paul begged God to remove the "thorn" in his flesh [2nd Cor.]. He suffered and yet chose to tolerate his pain in order to keep serving God.	I wonder how it would have helped Moses if he had screamed "I can't stand this anymore!" each time Pharaoh refused to free the Hebrews?	Imagine that God appeared to you and explained that He needed you to tolerate this circumstance for an important reason only He could foresee. Could you stand it then?	"For I have learned to find resources within myself whatever my circumstances" [Phil 4:11].
Therapist Self-Disclosure	In painful circumstances, I used to think God had abandoned me. However, it never made sense that my creator wouldn't know what I can stand!	I have never been able to find an example from the Bible in which God put someone in a situation that they truly could not *stand!*	I am always touched by Christ's words before his crucifixion: Father, not my will but yours be done. This seemed to prepare Jesus to *bear* the unbearable.	A man I know chose to get circumcised as an adult to show his commitment to God. The pain was remarkable. I now find *few* things I don't believe I can tolerate!	Frankly, I hate losing in life, feeling pain in relationships, etc., but I accept these as part of God's design for humanity and I pray that He will give me strength to endure.
Humorous	I guess we'll need to update St. Paul's words. They should now read: "I can do all things through Christ who strengthens me [Phil 4:13], EXCEPT THIS!!!!"	I'm confused. the Bible says we will all experience tribulation, and yet you say "In this world I can't stand tribulation!" Which is correct?	You and I wouldn't be here today if Noah had said "sorry God, I just *can't stand* lumber, pitch, boats, animals and neighbors who make fun of me!"	Don't you hate it when the author of the Bible gets it wrong? It should read "I can do all things through Christ, *except this one!*"	Come Lord God, be thou my guest, and help me *stand* this unpleasant mess!

TABLE 5.8
Examples Integrating Religious Material with Disputation of Self-Rating

Disputation Strategies

Disputation Styles	Theo-Logical	Religious Evidence	Religiously Functional	Religious Dissonance	Religious Alternative
Didactic	Look, if you're God's creation, it just doesn't make sense for you to call yourself a basket case or a weakling or a jerk or a pile of crap or some other insulting name.	Christ said, "If you have done it to the least . . . you've done it unto me" (Matt 25:40). That means that He considers all people to be of equal value with *Him*!	You know, when you call yourself names it *de*motivates you where right and wrong are concerned. You feel *less* like going to church and *more* like breaking commandments!	You forgive Peter for denying Christ—and remember, Peter saw miracles. So apply that kind of forgiveness to yourself. Be fair with yourself!	I suggest that you memorize and tell yourself, over and over again, what Peter said, "God hath showed me that I should not call any man common or unclean" (Acts 10: 28).
Socratic	If the Bible says "All have sinned and fall short of the glory of God" (Rom 3:23), help me understand how *you* are especially deserving of damnation when *you* sin?	What did Jesus say about the worth of sinners? The lost sheep? The lost coin? The prodigal son? What do these parables (all in Luke 15) say about your worth?	What does it do for you or for God when you down-rate yourself? Does it help you help others or pray or go to church or repent? Does it do any good for His works?	Do you believe what Christ said, "He who is without sin among you, let him first cast a stone" (John 8:7)? Why are you so set on clobbering yourself?	Instead of the unbiblical notion that you are no-good or less than human when you error (sin), what is a more truthful and biblically correct thing you could tell yourself?

Metaphorical	If God created and loved even Adolf Hitler, it seems to make very little sense that God would not love you when you fall short.	The Bible tells us repeatedly that the Shepard always pursues the lost sheep, never downing, degrading, or harming them. They have great value in His eyes.	Imagine identical twins in Hell. One rates only behavior, performance, or situation, and the other self-rates. One will be uncomfortable with the heat, and the other will have heat *and* the pain of self-damning!	The Prodigal son squandered his father's inheritance and lived a sin-filled life. Still, his father loved him just as much as the older ("good") son. What does this say about you?	Perhaps instead of self-downing, you could focus on the truth that you are created by God and saved by grace alone—REGARDLESS of your performance.
Therapist Self-Disclosure	When I fully understood that God loved me *in spite* of my faults, it made little sense to rate others as less than human when they disappointed or frustrated me!	I used to believe I would have more worth in God's eyes if I could act perfectly. Sadly, I couldn't find a *single* scripture to support this belief so I gave it up!	When I remember that I'm neither good nor bad (Mark 10:18), just a guy who does good and bad, I feel more encouraged to try to do good and less tempted to do bad.	I once believed I was *subhuman* when I failed. Then I remembered Jesus died on the cross for *me* and I figured he is a better judge of worth than I.	When I start really self-downing, I can always fall back on this: "Jesus loves me this I know, for the Bible tells me so . . ."
Humorous	You must think God is inept. You're so hard on yourself He doesn't need to judge you! It's nice of you to do His work for Him, but why not let Him earn His celestial salary?	That is interesting indeed. Could you show me that biblical passage in which God appointed you his chief assistant for damning self and others?	If self-downing is so helpful, I wonder why God didn't make it a commandment? "Thou shalt call yourself worthless and feel depressed!"	Does your mind ever wander when you sit in church? It does!?? Oh no. I guess that shows you are completely worthless!	When I err or fail to achieve what I would prefer, It gives me more opportunity to experience God's graceful forgiveness!

WBJ: So you'd rather be dead than feel depressed about breaking up with your girl friend?

Andrew: Sometimes . . . I guess.

At this point, it was apparent that Andrew was experiencing a secondary emotional disturbance as a result of low frustration tolerance in response to his depression about the break-up. It was decided to pursue his LFT about being depressed, because this appeared to undergird his suicidality:

WBJ: Well now Andrew I understand your girlfriend decided not to date you anymore, or at least not for now, and that you've become very depressed about that, but I'm not understanding how you got yourself from just depressed to deciding you must die rather than feel depressed.

Andrew: I don't know . . . [*long pause*]. I just can't take feeling this way. Everything sucks.

WBJ: I'd like to help you not be depressed about breaking up with Sarah, but before we talk about that, I'd like to spend a bit more time understanding why you think you should die. Is that okay?

Andrew: Yeah.

WBJ: Well, I guess I'm not convinced that because you've been suffering for three days that you can't stand to do it anymore. Can you convince me of that?

Andrew: That I can't stand it?

WBJ: Yes. That you cannot stand to be unhappy or even depressed for a while longer or even for a long time if you need to.

Andrew: I don't know . . . Its just that we went out for so long.

WBJ: Yes you did, and losing the relationship is very difficult and you've gotten quite depressed about it, but do you think you could survive even with feeling depressed?

Andrew: Yeah. I don't know how long though.

WBJ: Can you think of anyone in the Bible who really suffered?

Andrew: You mean like Job?

WBJ: Exactly. Job is a great example, and there are others, but lets talk about Job for a minute. What happened to him?

I (WBJ) find that when intentionally integrating religious beliefs in the disputational process, it is desirable to gauge the religious client's grasp of and familiarity with Scripture. In this case, Andrew offers a specific biblical figure as an example of one who suffered. Although there are many other biblical models of frustration tolerance, Job is an excellent model and I elect to use Job throughout the following disputation. Even if I had not been familiar with the story of Job, however, I would have asked the client to describe it for me:

Andrew: He lost everything. All his riches were gone and he threw himself down on the ground.

WBJ: That's right. He was a prosperous man who lost everything. All his possessions and all his children too. Do you remember that all of Job's children were crushed in an accident on the same day he lost all his wealth?

Andrew: Sort of . . .

WBJ: And do you remember what happened to old Job next?

Andrew: He got sores everywhere.

WBJ: Yes. I imagine them as huge boils all over his body. Incredibly painful sores. The Bible says he was covered from head to toe with painful sores. He then sat down in a heap of ashes. He loses everything including all of his children in one day and then gets hit with painful sores and sits alone in the ashes. Would it be safe to say Job's day sucked?

Andrew: [*laughs slightly for first time*] Yeah, that would suck.

WBJ: Okay, so Job's day really sucked, and he certainly got very depressed and could have killed himself but he didn't. Job was depressed enough to curse the day he was born, yet he didn't take his life. Instead, what did he do?

Andrew: He sat there and put up with his obnoxious friends.

WBJ: Yes, he sat there in intense pain, listening to his "friends" ridicule him day after day after day. Now if really really intense suffering means one has to commit suicide, wouldn't Job have done it? Killed himself?

Andrew: Probably . . . yeah, I'd say that would do it. [*laughs slightly again*]

WBJ: So, does it follow that you probably can stand working through this break-up with Sarah, even if it sucks and you feel quite down for awhile?

Andrew: Yeah. I hear what you mean. I know I can survive . . . I'm not going to kill myself.

WBJ: Even if you feel very unhappy and even feel miserable sometimes?

Andrew: Yes.

WBJ: Well that's sure good to hear! But what can you tell yourself the next time you feel depressed about the break-up. I mean, instead of "I'm hurting too much, I can't stand it, I better kill myself."

Andrew: [*smiles briefly*] . . . I don't know. Something like "I don't like this but I'm not going to kill myself?"

WBJ: Good. "This sucks and I'd really like not to feel depressed about this anymore, but I am feeling down right now and I can tolerate feeling this way even when I don't want to," or "this sucks but it won't kill me," or "If Job can do that, I can do this?"

Andrew: Yeah. I like the last two!

At this point, Andrew is making more eye contact and there appears to be more appropriate range in his affect. He appeared most helped by brief cognitive disputational self-statements that were less traditional and more idiosyncratically related to our session and the biblical example:

WBJ: All right Andrew. So we agree you *can* stand it. And that's a big relief 'cause now you don't have to kill yourself!

Andrew: [*smiles*]

WBJ: Well then the last thing to remember I suppose is what happened to Job . . . I mean at the end of that chapter in the Bible . . . Do you remember how things worked out for him in the end?

Andrew: Pretty good. He got everything back and lived happily ever after.

WBJ: Yep. I'm sure he never forgot the sores and the days that sucked on the ash heap, but I think the Scripture says he got twice as much back from God as he'd had before, including many children and great wealth. Does that sound right?

Andrew: Yeah.

WBJ: And if Job had killed himself?

Andrew: He'd miss out.

WBJ: Right. And what would killing yourself cause you to miss out on?

Andrew: Getting Sarah back?

WBJ: Well, whether it's Sarah or something better than before, I imagine God would be frustrated if you departed before he could show it to you.

Andrew: [*nods*] . . .

The remainder of this session and several subsequent sessions were spent on Andrew's primary emotional disturbance (depression) following his activating event and several demanding and catastrophizing irrational beliefs.

Religiously Oriented Disputation of Deborah's Demands. The same Deborah who told me (SLN) that my Socratic questioning wasn't working for her was overt in describing both her religious background and her ongoing devout commitment to her religious beliefs. During the first, session she reported that she had returned about 6 months earlier from a proselyting mission for the Church of Jesus Christ of Latter-day Saints in Brazil.

Her problem was that she had returned home 20 pounds heavier than when she left. She explained that she knew she would gain weight while on her mission, because she considered weight control a low priority compared with proselyting. She said that her weight went up because she "was too busy to fuss about dieting or exercise." Her weight gain was a relatively minor concern until her mother had begun to criticize her for it when she arrived home. Deborah's mother told her that she was ashamed of what she had become. She was also quite overt in favoring Deborah's younger sister Ruth, who was thinner than Deborah. The sisters, who had shared clothes before the mission, could no longer wear the same size clothes. Deborah reported that shortly after her return from the Brazil her mother gave most of her old clothes to Ruth. Deborah grew upset as she reported that her mother sent about $400 a month to Ruth to help out with expenses and told Deborah that she would not get any help until she could "measure up."

Deborah had some trouble explaining what she wanted help with. She knew that it would be difficult to change her mother, because her mother was in another state and she was in Utah. She agreed with my assessment that she was quite angry at both her mother and Ruth. She also agreed when I suggested that she felt discouraged. Additionally, she felt ashamed of herself for feeling angry with her mother and sister. I suggested that it might be good to work on not feeling so angry, and Deborah agreed. I also suggested that things would likely go better for her if she felt less discouraged, and she agreed. I suggested, quite didactically, that Deborah seemed to be demanding that her mother should be more fair and stop demanding that she lose weight. Deborah also agreed that she believed her mother should act more fairly. This caused at least one additional problem for her: First, her mother treated her badly. Second, she felt angry. Her anger caused her to suffer unnecessarily.

I told her, "Isaac favored Esau over Jacob. Then, ironically, Jacob unfairly favored Joseph over his 10 older brothers and gave Joseph the coat of many colors. Remember? The brothers were so angry about this unfairness that they sold Joseph into slavery. You're insisting that your mother *should* be fair, when parents, even parents with prophetic gifts like Isaac and Jacob, sometimes behave unfairly toward their children. Isaac treated Jacob unfairly compared to Esau, Jacob treated his 10 oldest sons unfairly compared to Joseph, your mother treats you unfairly compared to Ruth. Unfortunately, parents sometimes treat children unfairly. I think that telling yourself that she *should* treat you fairly—when she *doesn't* and may *not*—causes you to suffer from your own anger about it."

Deborah's religiosity opened a range of opportunities for disputing her demand that her mother stop demanding. It was possible to use the Scriptures to show her that she simultaneously believed strongly in two highly inconsistent things: First, although her mother *must* not treat her unfairly, it was okay that great biblical patriarchs (in whom she firmly believed) *could* and *did* treat their children unfairly at times. When Deborah began to understand this incongruence, I went on.

"I suggest that you begin to tell yourself that you really, really want your mother to treat you fairly, but then tell yourself that, if she chooses, she is utterly free to act as unreasonably toward you as Isaac and Jacob acted toward their kids. Some children get a bit of nutty parenting, others get a whole walnut grove FULL of nutty parenting!" I suggested that she begin talking with herself differently, telling herself that while she wanted fairness, she didn't NEED it. I further suggested that she call her mother several times during the coming week, preparing herself beforehand by "prophecying," by writing down what "nuttily" unfair things her mother would likely say when they spoke. But, I told her, "All the while—before, during, and after the call—insist to yourself that your mother may act just as nuttily as she wants to—just as nuttily or more nuttily, even, than Isaac and Jacob acted toward their children."

Deborah was skeptical that purposely calling her mother could help, knowing that speaking with her mother on the telephone was almost always an upsetting experience for her. We role-played what the calls might be like, first with Deborah taking her mother's role, saying what Deborah believed her mother would say or could say at her worst, with me generating rational coping statements and assertive responses to what she might say. We then switched, I said what Deborah predicted her mother could or would say, and Deborah practiced both rational coping statements and practiced new responses to what her mother might say. Deborah reported that she began to feel less upset even before she called and actually laughed when her mother said some of the things she had predicted. Some of what her mother said was a word-for-word match with what Deborah had "prophesied."

I made two attempts to get Deborah to laugh: First, I used exaggeration to compare her mother's "nutty" unfairness to a grove of walnuts; second, knowing that she was religious, I suggested that she "prophesy" about what her mother would say, rather than just asking her to predict or guess. She chuckled at both. Both attempts at humor carried a bit of risk; either could have offended some clients. Some clients could feel offended at my calling their mother's behavior nutty. Some religious clients might have thought that comparing their mortal predictions with divine prophesy was inappropriately glib talk about a sacred subject. Deborah had already laughed at some of my light humor, and she had already demonstrated that she was willing to tell me when my style wasn't working. My risks seemed, therefore, minor. Her laughter suggested that the risk had paid off. Trying combinations of different strategies and styles for disputing maximizes the chance of finding a meaningful, persuasive combination to help clients change their irrational beliefs.

Deborah's irrational belief was that her mother should and must act more fairly toward her. Her religious beliefs accepted that even Isaac and Jacob—two of the patriarchs—behaved unfairly toward their children. If God would allow the patriarchs (in whom she believed and whose prophetic calling she admired) if God would allow even them to behave unfairly toward their children, then it made little theological sense to demand that less prophetic souls like her mother should behave fairly toward her. Deborah's belief in the patriarchs was quite powerful, so the dissonance engendered by the inconsistency between her belief that her mother should be fair and the realization that even the patriarchs could be and were unfair to their children, reduced her demand that her mother (who was, after all more fallible than the patriarchs) should respect and be fair to her.

6

Behavioral and Emotive Interventions for Religious Clients

REBT has often been criticized for emphasizing cognitive (rational) disputation at the expense of behavioral and emotive approaches (Guidano, 1991; Mahoney, 1991; G. Neimeyer, 1993; R. Neimeyer, 1993). But REBT has always been a multimodal therapy derived from a holistic view of human experience, as I (AE) made clear elsewhere:

> The human being may be said to possess four basic processes–perception, movement, thinking, and emotion– all of which are interrelated. Thus, thinking, aside from consisting of bioelectric changes in the brain cells, and in addition to comprising remembering, learning, problem-solving, and similar psychological processes, is sensory, motor, and emotional. Then, instead of saying, "Jones thinks about this puzzle," we can more accurately say, "Jones perceives-moves-feels-*thinks* about his puzzle." Because, however, Jones's activity in relation to the puzzle may be largely focused upon solving it, and only *incidentally* on seeing, manipulating, and emoting about it, we may perhaps justifiably emphasize only his thinking. (Ellis, 1958, p. 35, italics in original).

After reading this and other descriptions of the theory of REBT, R. S. Lazarus (1999) concluded that REBT fits squarely "in the holist category"

(p. 60) as compared to theories of emotion which "are inclined to separate mental activity into independent systems" (i.e., separatists; 1999, p. 58). The view that emotion, behavior, and ideation are separable or discrete elements of human experience (Fig. 6.1a) probably arises as an artifact of analytic language. Furthermore, debates about the primacy of one process over another (emotion vs. behavior vs. cognition) especially when used to justify one intervention strategy over another (cf. L. S. Greenberg, Rice, & Elliott, 1993), may perpetuate such illusory notions about discrete elements in experience and serve to segregate rather than integrate treatment modalities.

REBT theory holds, and has always held, that psychological experience is inseparable, although it may for convenience be viewed from different perspectives, including emotional, behavioral, and cognitive or ideational perspectives (Fig. 6.1b). Because virtually every experience is an idea and a behavior and an emotion, any effective intervention, whether cognitive, behavioral, or emotionally evocative, will generalize across ideation, behavior, and emotion (Figs. 6.2a, 6.2b, and 6.2c, respectively).

An intervention may be more salient in a particular perspective, but the entirety of the client's experience will be affected in one way or another. For example, bibliotherapy is obviously ideational, because reading consists of translating symbols into meaning. Reading also usually includes the behavior of quiet sitting. That which is read will simultaneously evoke emotions. As another example, clients will often have positive emotional experiences when they encounter unconditional acceptance from their therapists. These emotions include behaviors and ideas. A client may experience a very pleasant emotion in association with an idea like, "I am worthwhile because my therapist accepts me." That emotion will be different from the emotion experienced in association with an idea like, "My therapist acts as if she really believes that I am worthwhile because I exist. She's right, I am worthwhile because I exist!" The positive emotion associated with the idea, "I am worthwhile because my therapist accepts me," is the riskier and more shallow of the two as I (AE) have noted in discussing client centered therapy (Ellis, 1994b, 1996b).

Remember Beth from chapter 4? Beth was having PTSD flashbacks and anxiety and guilt about having been the victim of her boyfriend's voyeurism. Her first homework assignment was to read repeatedly a paraphrased Scripture about the equality of human worth from the back of her therapist's business card. The paraphrased verse from her own LDS Scripture stated that all people, all of whom are sinners, have great worth in the

FIG. 6.1   (a) Separatist model of experience; (b) holistic model of experience.

Models of Experience

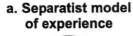

a. Separatist model of experience

b. Holistic model of experience

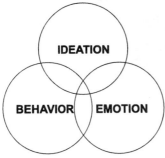

sight of God. The text she was asked to read for her homework assignment was written in this manner: "According to D & C 18: 10, the worth of MY soul is GREAT in the sight of God even if I DID sin!" This delivered an idea supporting a rational belief about unconditional self-acceptance, but did so in an emotionally evocative and behaviorally slightly more active manner. According to rational emotive behavioral theory, the more evocative the idea, the more likely it is that it is associated with core beliefs. Unconditional self-acceptance is, already, an emotionally evocative idea (Fig. 6.3a). Because Beth had declared herself to be religiously devout, I (SLN) guessed that using Scripture to dispute her human rating would make the idea of unconditional self-acceptance more evocative (Fig. 6.3b). Writing out a paraphrase emphasizing certain key words was an attempt to increase the evocative quality of this idea still further. Asking Beth to read the paraphrase outloud just as it was written, specifically to read with emotional emphasis in her voice matching the way the verse was written, was an attempt to increase the evocative quality of the idea still more and to integrate emotionally evocative thinking with the evocative style of reading forcefully, whether the reading was vocal or subvocal (Fig. 6.3c).

REBT practitioners rarely treat clients without using a combination of behavioral and emotive techniques in addition to a wide array of cognitive techniques (Ellis & Dryden, 1997, Ellis & Harper, 1997). Such an integrated, multimodal approach deals with multiple perspectives on experience (A. A. Lazarus, 1989). Beth, for example, carried out a range of therapeutic tasks in and between the sessions that followed her first

FIG. 6.2   Single modality intervention effects.

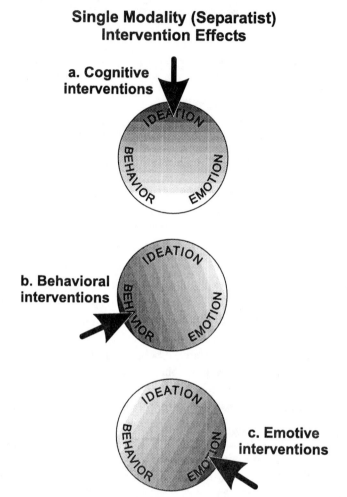

Single Modality (Separatist)
Intervention Effects

a. Cognitive interventions

b. Behavioral interventions

c. Emotive interventions

session. Remember that she felt panicky after experiencing a flashback, she was afraid of nightmares in which she saw her former boyfriend watching her undress, and she felt anxious about speaking with her parents because of worries about what they might be thinking about her. In subsequent sessions, she did rational emotive imagery in which she saw herself having panic attacks prompted by flashbacks—panics that other

FIG. 6.3   (a) Idea of unconditional self-acceptance (USA); (b) idea of USA delivered in scriptual version; (c) scriptual version of USA idea spoken in an emotionally expressive manner.

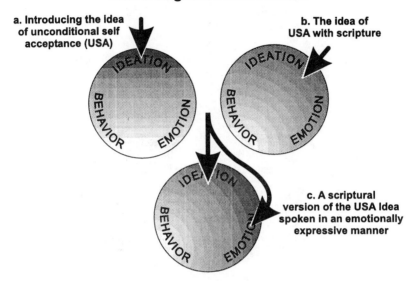

**Integrating Scripture and Emotion
with a Cognitive Intervention**

a. Introducing the idea
of unconditional self
acceptance (USA)

b. The idea of
USA with scripture

c. A scriptural
version of the USA Idea
spoken in an emotionally
expressive manner

people noticed. She imagined her former boyfriend peeking at her window while she walked around in various states of undress. Beth planned to study at her dormitory room window with the blinds open. She called and spoke with her parents more frequently and regularly than she wanted and on several occasions even asked them if they knew anything about what had happened to her former boyfriend. She planned out how she would respond to situations like those that had plagued her in her nightmares if she were to find herself in such situations when she was not dreaming. She especially did this just as she was preparing for bed. This kind of integrated selection of interventions in emotive, behavioral, and cognitive modalities was expected to have a broad impact on her symptoms, a more holistic impact like that depicted in Fig. 6.4. The core focus of the interventions reverted to her self-rating and her catastrophizing.

In addition to using a combination of interventions to change a broad range of target problems, *preferential* REBT coordinates these interventions around the core beliefs that usually fuel client upsets. Furthermore, preferential REBT incorporates emotive and behavioral interventions that

FIG. 6.4   Integrated cognitive, behavioral, and emotive interventions.

Effects of Integrated Cognitive, Behavioral, and Emotive Interventions

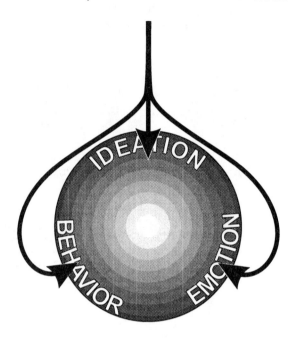

augment the essential goal of bringing about profound philosophic change in the client. For religious clients, preferential REBT will integrate religious ideas that support such rational philosophies for living. This was key to the success of the multimodal approach to treating Beth's PTSD. Remember that Beth felt depressed that it might mean she was some kind of seductress if her boyfriend believed he could watch her at her window, and she also felt anxious about what her parents might think of her because of what her boy friend had done. Both Beth's depression and her anxiety seemed to be linked with self-rating. Beth also felt panicky about her PTSD symptoms. Her panic seemed to be linked with catastrophizing about her symptoms; it would be awful if she could not control her senses and her anxiety responses.

When Beth did rational emotive imagery in which she imagined her boyfriend watching her, she was able to change her feelings from depression to concern and sadness by reminding herself that imperfect people make mistakes. Even if she had willfully done a striptease for her boyfriend (which she was sure she had not), it would be one of those sinful mistakes for which the atonement of Christ was designed–no more no less. She discovered while working on these images that she also lost her anger toward David, because she now saw him as a fallible sinner rather than as a creepy pervert. Before and after calls to her parents, Beth would read aloud to herself Scriptures focusing on equality of worth among God's children. She also reminded herself of Isaac's favoring Esau over Jacob, noting to herself that parents' opinions do not define their children. Thus, challenging Beth's core irrational beliefs formed the organizing principle around the interventions formulated for her treatment.

The cognitive disputational techniques discussed in chapter 5 are aimed at changing clients' erroneous beliefs through philosophical persuasion, didactic presentation, Socratic dialogue, and other verbal interventions. Behavioral and emotive techniques attempt to achieve the same ends through alternate therapeutic channels, all organized around changing core irrational beliefs. These approaches emphasize actual behavior change and modification of emotional responses, usually providing clients with experiences that run counter to their irrational beliefs (Ellis, 1998, 1999; Walen et al., 1992). Most of the behavioral and emotive techniques described can be carried out in session. Others will be most effective when applied between sessions in the client's own environment. REBT theory predicts that techniques focused on and coordinated around creating change in core beliefs will be more efficient and more effective than other interventions, as practiced with Beth and as depicted in Fig. 6.5.

This chapter describes those behavioral and emotive interventions that are used in conjunction with REBT's classic cognitive approaches to disputation. The following paragraphs describe the ways in which these techniques might be used with religious clients and how many of the techniques are, in fact, quite congruent with religious belief and behavior (Lasure & Mikulas, 1996). Most of the examples are *integrative*, as opposed to merely accommodative, in nature. Whereas an accommodative approach to REBT with religious clients implies intentional respect for a client's beliefs when applying an intervention, integrative REBT with religious clients implies direct and intentional use of spiritual or religious issues and resources in therapy (e.g., scriptures, sacred texts, prayer, or other religious practices). Tan (1996) made a similar distinction, referring to accommodative approaches as "implicit integration" (p. 368) and integrative approaches as "explicit integration" (p. 368).

Although some of the interventions discussed in this chapter are primarily behavioral or primarily emotive, others have both emotive and

FIG. 6.5   REBT disputation effects.

Preferred Form of REBT Disputation:
Belief Oriented, Cognitive, Behavioral,
Emotionally Evocative, and Integrative of
Client Experience, Including Religion

behavioral components. Take for example my (AE) widely used *shame-attacking* exercise (Ellis, 1969), in which a client intentionally behaves shamefully in public as a means of increasing tolerance for discomfort and developing a different emotional response to external events. In fact, shame attacking is very similar to the behavioral techniques of flooding and exposure, making shame attacking both an emotive and behavioral intervention. It is important to recognize that many of the interventions have both behavioral and emotive components and they are most effective when combined with cognitive disputational techniques.

RATIONAL EMOTIVE IMAGERY

Rational emotive imagery has been a critical component of REBT (Maultsby, 1975; Maultsby & Ellis, 1974) and other cognitive behavioral approaches (Beck & Emery, 1985; A. A. Lazarus, 1968; Meichenbaum,

1977; Wolpe, 1958) for decades. Images have a profound effect on emotions, thoughts, and behavior and they can be actively used in therapy. Religious clients may be especially responsive to intentional utilization of images, particularly religious images, for the purpose of changing emotions or coping with distress. Prayer, meditation, and other contemplative rituals are often rich in imagery and religious clients may find therapeutic applications of imagery to be especially powerful and easy to use.

Imagery can be used to assess distorted cognitions and irrational beliefs. Gross distortion of reality in the client's fantasies or images may be a clue to irrational evaluative demands. I (AE) (Ellis & Dryden, 1997; Maultsby & Ellis, 1974; Walen et al., 1992) have typically used imagery to teach clients to modify negative emotions and problem behaviors. There are two essential types of *imagery modification.* In *negative imagery*, clients are asked to picture themselves as vividly as possible in the unpleasant activating experience (A). They are instructed to experience the emotional turmoil and discomfort as intensely as possible. When they have achieved a clear image of this situation and the accompanying sense of upset (C), they are instructed to change the feeling from the disturbed emotion to a more constructive negative emotion (e.g., from anxiety to concern). When successful at making this emotional change, clients are asked to describe how they made this change. Invariably, clients describe changing their self-statements or beliefs about the situation. In the case of *positive imagery*, clients imagine themselves in the same problematic situation but picture themselves behaving and feeling differently. For example, clients who fear being assertive are asked to imagine themselves forcefully and clearly telling others what they want and how they feel. Clients may then be asked what they might say to themself in this imagery exercise in order to follow through with the avoided behavior.

There are several other useful imagery techniques, including *time projection*, in which clients are encouraged to project themselves into the future and imagine a feared (usually forthcoming) situation months or years after it has passed (A. A. Lazarus, 1968). This is especially useful for disputation of catastrophic irrational thinking (e.g., "If I go blank during that oral exam, I'll die"). Using a *repetition* approach to imagery, clients are asked to intentionally repeat fantasized images that have induced anxiety, anger, or depression and to deliberately modify components of the image each time in order to bring it more into line with reality (Beck & Emery, 1985). For example, the speech-phobic client is asked to repeatedly imagine a forthcoming speech until his image of the event is more accurate (e.g., instead of fainting and being forever banned from the organization, the client may simply be very uncomfortable and feel anxious at points). Of course, the client must also modify his cognitive evaluation of the worst case scenario from catastrophic to merely unpleasant. This is quite similar to Raimy's (1975) *emotional review* strategy in which clients are asked to imagine the A repeatedly, regardless of how they feel about A. The assumption is that repeated exposure to the image results in lowered levels of distress. With less intense levels of distress, disputation can then be introduced more effectively into the imagery scenario.

Kelly's fixed-role therapy (Ellis & Dryden, 1997) is another frequently utilized REBT imagery technique. Here the client is requested to imagine, in vivid detail, what they would look, act, and feel like if they actually behaved and believed the way they would prefer. For example, the angry spouse is asked to imagine how she would respond to her husband if she truly believed his behavior was merely annoying and not awful and intolerable. Fixed-role therapy is similar to *coping imagery* (Meichenbaum, 1977) in which clients are asked to imagine themselves actively disputing IBs in the key activating context (A) and thereby coping effectively with the previously overwhelming situation.

Propst (1980, 1996; Propst, Ostrom, Watkins, Dean, & Mashburn, 1992) pioneered tailoring imagery to the worldview of religious clients. Using an integrative strategy, Propst encouraged clients to modify their depressive images by using images of Christ alongside them as they face difficult situations. By imagining Jesus present with them as they revisit a traumatic memory, many Christian clients will be more fully able to respond to and evaluate the event. This strategy can be implemented with each of the imagery approaches outlined here. Ask clients if they would feel better if accompanied by God (Jesus, a Saint, or an important figure from their Scripture) to relive the difficult memory or face the future feared event. As you begin the imagery exercise, ask them to imagine God, or the other faith-relevant figure, accompanying them. Ask them to imagine God comforting them in the midst of their difficult time. What would He/She say and do? The client can be encouraged to practice this imagery routinely.

In addition to this *God-present imagery*, the client may benefit from using negative or positive imagery with the addition of Scriptures that support changing their thinking about an event or engaging in a behavior they have been avoiding. There are also many Scriptures in the Bible that support the notion of carefully choosing what one thinks about and how one thinks about it. For example, consider Philippians 4: 8, "Finally brethren, whatever is true, whatever is honorable, whatever is just, whatever is pure, whatever is lovely, whatever is gracious, if there is any excellence, if there is anything worthy of praise, think about these things."

REINFORCEMENTS AND PENALTIES

Most religious clients will be familiar and comfortable with the concept of "sowing and reaping," or receiving consequences (good or bad) as a direct result of one's behavior. In fact, the Bible is full of operant conditioning-congruent examples of consequence (Lasure & Mikulas, 1996). Of course, Heaven may be the ultimate reinforcement in the mind of the religious client, but Scripture is also replete with specific examples of God providing direct reinforcement for righteousness, adherence to God's law, and obedience (e.g., prosperity, numerous children, joy, etc.). In REBT, it is often helpful to have the client self-administer reinforcements after homework is completed each day or after the client engages in a feared behavior (Wilson, 1995). It is important that the behavior be contingent on the target behavior, rather than on clients' performance. Of course, clients need to select their own reinforcements, which can range from commodities to activities or socializing. Although religious clients often choose the same kinds of rewards as nonreligious clients, it is important that the therapist allow the client to select reinforcers and not recommend any that might run counter to the client's values (e.g., sleeping with an attractive stranger).

Punishment is also likely to be quite familiar to religious clients. Part of the reason for this is the prevalence of punishment in Scripture. In the Bible, the apostle Paul recommends that an adulterer be cast out of the church so that he might repent and avoid punishment in the afterlife (1 Corinthians 5: 5). Christians are taught to regard punishment or "discipline" with reverence as it is linked with being cared for (e.g., "The Lord disciplines him whom he loves," Hebrews 12: 6). One self-applied penalty technique for use with religious clients involves having them commit to sending an amount of money (e.g., $20) to an antireligious organization or one they view as working at cross purposes with their church. So a Baptist woman might be asked to send $20 to Larry Flint (owner of *Hustler* magazine) or an organization for witchcraft each time she fails to complete the homework she has agreed to for the following week.

Many clients may be so prone to self-punitive cognitions and behaviors that the REBT therapist must use judgment in deciding whether they can be expected to reasonably self-apply punishment following failure to complete homework or whether they are too prone to punish themselves and subsequently engage in self-downing cognitions (often linked to shame).

SHAME ATTACKING OR FLOODING

The rational emotive technique of *shame attacking* (Ellis, 1969; Ellis & Becker, 1982) is quite similar to the behavioral technique of *flooding* (Wolpe, 1990). Both are substitution techniques that rely on substituting an adaptive behavior or reaction for a maladaptive behavior or reaction. REBT prefers these techniques to gradual desensitization approaches because REBT emphasizes frustration tolerance and in vivo exposure to feared situations and objects (Ellis & Dryden, 1997). Shame attacking is especially useful for the client with unrealistic, exaggerated, negative reactions (e.g., anxiety, disgust, self-defeating avoidance) to objectively neutral or even positive situations or objects. Shame attacking involves encouraging clients to deliberately act "shamefully" in public in order to accept themselves and to tolerate the ensuing discomfort. Because it is important that clients not harm themselves or others, shame attacking typically involves intentional infractions of minor social rules. Examples include calling out the time in a crowded store, wearing bizarre clothing, or asking loudly for extra small condoms in a crowded drug store. The point is that clients, on their own initiative, elect to expose themselves to an anxiety or shame-provoking situation and agree to remain in the situation while practicing cognitive disputations focused on self-acceptance and discomfort-tolerance.

   Jewish and Christian clients may be encouraged to face feared situations head-on using Scriptures such as these from the Psalms as encouragement: "Because you have made the Lord your refuge, the Most High your habitation, no evil shall befall you" (Psalm 91: 9), or "Even though I walk through the valley of the shadow of death, I fear no evil; for thou art with me; thy rod and thy staff, they comfort me" (Psalm 23: 4). Certain clients will be particularly shame prone as a direct result of their religious education or upbringing. They may present as intensely self-downing for any perceived shortcoming and may have little toleration for any deviation from religious group norms in themselves or others. For these clients, shame attacking may be especially useful, particularly when it involves imperfect behavior at church. Wearing something bizarre or inappropriate to a worship service, beginning a hymn before anyone else, or intentionally dropping the offering plate may be good exercises. Of course, simply sharing personal problems with other parishioners may be shame inducing enough for many clients, and this may provide a good starting point.

UNCONDITIONAL SELF-ACCEPTANCE

Religious clients often have every reason to be unconditionally accepting of themselves—that is, their religion's theological tenets will often embrace the idea that each human being is a divine creation and their sins are forgiven such that in God's eyes, they are without blemish. For example, Christian clients will believe that their salvation and assurance of life hereafter is predicated exclusively on Christ's death for them on the cross. They themselves cannot "earn" their way into heaven through good behavior. If Christ was willing to die on the cross for them, then how is it that they themselves cannot fully accept themselves in spite of their shortcomings?

Not only will the REBT therapist demonstrate unconditional acceptance of clients, the therapist will also look for opportunities to teach clients to only rate their acts and behavior patterns, and never their core being (Ellis, 1962, 1973a, 1973b). In contrast to what they have heard and believed in the past, there is nothing they can do or say to make themselves bad or unworthy in any way. They can only choose to do bad things. So, when a Mormon client has "lustful thoughts" and creates irrational beliefs about them (i.e., "I absolutely must not have those sorts of thoughts!"), the REBT therapist would model unconditional acceptance of the client, emphasizing that his undesired thinking has nothing to do with his value as a person. The therapist might also add some cognitive disputations, such as "If God were to find out about this, He'd probably think you were no good?" or "I wonder how Jesus would rate you now? Do you suppose He has second thoughts about dying on the cross for you?" Most Christian or Mormon clients will quickly see that such irrational statements are incongruent with the concepts of grace and salvation by faith.

FORCE AND VIGOR IN DISPUTATION

REBT has long held that clients who learn to use vigorous and forceful disputations are more likely than other clients to overcome their irrational beliefs (Ellis, 1979). Although many clients seem to achieve reasonable cognitive understanding (*intellectual insight*) regarding the ways they disturb themselves, unless this knowledge is translated to *emotional insight* and steadily used to help themselves, change tends to be less enduring. REBT therapists often teach clients to dramatically and energetically take the role of their "rational" self in disputing self-defeating beliefs.

Many Jewish and Protestant clients may be especially receptive to using vigorous-active disputations in therapy. Old Testament prophets were known for high-volume and confrontational prophesying and preaching, which made people around them quite uncomfortable. Yelling out God's word to all who would listen was their primary calling. Many of the great Jewish martyrs forcefully reaffirmed their faith even in the face of death (e.g., "Here O Israel, The Lord our God, The Lord is One . . ."). Many Protestant denominations also value "fire and brimstone" preaching styles. Loud, direct, and uncompromising proclamations of God's word from the pulpit and elsewhere are common. Many African American congregations are particularly fond of vigorous verbal interaction and affirmation of biblical truth during services. For these reasons, religious clients may find the use of force and vigor in disputation particularly familiar and helpful.

Consider, for example, a Jewish client who wishes to gain more autonomy from his parents. In the past, he has indoctrinated himself with beliefs such as "I must not disappoint my parents! It would be awful if my parents thought I was rejecting them. I would be a failure as a son if I didn't obey my parents." After the therapist disputes these beliefs to the point that the client understands their irrational nature, the client may be instructed to "attack" these falsehoods with the voice of Joshua, Daniel, Isaiah, or Jeremiah. For extra impact, he might even be encouraged to stand and point or shake his fist dramatically as if directly confronting the irrational beliefs. The therapist might role-play "being" his irrational beliefs, while the client practices forceful and vigorous disputation of these beliefs until both he and the therapist are convinced. Religious clients may also find it helpful to practice this technique at home, first stating their irrational beliefs, then forcefully arguing against them using a range of disputational approaches. It is often useful for clients to tape these practices and to bring the tapes to sessions for the purpose of receiving feedback from the therapist (Ellis & Becker, 1982).

ACTIVITY HOMEWORK

From its inception, REBT has advocated the use of behavioral homework assignments to help clients make and sustain lasting change (Shelton &

Levey, 1981). In nearly every case, clients must confront those situations, people, and tasks that they have previously avoided due to unpleasant anxiety, anger, or depression. Because REBT therapists have learned there is "little gain without pain," clients are asked to do exactly what they would usually avoid (Ellis & Dryden, 1997). Activity homework may involve listening to tapes of REBT sessions, reading relevant self-help material, practicing various disputational techniques learned in session, engaging in rational emotive imagery, applying rewards and penalties for various behaviors, an so on. Some of the most effective homework assignments, however, are those that involve self-induced exposure to feared situations. The shame-attacking technique described earlier in this chapter is an excellent example of an exposure technique. Self-monitoring procedures (Bandura, 1997) may also be useful homework assignments. Here, the client is asked to carefully monitor thoughts, behaviors, and emotions as a means of comparing subjective evaluations with more objective frequencies. Often, monitoring alone will produce considerable therapeutic change.

Convincing clients of the value of between-session activity and getting them to follow-through with homework is a challenge REBT therapists take very seriously. Beck and Emery (1985) recommended presenting homework activities as "real world experiments" in which the client is asked to engage in in vivo exposure to feared events and stimuli for the purpose of objectively evaluating them and the catastrophic consequences the client normally predicts. Several authors offered strategies for instilling motivation for and increasing compliance with homework assignments (Beck and Emery, 1985; Ellis, 1985; McMinn & Lebold, 1989): (a) Begin therapy sessions by reviewing the client's homework assignment and exploring the causes of successes and failures; (b) develop specific homework assignments collaboratively with clients instead of assigning them in authoritarian fashion; (c) ensure that the client is capable of actually doing the homework and the homework will not prove destructive or dangerous in any tangible way; (d) make sure the homework assignments flow logically from material covered and skills learned during the actual therapy sessions; (e) have clients commit to each homework assignment; (f) install a system of self-administered or therapist-administered (with the client's cooperation) rewards for follow-through and penalties for lack of follow-through; and (g) attempt to anticipate potential sources of resistance to homework assignments (see chap. 7).

Religious clients may also benefit from linking activity homework with other daily rituals, particularly those of a religious nature. Muslim clients might be asked to link a 10-minute session of rational emotive imagery practice to their daily prayers (this could occur up to five times per day and would provide substantial practice). This may be especially helpful if they practice an integrative form of imagery in which Allah or Muhammad are part of the image. Or a Catholic client may be asked to conduct a shame-attacking exercise around the ritual of confession, perhaps confessing an embarrassing thing to the priest. We have also found it useful to use the principle of "covenant" with Christian, Jewish, and Latter-day Saint clients. A covenant often refers to an agreement between God and His people in both the Old and New Testaments. It can also refer to solemn agreements between people, typically with the implication that the agreement is observed and honored by God. Religious clients will often regard a "covenant" as a solemn agreement that is not to be broken. It may be useful in therapy with devout clients to ask "I wonder if you are willing to make a covenant that you will follow-through with this difficult assignment? Making this kind of serious commitment to follow-through signifies that you are really ready to make some change in your life, even if getting there is difficult." Of course, regardless of whether or not the client actually completes the homework assignment, the therapist should be unconditionally accepting and reinforce the client's willingness to covenant and his or her attempts at the homework activity.

MODELING

Intentional modeling, especially with role-playing, constitutes an important behavioral and emotive technique in REBT. Bandura (1997) pointed out that intentional modeling in therapy provides clients with examples of new behaviors, provides cues to prompt behavior they already know how to perform (e.g., when to laugh or when to listen in a social situation), and serves to disinhibit by facilitating those behaviors the person can perform but does not because of anxiety. *Behavioral rehearsal,* or role-playing, is the common approach to modeling in REBT. Here, the therapist models various forms of disputation of the client's main irrational beliefs. Following this, clients are instructed to dispute their own irrational self-statements using those disputations which they find most useful. Very often, the therapist will take the role of the client's irrational beliefs at this point and the client is encouraged to vigorously dispute the therapist's statements. Following this exercise, clients can critique their own disputing performance, receive reinforcement from the therapist, and observe as the therapist again models those techniques requiring fine-tuning.

Religious clients will often find modeling both useful and faith-congruent (Lasure & Mikulas, 1996). Regarding the Ten Commandments, the Bible says "impress them on your children. Talk about them when you sit at home and when you walk along the road, when you lie down, and when you get up" (Deuteronomy 6: 4–7). Similarly, Jesus intentionally modeled for his apostles, and Christians are encouraged to model desired behavior for others: "I have set an example that you should do as I have done" (John 13: 15), and "Therefore I urge you to imitate me" (1 Corinthians 4: 16). In this regard, it may be exceptionally helpful for religious clients when the REBT therapist is able to refer to specific biblical or scriptural examples of God or another religious figure performing the target behavior of interest. So, a client facing a threatening oral examination might be encouraged to consider the story of Daniel facing the Lions, or a Catholic client might be asked to describe the behavior of a favorite Saint in a difficult or unpleasant situation (e.g., torture) with emphasis on how the person weathered an activating event without becoming disturbed. Here the therapist might insert statements, such as "and what might Daniel have been saying to himself in the lion's den in order to not become depressed or anxious?"

SKILLS TRAINING

REBT therapists often provide direct training in specific skill areas as part of the therapy process. For example, a client with social anxiety may be helped by the disputation of her irrational beliefs about speaking in social situations, but the therapist may also provide her with direct skills training in social encountering, communication skills, and even resume writing tips (Ellis & Dryden, 1997). Religious clients are often extremely receptive to such educative interventions. Jesus was referred to as a "teacher" in his day, and indeed much of his activity could be described as instruction and teaching to both groups and individuals. So too, other religious faiths place substantial emphasis on learning Scripture and theology as well as honing spiritual skills and disciplines. Clients are prone to be more receptive to "skill building" than "psychotherapy." This is particularly true of many Christian clients, who have been taught to fear or distrust mental health professions as being too secular or humanistic.

A wide range of skills might be relevant to any specific REBT case. They may include communication skills (e.g., active listening), social skills, presentation skills, and assertiveness skills. Skills training might also include basic educational approaches. For example, clients with anxiety reactions may benefit from information about the physiology of anxiety, as well as disputational techniques aimed at those beliefs that produce their anxiety reactions. In this case, the REBT therapist may describe the biology of anxiety reactions—including the evolutionary and adaptive qualities of fear. Such information may help the client objectify and normalize the symptoms themselves (e.g., it may be very helpful merely to learn that death from heart attack is rare during public speeches). For a religious client, it may be even more helpful to hear that fear is simply one important function of their God-given body. Further, the REBT therapist might go on to note that although fear helps keep us alive, anxiety is almost always counter to our purposes and God's as well. For example, Christian Scripture says "Do not be anxious about anything . . . the peace of God that transcends all understanding, will guard your hearts and minds" (Philippians 4: 6–7).

With religious clients, it is always wise to consider the broader implications of skill development. Among fundamental Christian women, for example, expression of "appropriate" assertiveness may lead to marked conflict with husbands, peers, and the church more generally. As another example, providing an adolescent Latter-day Saint client with research-based information about the prevalence of masturbation in the population and the lack of data supporting any harmful physical or emotional consequences as a result of this activity, may possibly be seen by the client's parents or church elders as an act of disrespect to religious prohibitions against masturbation. The point is that delivery of educational and skill-focused interventions should take place with attention to religious implications for the client.

OTHER EMOTIVE AND BEHAVIORAL TECHNIQUES

There are several other emotive and behavioral techniques in REBT that are likely to be useful with religious clients. REBT therapists have often used stories, mottoes, parables, witticisms, and poems as adjuncts to disputing techniques (Wessler & Wessler, 1980). Moreover, religious Psalms, parables, stories, and rituals can be added to traditional REBT interventions to enhance the effect of disputational work. For example, contemplative silence at the start of each therapy session may be especially helpful with Buddhist, Hindu, or Quaker clients. I (SLN) have used many parables with Mormon clients to good effect. Parables such as the Prodigal Son, the Lost Sheep, and the Lost Coin (Luke 15) have been especially helpful for disputing self-downing beliefs on the part of devout clients who view their sins as evidence of their own worthlessness.

Albert Ellis has written many rational-humorous songs designed to present the REBT principles in an amusing and memorable format (Ellis, 1977b, 1981, 1989b). Because many religious clients routinely incorporate hymns and other religious devotional music into their weekly worship and daily lives, using rational-humorous songs may be especially helpful. I (SLN) have even created a few that are specifically tailored to my religious clients. Here is an example:

A Mighty Prison Is The Must
(Tune: A Mighty Fortress Is Our God)

A mighty prison is the must!
A pit of spit never draining.
Our joys and fun will surely go bust,
When shoulds and oughts are prevailing.

We could replace our shoulds
With wants for our own good,
Drop oughts in place have hopes,
Stop acting like such big dopes.
Have peace in place of our musturbation.

Finally, appropriate use of self-disclosure in therapy can be quite useful for religious clients. REBT advocates admission of one's own foibles, shortcomings, and irrational tendencies to clients when this disclosure is apt to provide an effective *coping* model—that is, an example of how another person has managed to cope with (not overcome, as 100% mastery is rare indeed!) their irrational tendencies. For example, I (WBJ) have described the speaking anxiety I experienced as a college student and how the techniques of forcing myself to speak more often and religious rational emotive imagery (Jesus calmly standing beside me with his hand on my shoulder while I spoke) were both important components in effectively reducing my anxiety. When the REBT therapist happens to share the client's faith, this kind of disclosure can be even more effective. For example, as a Bishop in the Church of Jesus Christ of Latter-day Saints, I (SLN) find that my self-revelations and coping examples are more impactful for my Brigham Young University student clients than would be the case if I were not a leader in the church.

7

Obstacles to Effective REBT With Religious Clients

For clients to really benefit from REBT, it is highly desirable that they achieve the following three insights (Ellis & Dryden, 1997): (a) Their psychological problems mainly stem from irrational absolutistic beliefs that they rigidly hold about themselves, others, and the world; (b) although these beliefs may have been created in various ways at various times in their lives, they perpetuate and worsen their disturbance by currently reindoctrinating themselves with them; and (c) only by constantly working and practicing in the present and future to think, feel, and act against these irrational beliefs are they likely to make themselves significantly less disturbed.

Unfortunately, human beings (or at least those we have treated) often refuse to or remain unable to achieve one or more of these critical insights. In fact, many clients appear uniquely prepared to resist change and growth. A foundational paradox for therapists practicing REBT or any other psychotherapy is that no matter how strongly and sincerely clients state a wish to overcome their problems, they persistently engage in efforts to avoid experiencing discomfort or pain, to fight the therapist's interventions, to resist change and growth, and to cling desperately to maladaptive beliefs and behaviors (Narramore, 1994). Most client resistance is motivated and perpetuated by the belief that no matter how painful or frustrating their current turmoil, it is in some way preferable to what they fear might be experienced if the resistance were relinquished and they had to face the fact that they created their own disturbance.

Traditional psychoanalytic authors have long noted the pervasive human tendency to resist change. Freud (1912) described resistance as a constant part of treatment at all phases. Menninger (1961) described the "never ending dual between the analyst and the patient's resistance" (p. 102). REBT therapists have also described the difficulties presented by client resistance (Ellis, 1962, 1985; Walen, et al., 1992). However, unlike other approaches, REBT favors rapid, directive, and vigorous disputing of therapeutic roadblocks created by client resistance.

Resistance is a way of life for most disturbed people, and is deeply rooted in their innate human propensities. It seems that all people are born highly "disturbable" and have a biological tendency to self-disturb (Ellis, 1987a). In fact, most clients appear amazingly adept at avoiding difficult work, refusing to do what is good for them in the long run, and putting off what would be best done immediately. We humans often have abysmally poor frustration tolerance and demand that change (both in and outside of the therapy room) be easy, interesting, rapid, and free of discomfort. We are also masters of procrastination, avoidance, and inertia and often strongly resist independence and action. Furthermore, even when we do recognize our own resistance and avoidance, we may use this awareness merely to further damn and disturb ourselves.

It is not surprising that religious clients are just as skilled at resisting change as most other human beings. Religious clients often express conflicts, anxieties, and resistances through the language of their faith (Lovinger, 1979; Meissner, 1996; Narramore, 1994; Nielsen, 1994). Religiously based resistances are often particularly resilient and difficult to dissolve, requiring particular care on the part of REBT therapists, especially those with little religious background. This chapter explores obstacles to effective REBT with religious clients and approaches to overcoming such resistances. It first explores client-based obstacles, then those stemming from the therapist's behavior, and finally those that appear rooted in the match or relationship between therapist and client. We then offer some general strategies for minimizing the development of resistance in REBT and conclude with several ethical cautions when using REBT or other cognitive behavioral approaches with religious clients.

CLIENT-BASED OBSTACLES

Although most religious clients are exceptionally receptive to REBT and successful in using it to overcome their various disturbances, some clients with deeply held religious convictions may be extremely difficult to help with REBT or any other approach. When REBT clients are, for whatever reason, highly resistant to therapy, they are often described as *difficult customers* (DCs;Ellis & Dryden, 1997). Those clients whose religious beliefs or practices appear to contribute to or worsen their resistances are referred to as *difficult religious customers* (*DRCs*). In addition to the more common reasons for therapeutic resistance, religious clients may have several motivations for evading change that are uniquely tied to their theistic beliefs and religious lifestyle (D. Greenberg & Witztum, 1991; Lovinger, 1979; Rayburn, 1985). To be most successful with religious clients, REBT therapists had best remain aware of these causes and indicators of client resistance.

Common Reasons for Resistance by Religious Clients

Fear of Discomfort. At some point in therapy, nearly all clients will demonstrate low frustration tolerance and anxiety about the effort and discomfort required for change (Ellis, 1962, 1985). Humans by nature appear to have a fundamental opposition to change and growth. Many clients live by a philosophy of short-range hedonism, which holds that "because it is uncomfortable and even painful to work hard to change, it is best that I not do so and instead, that I find the easiest and most immediately pleasurable solutions to my problems." Ellis and Dryden (1997) reported that those clients most likely to "fail" in REBT treatment are those who (a) fail to consistently complete between-session homework assignments involving cognitive disputation, refuse to accept responsibility for their disturbed emotions and consequently refuse to forcefully work at changing their beliefs and actions, and often do poorly in behavioral assignments because of their low frustration tolerance.

When religious clients resist work and change, the REBT therapist attempts to quickly convince them that no matter how hard it is for them to change, it will be much harder for them if they do not. The therapist may show them that neither their own religious beliefs, nor those of most other religions, support the notion of gain without pain and, in fact, most religions hold hard work and commitment to be great virtues.

For example, a Christian or Jewish client with low frustration tolerance may resist REBT exercises and homework assignments requiring work at changing beliefs and behaviors that contribute to marital turmoil. This client may be confronted with the Old Testament story of Jacob (Genesis 29), who toiled as a laborer for his dishonest uncle for 14 years in order to have the privilege of marrying his daughter, Rachel. Clients may also be given several Proverbs to be read as homework assignments when they are tempted to avoid the hard work associated with therapy (e.g., "In all toil there is profit," Proverbs 14:23). Peck began his immensely popular book, *The Road Less Traveled* (1978), with the striking sentence "Life is difficult." Peck noted that one of Buddah's Four Noble Truths was "Life is Suffering." In fact, most religions share respect for the notion that nothing guarantees or even recommends an "easy" life. It is certainly true that most of the central figures in the Judeo-Christian Scriptures suffered and faced immensely difficult and often physically painful circumstances (Jesus, Job, Joseph, Paul, etc.). At times, a client may suggest that no one, not even God, can understand her unique experience of discomfort or suffering. Here, it is often helpful to refer to the story of Job, who lost everything he owned and all of his loved ones. Job was left friendless, laying on a mound of ashes with painful boils covering his body. Clients may be asked to compare their discomfort with Jobs. It may also be helpful to point out that Jesus was very familiar with suffering (cf. Isaiah 53: 3, "He was despised and rejected by men; a man of sorrows and acquainted with grief and as one from whom men hide their faces he was despised, and we esteemed him not"). Other examples include Hebrews 12:1–3, and Romans 5: 3–5.

Perfectionism and Shame.   Many religious clients hold excessively rigid and perfectionistic standards regarding their behaviors, emotions, and thoughts. These clients constantly rate their worth in accordance with their "performance" in life and in REBT treatment. Such clients may have strong compulsive tendencies to begin with or may be driven by anxiety and fear of punishment. In any case, they are often lopsidedly focused on scriptural exhortations to "be ye perfect" and to "hunger and thirst after righteousness" at the expense of other passages promoting acceptance of one's fallen human condition ("All our righteous acts are like filthy rags," Isaiah 64:6; "The heart is deceitful above all things and beyond cure, who can understand it?", Jeremiah 17:9; or "There is none righteous, no not one," Romans 3:10), and the need to accept grace for inherent imperfections. Perfectionistic religious clients may actively or subtly resist REBT secondary to fear that their imperfections will be discovered or their performance in therapy will be less than flawless. The skilled REBT therapist will patiently work to convince these clients that all human beings think both rationally and irrationally, behave badly and very well, and create healthy emotional responses as well as highly disturbing states such as rage and suicidal depression (Walen et al., 1992).

At times, it may prove helpful to briefly examine the basis of clients' inherent value from within their own faith. So, for Jewish or Christian clients who believe themselves to be worthless or fully damnable because of bad behavior or (more often) failed attempts at perfection, the therapist might point out that their value in God's eyes is based simply on their belief in God (faith) and not on any thought, emotion, or behavior. For example, Genesis tells us that "Abraham believed God and it was *credited to him* as righteousness" (Genesis 15:6). Similarly, the New Testament is full of references to grace and the notion that our own "works" are irrelevant and only our acceptance of God's grace really matters (e.g., "For by grace you have been saved through faith; and this is not your doing, it is the gift of God—not because of works, lest any man should boast," Ephesians 2:8–9). Clients, therefore, may be challenged to reconcile these Scriptures with the sometimes dogmatic belief that they are worthless unless they perform well.

Related to perfectionistic demands of themselves, others, and the world around them, is the tendency for many religious clients to be highly prone to the experience of *shame*. Shame is a C (consequence) of awareness of their own personal weakness (Activating Event) and a core belief (B) that they are therefore flawed and worthless. In REBT, shame is typically a secondary emotional problem that keeps the client from focusing fully on primary emotional disturbance (Dryden et al., 2000; Ellis, 1985). Thus, some religious clients may be appalled by and highly resistant to the therapist's suggestion that they are depressed, anxious, or angry. The client believes firmly that such emotions are unholy, incongruent with their religious ideals, and/or clear evidence of their failure to be adequate or worthy. They, therefore, perfectionistically demand that they must not be disturbed and deny that they are. For this reason, the client may vigorously resist "confessing" certain thoughts, behaviors, and emotions to the therapist and may actively deny them when hypothesized by the therapist. As a general rule, until the REBT therapist helps religious clients work through their secondary disturbance (most often shame) about their primary problems, therapy will be stymied.

For these reasons, it is desirable for the REBT therapist to carefully assess how their religious clients *feel about* being angry, anxious, and so on. One may begin by simply asking the client "but how do you feel about being that angry?" Or, if clients are unable even to acknowledge their anger, the therapist may have to start with some exploratory inference chaining, such as "well, lets assume you *were* angry at so and so, what would that mean or what would happen then?" When religious clients view themselves and their behavior as abhorrent and unforgivable, they may only present the REBT therapist with surface or tangential issues in treatment, withholding those most shame-producing experiences until the therapist demonstrates unconditional acceptance of the client in spite of such shortcomings.

When clients are disturbed about their primary emotional disturbances, it is useful to invoke biblical examples of strong emotional reactions on the part of well-known saints or even God Himself. For example, in the New Testament, Jesus became so angry with the wicked behavior of money changers in the Temple, that he overturned their tables and threw them out! If God's own son could become angry, why can't they? If the client responds with something like "because Jesus' anger was righteous and mine isn't," then refer the client back to those Bible passages stating they are righteous in God's eyes merely on the basis of their faith, not their behavior. Other Scriptures that might be helpful here include Psalms 4:4, "In your anger, do not sin; when you are on your beds, search your hearts and be silent." This Scripture suggests people are likely to be angry at times, but when they are, it would be best not to harm themselves or others, but rather attempt to resolve their anger—perhaps through disputation of their anger-producing demands. Likewise, Ephesians 4:26 cautions, "In your anger, do not sin: Do not let the sun go down while you are still angry." Also, even when individuals fail miserably at good or desirable thinking, feeling and acting, they may still be of great service to God. After all, even though Peter denied Christ three times, he was later described as the "Rock" on which the church was built.

In addition, it will often be useful to confront the clients' tendency to harshly condemn themselves for their less than perfect behavior. I (WBJ) once worked with Paul, a seminary student who was experiencing bouts of overwhelming anxiety in the year before he was to graduate and assume his first job as a pastor. Paul was extremely intelligent and successful in school and in the pulpit. He was also very kind and inherently grace-filled and forgiving toward others. However, as Paul's anxiety worsened and he began to experience some public episodes of panic, he became deeply ashamed and nearly immobilized professionally. By the time Paul entered therapy, he was staying in his room, missing classes, and avoiding friends. In this case, our REBT sessions focused nearly exclusively on his disturbance about the primary disturbance (anxiety). The irrational beliefs driving Paul's shame went something like this: "I must not be anxious or weak in any way and if I am, I will be worthless to God and unable to serve the Church. Furthermore, if I am anxious, it must be the result of some sin and if others see me panic, they will despise me and I couldn't stand to be rejected like that." Paul worked diligently to dispute and relinquish perfectionistic demands of his own performance. He completed behavioral assignments in which he told as many people as possible about his anxiety and gave presentations in his ministry classes on anxiety, always including some personal experiences. Once his shame about anxiety abated, Paul's anxiety was rather easily and quickly addressed in therapy.

When Jesus was given opportunities to condemn and punish others, he declined. With a Christian client experiencing shame about some transgression or disturbing emotion, the therapist might say, "Have you heard the story from the Bible about the men who brought the woman caught in adultery to Jesus, expecting him to condemn her to be stoned (as was the law at that time)?" Most Christians will be somewhat familiar with this and will also know that Jesus said, "Let he among you who is without sin cast the first stone"(see John 8:7). Of course, no one present in the story was perfect and the woman was spared. In general, shame and the perfectionistic demands that produce shame are best confronted with the pervasive biblical message that although "all have fallen short of the glory of God, God has chosen not to condemn, but to redeem" (Jeremiah 31, John 3:17). Until the religious client can effectively dispute and surrender such disturbances about their thoughts and feelings, progress in treatment will likely be compromised.

Self-Punishment (Seeking to Suffer). One obstacle to REBT with some religious clients is the firm belief that people deserve to be punished for some transgression or shortcoming, and they therefore deserve the problems or symptoms they currently experience. Some fundamentalist Christians, for example, may assume that their symptoms are direct punishment for sin and these sinful actions, thoughts, or feelings provide irrefutable evidence of the person's failure, "evilness," or low value in

God's eyes. Ellis (1985) described how such reasoning may occur: "Because I have done evil acts, which I *absolutely should not* have perpetrated, I am a *thoroughly worthless individual* who deserves to suffer. Therefore, I *rightly ought* to be punitively disturbed and will make little effort to overcome my handicaps" (p. 14). One helpful technique to keep in mind with clients who insist they are worthless for one reason or another is to ask them to reconcile their self-proclaimed "shithood" with biblical references to their creation by God's own hands. So, the therapist might say, "Now I'm a bit confused, you say you are a miserable failure, yet the Bible says we are the treasure and God is the man, we are the pearl and God is the merchant (Matthew 13:44-45). Scriptures also say you were created by God: "For you created my inmost being; you knit me together in my mother's womb. I praise you because I am fearfully and wonderfully made" (Psalms 139: 13-14). Now, how is it that God made you wonderfully with his own hands, and values you like a 'pearl' and yet you believe you have no value?" Similarly, a Latter-day Saint client might be reminded that in the LDS Book of Moses, the Lord is recorded as having said, "This is my work and my glory—to bring to pass the immortality and eternal life of man" (Moses 1:39).

For some clients, emotional disturbance may be proof of inadequate religious faith (Lovinger, 1996) or a clear sign of spiritual failure (W. B. Johnson & W. L. Johnson, 1997). In such cases, clients will likely become self-damning and heap self-deprecation on top of their primary symptoms, so much so that they may remain quite disturbed and minimally responsive to treatment. Again, the therapist may need to spend more time on the concept of grace and incorporate it into disputations of the client's self-downing rating. Christians may neglect biblical evidence that Jesus took the punishment for their spiritual failures. For Jewish clients, Passover symbolizes God's acceptance of a sacrificial atonement for one's transgressions.

Related to this is the tendency for some religious clients to view self-punishment as noble or "holy" (self-atonement). In the fourth and fifth centuries, ascetic Christian monks practiced extreme austerities:

> There were the "pillar saints," those who lived on the top of pillars. One of the earliest and quite the most famous of them was Simeon Stylites, who died in 459. He dwelt on his pillar east of Antioch for thirty-six years, is said to have touched his feet with his forehead more than 1244 times in succession, and to have dripped with vermin. . . . Other monks were immured in cells, some of them so small that they could neither lie

at full length nor stand at full height. In one group the monks are reported to have subsisted on grass which they cut with sickles. Some monks passed many nights without sleep. Others went for days without food. The extreme ascetics were popularly known as "athletes of God." (Latourette, 1975, p. 228)

At times, clients' beliefs about the virtues of intentional suffering can be challenged from within their own religious framework. The therapist might challenge them to show where it is written that God prefers or enjoys it when they suffer. And, how do clients handle passages such as "The Lord is gracious and compassionate, . . . He does not treat us as our sins deserve . . . (Psalms 103:8–12). A Christian client could be asked why Jesus spent so much time healing people of various afflictions (physical and emotional) if suffering were so beneficial. Or, the therapist may encourage clients to explore their distorted beliefs about disturbance by conducting some inference chaining (e.g., "Lets imagine you woke up tomorrow and you were no longer depressed, I wonder what would happen then? How would you feel about that? What would God think?"). Of course, if clients remain firm in the view that suffering is an important sign of spiritual purity or a demonstration of their commitment to faith, motivation to relinquish their disturbance will be understandably poor and the REBT therapist will need to determine the potential value of continuing treatment. More often, however, the therapist will find clients who are invested in suffering or discomfort to legitimize their dysfunctional behavior and emotional reactions. In such cases, it is relatively easy to show that no activating event (no amount of suffering) is sufficient to cause disturbance emotionally or otherwise. The apostle Paul was happy and even rejoicing while suffering in prison and the "fruits of the spirit," including joy and peace, are available to all who believe regardless of the activating event(s) at hand.

Secondary Gains and Hidden Agendas.   Self-punishment is related to the concept of secondary gain. It is important to explore the potential payoff clients receive from their disturbance. If the divorced father of three becomes less depressed and appears more functional, then will the church continue to provide him with special care and financial support? Will the pastor continue to meet with him weekly for prayer and counseling? And will he be expected to take his turn in various church ministries? What will the Muslim housewife stand to loose if she becomes less dependent and more assertive with her abusive husband? Will her less compliant and deferential behavior cause her to lose standing and peer support in her religious community? Will she be at greater risk for victimization and loss of community? The point, of course, is that the careful REBT therapist will explore the potential secondary gain driving the religious client's lack of progress in therapy (Ellis, 1985).

In addition, treatment may be thwarted by an agenda that is entirely different from the one presented to the therapist. A common scenario involves a religious couple coming for counseling ostensibly for the purpose of enhancing their marriage. After minimal progress, the therapist begins to discern that they have very different agendas. The husband is interested in the therapist's ability to "rebuke" his wife and recommend she become more compliant with his leadership in the home. The wife, on the other hand, is ready to divorce and minimally interested in reconciliation. When hidden agendas are suspected, it is best to actively explore them and address them openly. The therapist then highlights the importance of their interests and wishes and honestly evaluates the extent to which REBT may be helpful in helping them achieve those goals and agendas.

Common Symptoms of Resistance in Religious Clients

Narramore (1994) suggested that there really are no unique "religious resistances," but among religious clients, common defense mechanisms may merely have religious content, be framed in religious language, or be connected to the client's religious experiences. Although we concur that common resistances can become religiously flavored and reinforced, we have also noted several unique indicators that religious clients are resisting change.

Theological Debates.   Meehl (1959) found that some clients introduced religious material as a form of resistance, as an intellectualized defense style, or as an effort to seduce the therapist into cognitive combat. Indeed, some religious clients will have a great deal of familiarity with the texts and scriptures of their faith. In fact, it is not uncommon for such clients to bring Bibles and other religious material to the session. They may routinely attempt to engage the REBT therapist in discussion and debate about the meaning of specific texts or stories, and in so doing, draw the focus away from the hard work of disputing and giving up their own irrational beliefs. In addition, some clients will spend more time scrutinizing the therapist's "theological credentials" than they will getting to the business of working on their primary problems. Such clients tend toward intellectualizing as a defense and a way of life. For example, a devoutly religious man struggling with his self-identified "pornography addiction" may experience intense depression and shame about using pornographic materials regularly. When the savvy REBT therapist attempts to dispute this man's self-damning beliefs about his behavior, by drawing his attention to the Apostle Paul's self-admission of a "thorn in the flesh" (typically considered by some biblical scholars to refer to some form of sexual desire or "lust"), the intellectualizing client may strongly object to this interpretation of the Scripture, take great offense at such, and insist on discussing the text's alternate interpretations and historical context.

Related to the debating client is the "argumentative" or "yes but" client described by Walen et. al. (1992). Again, these clients may spend a great deal of energy arguing with the therapist or avoiding responsibility for their disturbance by searching desperately for reasons why therapists and their interventions are misguided or theologically incorrect. Argumentative religious clients may benefit from a paradoxical intervention, such as "You're right Frank, because you sometimes view pornographic material, it proves you are entirely without value, and Satan will certainly spend eternity making sure you suffer more than anyone else for such an awful sin."

Preoccupation With a Single Text.   At times, religious clients may resist giving up a particularly disturbing irrational belief that is linked in some manner to a verse or passage from the Bible (W. B. Johnson & W. L. Johnson, 1997). Invariably, their interpretation of the text is quite idiosyncratic and highly disturbing. They may also engage in "selective abstractions" (DiGiuseppe et al., 1990), the tendency to selectively abstract certain meanings from religious doctrine or Scripture to the exclusion of other, often incongruent meanings. For example, it is strikingly common for Christian clients to have disturbing beliefs about their own worthlessness in light of their reading of certain Scriptures highlighting the eternal consequences of certain behaviors. However, they have often neglected the foundational message of grace and forgiveness contained throughout the New Testament. So Scriptures such as 1 Corinthians 6:9 ("Do you not know that the unrighteous will not inherit the kingdom of God?"), Hebrews 10:26 ("For if we sin deliberately after receiving the knowledge of truth, there no longer remains a sacrifice for sins"), and Matthew 7:14 ("For the gate is narrow and the way is hard, that leads to life, and those who find it are few") have consumed their attention, while Scriptures such as Psalms 103:8 ("The Lord is merciful and gracious, slow to anger and abounding in steadfast love"), John 3:16 ("For God so loved the world that he gave his only Son, that whoever believes in him should not perish but have eternal life."), and 2 Peter 3:9 ("The Lord is not slow about his promise as some count slowness, but is forbearing toward you, not wishing that any should perish, but that all should reach repentance.") have been ignored or relegated to a place of relative insignificance.

When combating problems related to a specific Bible text, Lovinger (1996) attempted to determine when the specific textual point became a problem for the client. He then asked the client to show him the specific verse (which they often cannot), and evaluated the context in which the verse exists. He then drew the client's attention to alternative translations or considered consulting other sources about the text. In this way, the therapist may model for the client a respectful but scientific and methodical approach to evaluating the value of a particular text. If the client resists this sort of objective exploration of scripture or doctrine, then this resistance should be quickly addressed.

Relinquishing Responsibility. A small proportion of clearly religious clients will, knowingly or not, use their religious faith and doctrinal beliefs to relinquish responsibility both for the creation of their disturbances and responsibility for the hard work of undisturbing themselves. In the most benign (and common) scenario, the client may adopt a derivative of the classic "the devil made me do it" defense when confronted with their active contribution to their problems. These clients may be adamant about the role of external supernatural forces in causing both unfortunate activating events and their emotional responses to these events. For example, a couple in REBT marital therapy may bring out a primary complaint regarding the husband's episodes of angry verbal abuse directed at his wife. When confronted with his own anger-generating beliefs about his wife's behavior (e.g., "She *should* not have humiliated me in front of the children and she *must* suffer for this *terrible* offense"), the "relinquishing" client might insist that a demonic presence or possession is the only explanation for his anger. He might refer to several popular books on the topic, sermons his pastor has delivered about the activity of demons, and so on. Unfortunately, his spouse, who may also be deeply committed to her faith, may feel compelled to consider this a viable explanation for his explosive anger. This case and others like it may present a significant challenge for even the most savvy REBT therapist. It may at first appear that there are very few therapeutic options that allow respect for the client's faith, as well as hope for a breakthrough in the resistance.

One option in such a case is to quickly explore faith-congruent treatment options for the client, with questions such as "Well, I've never seen a case of demon possession. And, I'm not sure that is the best explanation for your outbursts, however, if a person was possessed by a demon, what would your church recommend?" At this point, prayer, sacraments, or even exorcism may be mentioned. Rather than belittle these as viable alternatives, the therapist might try the following: "Well, I'm certainly not familiar with how to do those things and I'm not convinced they will help you become less angry at your wife. However, it seems to me that as long as you believe you are demon possessed, you are not likely to work very hard at changing the way you make yourself disturbed. So, I propose that we discontinue our REBT sessions briefly while you attempt an exorcism or other strategy with someone you trust to do those things. If, afterward, you decide working hard in therapy may be helpful, then let's continue working together at that time."

At times, this intervention alone may be enough to help clients to take responsibility for themselves. Of course, if the client is merely disturbed about an activating event (car accident, relationship failure), which she blames on a demon, Satan, and so on, then the intervention is much clearer and fits nicely within the REBT model: "Well, okay, lets assume your boyfriend did leave you because of some demonic influence or even because Satan himself wanted you to be alone, what are you telling yourself *about* Satan doing that to get you depressed and suicidal? Is it actually *100% awful* or could Satan have also done some other things which would have made your life even more unpleasant?" The therapist may also wish to consider invoking some relevant Scriptures that clearly refute the notion that Satan has any "power" at all (cf. 1 John 4:4).

Of course, some clients will be more conscious and intentional in their avoidance of therapeutic work. Some clients are simply reactive and rebellious and tend to see therapy as an impingement on their freedom (Ellis, 1985). They rather perversely fight therapy even when they have voluntarily asked for it. Such clients will typically present with demanding irrational beliefs about the need to control their destiny and will find it awful if an REBT therapist, or anyone else for that matter, directs them to modify their beliefs or behavior. Now these clients are not likely to find any help to support their resistance in the Bible or other Scriptures. Most faiths honor the notion of submitting to proper authorities and yielding to wisdom (cf. Romans 13). The Proverbs are full of references to "fools" who despise or ignore wisdom only to find themselves suffering greatly for it later. The therapist might ask, "Help me understand where the Bible suggests that you shouldn't have to change or do what is unpleasant?"

Vague or Incompatible Treatment Goals. At times, a client may express the desire to feel neutral, indifferent, or calm in response to events about which it would be rational (and perhaps quite healthy) to experience negative emotions. Among religious clients, such goals may stem from a misunderstanding of Scripture or a selective focus on certain passages that highlight the virtues of patience and moderation. For example, the New Testament notion of "turning the other cheek" when wronged could suggest a nonreactive and staid response to a very provocative activating event. Similarly, the example of Jesus' quiet suffering prior to his crucifixion could be wrongly interpreted as evidence that the ideal emotional state is one of mild anesthesia or detachment. Of course, there are two problems when the REBT therapist accepts treatment goals that include such emotional neutrality. First, rational emotive behavior theory does not endorse emotionlessness as feasible, healthy, or desirable and strongly encourages clients to accept the wide range of adaptive human emotions, both positive and negative. The client experiencing irritation when assaulted, sadness following a loss, or some anticipatory nervousness prior to a major speech, would be viewed as responding normally to life's activating events. REBT sees life without emotional responsiveness as not only highly unlikely, but also not particularly desirable. Second, it is unlikely that the client's own religious Scriptures or doctrine supports such robotic functioning. It has been mentioned elsewhere that Jesus became angry at the money changers. He was also seen to grieve publicly and privately for others and for himself as the end of his life approached. Although Jesus did not become depressed or disabled by his emotional experience, it would be a misinterpretation to suggest that he did not experience strong emotions.

It would also be a mistake for the REBT therapist to accept treatment goals suggesting a client wishes to experience positive feelings about a negative activating event. For example, the client who says she wishes to simply feel "love" for a man who recently assaulted her or the client who wishes to "experience joy" about the recent loss of his child may be operating on some incomplete or distorted interpretations of their humanness and the extent to which it is acceptable for them to have a range of emotional experiences. So, although it would certainly be preferable following the loss of a child to feel joy secondary to the client's belief that the child is now with God in heaven, and whereas such "joy" may become a real experience for the client at times, it is also likely that the client will feel very sad, perhaps even grief stricken initially.

The therapist's job then is to create permission for healthy negative emotion within the clients' belief systems. Asking for evidence that they should feel "nothing" or experience joy following very difficult life events is often a good place to start. There are numerous examples from the Bible to dispute such beliefs. For example, the book of Ecclesiastes explains "there is a time to mourn and a time to dance," and Matthew (5:4) says "Blessed are they who mourn for they shall be comforted." Romans (12:15) says "rejoice with those who rejoice, mourn with those who mourn." In addition, many of Paul's letters suggest he experienced intense emotions, including anguish, anger, and depression.

Finally, it is wise for the therapist to be attuned to vague or incompatible treatment goals. The client who states a desire to become more "righteous," "Christ-like," or "pure in heart" could be struggling with a range of issues that will not become evident to therapists until they push for a clearer articulation of the therapy goals. For example, clients who wish to become more "pure in heart" may actually be experiencing tremendous shame about emotions and behaviors which they find shameful or unacceptable, such as homicidal rage at a delinquent child or compulsive sexual activity of some sort. As long as the therapist accepts the original goal of purity in heart, the goal will never be operationalized, clients will never articulate their actual disturbance, and the probability of a positive treatment outcome will be strongly diminished.

Also, there are some "goals" that are really not well suited for REBT or any other kind of psychotherapy. For example, spiritual maturity, spiritual wisdom, and spiritual discipline may all be very desirable and health-facilitating goals in the lives of religious clients. However, unless the client's emotional disturbances are somehow inhibiting the aforementioned, it is unlikely that the REBT therapist will be most helpful to the client in achieving these goals (unless of course the REBTer is also a priest, rabbi, pastor, church elder, etc.).

Objections to Psychotherapy. Some religious clients will simply resist the process of psychotherapy from the start and may seem particularly resistant to the active-directive approach advocated by REBT. At times, such resistance may stem directly from the client's realization that it is they who are responsible (rather than their environment or history) for creating and perpetuating their disturbance (Ellis, 1985). At other times, resistance may be more closely linked with seemingly legitimate fears that their faith may be threatened or compromised by the therapist or the experience of treatment. Such fear may be institutionalized within the client's religious community and perpetuated by objections to the client's treatment participation by family members, friends, and even religious leaders. Rather than openly articulate these fears or wishes to avoid accepting responsibility, some religious clients may present the REBT therapist with a range of reasons why REBT (and presumably most other forms of treatment) is unlikely to be helpful for them.

These clients may emphasize the incompatibility between their own faith commitments and those of the therapist (particularly if the therapist is less devout or a member of different religious group). They may say that unless the therapist shares their strong faith perspective, nothing good could come of treatment. In such cases, the client may (while ardently avoiding their own responsibility for change) work overtime to show how the therapist's expertise, training, or skill is nullified by a lack of religious commitment. They may demand that prayer alone be used as an intervention or that the Bible should be used as an exclusive and moment-to-moment guide to life and change (Lovinger, 1996). When the therapist questions these demands, this may be taken as further proof of the futility of working together in treatment. Similarly, these clients may work much harder gathering outside support (from friends, pastors, or religious materials) to prove that the therapist's recommendations are incongruent with their faith, than they will addressing their own disturbance! When the client's resistance is deeply entrenched in this manner and convictions about the dangers of psychotherapy with a secular therapist or secular treatment are pronounced, a referral is likely to be the most effective approach. When clients believe devoutly that they must have a therapist with precisely the same religious convictions as they, therapy is unlikely to result in significant gain until such a match is made.

THERAPIST-BASED OBSTACLES

At times, both the process and outcome of REBT may be stymied and diminished by the behavior of the therapist. These "therapist-based" or "therapist-originated" treatment obstacles may be considerably more subtle than the client-generated problems noted earlier. A significant concern is that when an REBT therapist elicits resistance from a client, the therapist's contribution may not be immediately discernible. Thus, not only are clients provided with unhelpful therapy, they may be additionally "blamed" by the therapist for resistance or avoidance when in fact the therapist has encouraged precisely that behavior. Two major categories of therapist-based treatment obstacles when working with religious clients are described. First, those obstacles stemming directly from skill and knowledge deficits are considered, then therapy problems generated by the therapist's own disturbance are explored. Both types may pose serious impediments to successful treatment outcomes.

Therapist Skill/Knowledge-Based Obstacles

Certain obstacles to client progress emanate from the therapist's lack of knowledge and general clinical acumen. Among these skill or training-based deficits are some that are most likely to impact the practice of REBT. Ellis and Dryden (1997) offered the following list of ways in which REBT therapists impede client progress:

1. Improperly inducting clients into therapy and failing to correct unrealistic expectations, such as "my therapist will solve my problems for me."
2. Incorrectly assessing client's problems and thus working on "problems" that clients do not have.
3. Failing to show clients that their problems have ideological roots and that C is largely (but not exclusively) determined by B and not by A. Inexpert therapists often fail to persist with this strategy or persist with an ineffective strategy.
4. Failing to show clients that the ideological roots of their problems are most frequently expressed in the form of devout, absolutistic "musts" or one of the three main derivatives of "musturbation." Instead, inexpert REBT therapists frequently dwell too long on their clients' antiempirical or inferentially distorted thinking.
5. Assuming that clients will automatically change their absolute thinking once they have identified it. Inexpert REBT therapists either fail to dispute such thinking at all or use Disputing methods sparingly and without sufficient vigor. In addition, inexpert therapists routinely fail to (1) give their clients homework assignments, which provide them with opportunities to practice Disputing their irrational Beliefs, (2) check on their client's progress on these assignments, and (3) help their clients to

identify and change their philosophic obstacles to continually working at self-change.

6. Failing to realize that clients often have problems about their problems and thus working only on a primary problem with the client is preoccupied with a secondary problem.

7. Frequently switching from ego to discomfort disturbance issues within a given session so that clients get confused and thus distracted from working on either issue.

8. Working at a pace and a level inappropriate to the learning abilities of clients so that these clients are insufficiently involved in the therapeutic process due to confusion or boredom. (pp. 58-59)

Each of these therapeutic errors could quickly hamper effective treatment with religious clients. In addition, there are several skill-related deficits that are unique to work with religious clients.

Lack of Experience With and Knowledge About Religion. Gallup surveys and other opinion poll data consistently suggests that the vast majority of Americans affiliate and involve themselves in organized religion and find this involvement important. In contrast, psychologists, and to a lesser extent other mental health professionals, are consistently among the least likely to affiliate with a formal religion (Shafranske, 1996). Although many psychologists value and respect the religious dimension, they are considerably less likely than the general population to endorse a personal, transcendent God orientation and considerably more likely to state a more nonspecific transcendent/spiritual belief. Among mental health practitioners, there exists a wide range in the approaches used in dealing with religious or spiritual issues in therapy. Surveys suggest that from 25% to 50% of psychotherapists acknowledge ever having used religious language or concepts with clients (Shafranske, 1996). Further, religion is seldom a topic during graduate training and it is not surprising that many clinicians are ill prepared to confidently handle religious concerns emerging in the therapy hour. The net effect of this lack of experience may be a poor understanding of the client's religiousness and subsequent communication to the client, overtly or subtly, that one is uncomfortable with religion (Lovinger, 1984; Spero, 1985). Therapeutic inefficacy or, worse, outright conflict may stem from the therapists' failure to attend to or grasp the significance of the client's organizing religious system. This would be equivalent to entirely overlooking the potential salience of a client's gender or racial identity.

Failure to Convey Respect for Client Religious Beliefs and Practices. A good number of religious clients fear their faith will be discounted by mental health professionals (Rayburn, 1985; Worthington, 1988). In general, REBT therapists are likely to be more helpful to their religious clients when they work to ameliorate this fear early in treatment by skillfully conveying genuine interest in and respect for the client's specific (even when apparently odd and idiosyncratic) religious convictions (Lovinger, 1984; Stern, 1985). Failure to do so may present a therapeutic obstacle to clients who fear their faith may be jeopardized by the treatment process.

Lack of authentic valuing of the client's religious faith may take several forms, but it nearly always stems from both lack of experience with healthy religious persons and a range of misbeliefs and stereotypes about religious belief. For example, psychologists tend to assume that clients' spiritual orientation may have direct bearing on their disturbance (K. N. Lewis & D. A. Lewis, 1985). They may additionally assume that religious belief and commitment are synonymous with mental disturbance and mention of religion or spirituality in therapy indicates either disturbance or resistance. Of course, reviews of relevant research on religion and health suggest quite the opposite (Bergin, 1983, 1991; Donahue, 1985; Gartner et al., 1991; Pargament & Park, 1995). For instance, Pargament and Park (1995) reviewed empirical literature relative to religion and found no evidence to confirm the notion that religiousness serves merely as a defensive reaction to trouble or dysfunction. Instead, religion appears to serve as an active and often very effective means of coping with a range of activating events.

This obstacle may be markedly reduced merely by carefully listening to the client's discussion of religious topics while actively eliciting further information about specific religious convictions and scriptural interpretations (W. B. Johnson & W. L. Johnson, 1997). In the process of actively gathering this information, REBT therapists help to increase the chance of a favorable therapeutic alliance regardless of their actual religious belief. Active and respectful therapists further arrange to collect critical information about the client's cognitive style and most descriptive irrational/disturbing beliefs (those that may transcend specific religious content).

In addition to active interest in the client's religious experience and commitment, the therapist might work at understanding components of the client's larger religious milieu and faith tradition. For example, orthodox Christian clients tend to highly value clear belief, prayer, meditation, biblical teaching, and counseling that emanates from an explicitly Christian framework (Gass, 1984). Nonetheless, each denomination or religious sect may harbor very distinct forms of doctrine and practice. For this reason, it is always wise to actively inquire about the client's faith when it is introduced in therapy. Assured of the clinician's commitment to honoring their faith, clients may turn quickly to the disturbance at hand, never mentioning religion again. Or, if religious conflicts are salient in the clients' disturbance, they are more likely to continue in REBT with the respectful therapist regardless of the therapist's actual knowledge of their religion.

In REBT, one specific danger related to failure to understand the client's religiousness is inappropriate (and ineffective) disputing of irrational beliefs. For example, with a deeply spiritual Muslim or fundamentally devout Christian client, reliance on illogicality and empiricism as dispute strategies may be flawed. The client, in this case, may place little value on logic and empirical groundedness (Dryden et al., 2000). Instead, she may note that it is so because the Koran or Bible "tells her so." At this point, less sensitive REBT therapists may be tempted to dispute or otherwise devalue the client's faith commitment or scriptural belief, which, of course, will help to ensure resistance, an impasse in treatment, and perhaps termination of therapy.

In such cases, relatively healthy religious clients, in an effort to safeguard cherished beliefs, may terminate treatment and experience prolonged suffering (Nielsen, 1994). Alternatively, the more sophisticated REBTer may focus broadly on the client's irrational demands and methods of self-disturbance. When there is convincing evidence that the client's actual religious beliefs are inherently disturbing, the therapist might request clarification regarding the client's specific belief, request a clearer analysis of related Scripture, consult with religious leaders of the client's faith, and point out discrepant or incongruent scriptural evidence or doctrine refuting the dysfunctional belief.

Use of Profanity.   I (AE) have at times encouraged judicious use of obscenities with clients. In fact, it is not unreasonable to say that among the notable psychotherapists of this century, I have probably used four-letter words more frequently and with more good effect than most others. During an interview in 1960 I noted that "my own standard is that certain modes of expression, including the use of many of the famous or infamous four-letter words, are unusually appropriate, understandable, and effective under certain conditions and at these times they can be unhesitatingly used. Many common obscenities are most incisive and expressive

when properly employed" (Ellis, 1983a, p. 4). Also, I have often used profane words in the rational-humorous songs, which I create and then occasionally sing with some clients, especially those I refer to as "difficult
customers" (DCs).

Quite often, I find that the "sprightly use of obscenity" may serve two
therapeutic purposes. First, it may facilitate rapport building with many
clients, and second, it is quite common for clients to awfulize and disturb
themselves in four-letter expletives (even when they rarely indulge in
such language in public!). For many religious clients, even those with
very devout lifestyles and commitments, profanity may very well facilitate the therapeutic relationship. It may also normalize and help them de-
catastrophize their own disturbing thoughts. Religious clients may find
particular relief in the implicit permission–conveyed by the therapist in
the use of profanity–to be more authentic and self-disclosing.

Nonetheless, for some religious clients, obscenities may neither
"match" their typical awfulizing verbalizations, nor serve to build rapport
(Nielsen, 1994; Walen et al., 1992). I (SLN) have elsewhere (Nielsen,
1994) described both the advantages and liabilities of using profanity in a
therapy group at Brigham Young University:

> The group members were Mormon BYU students. A law student was
> upset about her poor academic performance—I believed she exagger-
> ated this, as she was actually in the top third of her class. I told her, "a
> famous psychologist, Albert Ellis, has a technical term for this. Your less
> than perfect performance is proof to you of your shithood!" Tears ran
> down her face she laughed so hard. She was quickly able to dispute her
> self-rating, in part because of my profane satire of what she believed
> about herself. She soon seemed comfortable with her level of achieve-
> ment. Other group members laughed, too, but not everyone. Two other
> group members seemed offended. Luckily, they were offended with Dr.
> Ellis, not me, and we were able to cooperatively continue with therapy
> as long as I avoided profanity. I have since discovered that about 30% of
> my BYU clients will be offended by this particular REBT technical
> term. However, none has been offended by the BYU modification of the
> term, "manurehood," which often provides a satirical inroad to helping
> them dispute their self-rating. (p. 319)

Thus, a good many of my devoutly religious, returned missionary
LDS clients report that disputing with profanity has helped them. I now

attempt to ease into profanity disputing, saying "manure-like" and watching carefully for reactions. Several clients strike the compromise of inner profanity in their own disputing.

Because profanity, or "cursing," is explicitly or implicitly prohibited by many religious cultures, REBT therapists would be well served to adjust their approach to account for such religiously based sensitivities in the clients they serve. Also, newly minted REBT therapists may be most inclined to use profane language–not because it is an essential component of the therapy–but because profane language is so characteristic of my (AE) work. It is quite likely that REBT therapists who attempt to broadly use profanity with religious clients will be punished (in the form of negative client reactions or treatment failures).

Premature Use of Spiritual Interventions.   A final therapeutic obstacle related to lack of skill or experience on the part of the REBT therapist is premature introduction of uniquely religious or spiritual interventions with clients. There are many potential problems when the therapist begins quickly introducing spiritual interventions with a client (Richards & Potts, 1995). First, religious and spiritual issues may not hold substantial significance for the client, and although they may introduce some religious content early in treatment, this may be irrelevant to their primary disturbance or merely an attempt to determine whether the therapist will be "safe" or respectful of their faith commitments. Until the therapist has thoughtfully assessed the salience of religious commitment in the life of the client, it is wise to refrain from introduction of religious material.

Second, some therapists may introduce religious disputations, prayer, imagery, and so on, without adequate assessment of the client's specific beliefs and doctrinal understandings. So, conducting guided religious imagery or disputing irrational beliefs with specific scriptures when the client is a "Presbyterian by birth" and may not have practiced any sort of religion for his entire life, could be quite sabotaging to therapy progress. In this case, clients may feel misunderstood by the therapist, offended by the introduction of religion, or worse, further depressed at the thought that they must also be spiritually inadequate secondary to not knowing or understanding the practices or scriptures introduced by the therapist.

I (WBJ) once wrongly assumed that religious faith would be an important value in the life of a divorced Mexican-American woman. Although she noted in the first session that she attended a very conservative church on a weekly basis, I failed to assess how personally important her faith was or how much it impacted her central disturbance. Had I done so, I would have quickly learned that she attended church primarily for social purposes and she rarely gave thought to religious or spiritual matters herself. When, in the first session, I began introducing biblical challenges to the belief that she was worthless for being the mother of two delinquent sons, the client rightly stated, "I don't really care what God thinks about that. In my family, the only thing that matters is how your children turn out." Standing corrected, I was able to refocus therapy on the client's demands for different behavior on the part of her children and her pattern of self-downing using more traditional (nonreligious) REBT techniques.

Third, therapists may introduce religious interventions in REBT prior to establishing a therapeutic relationship with the client. In general, infusing religious material into REBT interventions is not recommended during the first session. Exceptions would be when clients explicitly request such an approach or when a treatment facility is recognized for pastoral or religiously oriented treatment. By waiting until after a careful assessment of the client's experience of primary disturbance(s), the therapist increases the probability of introducing religious material or interventions in a manner that matches the client. This, of course, does not mean the therapist should not actively explore material introduced by the client. Clients often note religious affiliation or core religious beliefs in the first session. Trust and rapport are markedly facilitated when the therapist respectfully encourages elaboration of this material and communicates genuine interest in how it may undergird certain of their presenting problems. When asked about the role of religion in their disturbance, clients will often invite exploration of religious issues.

If the clinician determines that use of a religious intervention may be beneficial for the client early in treatment, it should be used in a very collaborative manner. For example, the therapist might say something like "You know, talking about this with you, I get the feeling that your faith is fairly important to you. Is that accurate?" or "Am I misunderstanding how important religion is to you?" If the client responds positively regarding the salience of religion, then the therapist may continue with "Well, as I hear you talk, I'm remembering something I heard from the Bible that would suggest just the opposite. Would you like to hear it?"

Finally, it may not be appropriate to introduce religious interventions with seriously disturbed clients. In fact, introducing religious material with psychotic clients could conceivably worsen their condition. Unless therapists are certain that the client is free of paranoid thinking, delusional beliefs, and hallucinations, they should use religious techniques with extreme caution.

Therapist Disturbance-Based Obstacles

Some REBT therapists may disturb themselves about their clients or about their performance as psychotherapists to such an extent that they are minimally helpful to those they serve. I (AE) commented before that psychotherapists, in spite of their aspirations to godliness, are still human, and as human beings, they often indulge in the same kind of irrational absolutistic beliefs that other people hold (Ellis, 1983b, 1985). In general, therapists run the risk of disturbing themselves in two primary ways. Both forms of disturbance are counterproductive and potentially harmful to the religious client.

Countertransference: Disturbance About the Client. At times, therapists may avoid religious material in therapy or may elect not to treat religious clients secondary to an awareness of their own limited grasp of religious doctrine or practice. Ideally, they are open with clients about deficits in experience or training when religious material emerges as critical to the client's central disturbance. However, others may hold intensely negative attitudes toward specific religious beliefs, particular religious groups, or religion more generally. Due to some unresolved negative religious experience or a dichotomous perspective on religious belief (religion is nearly always healthy or pathologic), the therapists project their conflicts about religion on to the client, which may ultimately have a destructive impact on the client and treatment progress (Lannert, 1991; Lovinger, 1979; Narramore, 1994). Negative countertransfernce toward religious material may be evidenced when the therapist responds with hostility (subtle or overt) toward the client or the client's fundamental beliefs, or when the therapist actively ignores religious material that the client suggests is meaningful or important to his or her understanding of the problem. In both cases, the therapist's unexamined or unresolved issues with religion hinder treatment. Such therapist disturbance may reinforce the client's fear about the danger of psychotherapy.

Some examples of irrational beliefs that may undergird negative countertransference toward religious clients include the following:

"I *should* not have been abused or slighted by a religious person or group during my own development.

"Because some religious people seem exceptionally nutty and do bad things to others, they *should* be punished and suffer."

"I can't stand it when clients adhere to empirically unverifiable religious beliefs."

"My clients *must* give up religious beliefs in order for them to overcome their disturbance."

"Since I am doing my best and working so hard as a therapist, my clients *should* quickly see that their religious beliefs are misguided, *should* easily give them up, and *should* be appreciative that I have helped them relinquish these harmful beliefs."

When the REBT therapist strongly dislikes religious clients, evaluates them in a negative manner, and becomes insensitive to important elements of their belief and experience, the therapy relationship is likely to be compromised.

Performance Demands. The second way that therapists may easily disturb themselves is through irrational absolutistic demands about themselves and their performance as therapists. I (AE) have previously described some popular irrational beliefs among psychotherapists:

"I *have* to be successful with all my clients practically all of the time."

"I *must* be an outstanding therapist, clearly better than other therapists I know or hear about."

"I *have* to be greatly respected and loved by all my clients."

"Since I am doing my best and working so hard as a therapist, my clients *should* be equally hardworking and responsible, *should* listen to me carefully, and *should* always push themselves to change."

"Because I am a person in my own right, I *must* be able to enjoy myself during therapy sessions and to use these sessions to solve my personal problems as much as to help clients with their difficulties." (Ellis, 1983b, p. 4)

Such beliefs are unfortunately common among even the most skilled therapists and may serve to prevent them from confronting their clients, distract them and their clients from getting to the core therapeutic issues, foster undue therapist anxiety and anger, and encourage inappropriate therapist behavior (Ellis & Dryden, 1997). Some religious therapists may be prone to have very harsh judgments of their own performance with clients. Unique irrational beliefs among devout therapists might include:

"I *must* heal all my clients or I will be *unworthy* to God."

"My clients have failed to get better because I have *failed* spiritually."

"God *should* have helped me cure all of my clients and because he didn't, it proves that he hates me or that I am being punished for some transgression."

When therapists are moralistic, or prone to self-condemnation and condemnation of others, they are likely to demand that both they and their clients be other than they are. When this does not occur, they easily condemn themselves for their "failures" and help their clients damn themselves as well. In such cases, the therapist will need to actively dispute the related irrational beliefs and perhaps even model such disputation for the client. When therapists have offered themselves unconditional self-acceptance they can better offer unconditional regard to clients.

CONTEXT- OR RELATIONSHIP-BASED OBSTACLES

At times, religious clients may be poorly matched with therapists, either because of a perceived disparity in religious belief or because of excessive commonality in religious status. There may also be times when the religious community or context may pose a challenge to effective psychotherapy. Each may present a salient treatment obstacle.

Therapist–Client Disparity

Therapists and clients will seldom share precisely similar religious experiences and beliefs. Even when they are members of the same religious denomination, it is unlikely that they will concur on all doctrinal matters within that faith. More often, REBT therapists will not share the religious beliefs of clients and this need not pose an obstacle to effective treatment. However, clients may present with idiosyncratic preferences or demands about the therapist and the therapist's religiousness (Ellis, 1985; Ellis & Dryden, 1997; Lovinger, 1996).

Certain religious clients may demand that their therapist confess a belief in God and often begin therapy with questions such as "Do you believe in God?" or "Are you saved?" Of course, in such cases it is wise for therapists to be honest about their religiousness while at the same time questioning how this will be important in helping the clients work hard on overcoming their primary disturbance. The therapist might respond, "Well, actually I do (or do not) believe in God, but help me understand how that is important to you" or "what are you telling yourself *about* my religious beliefs?" Often, direct discussion of the dissimilarity in religious beliefs between therapist and client can strengthen the therapeutic relationship.

More problematic are clients who hold rigid beliefs about the credentials of the therapist who can help them. For example, a male client might state, "I can only see a male United Methodist therapist who has been an elder in the church and believes in divine creation and the inerence of scripture!" In this case, the client may believe that "if the therapist does not share my precise religious beliefs, then it is awful or even highly dangerous for me to continue in treatment with him or her." I (SLN) have found that some of my religious clients develop very intricate scriptural foundations for their distress and they then become resistant and anxious when this foundation is questioned or challenged (Nielsen, 1994). Such resistance may be heightened when the client is faced with a therapist who cannot (due to lack of familiarity) or does not (due to doctrinal disagreement) share their idiosyncratic beliefs.

This may additionally be evidence of resistance to change. If the client's requirements for "adequacy" in a therapist are so restrictive that few would meet the criteria, then the therapist must consider strongly the hypothesis that the client is not sincerely interested in change. Here the therapist may choose one of two alternatives. The therapist may attempt some disputation of the client's demanding beliefs about the therapist (e.g., "Where is it written that you cannot be helped by someone with somewhat different beliefs about God?" or "Do you believe that God ordains or oversees things that happen to us? [if yes], then I wonder why God brought you to me in the first place?"). If the client proves unwilling or unable to get past concerns about the match between themselves and the therapist, then simply offer to refer the client to a therapist with religious credentials which more closely match the client in that regard.

Therapist–Client Similarity.   With the forgoing concern about therapeutic obstacles posed by therapist-client dissimilarity, it may appear rather paradoxical to now focus on the problems inherent in excess similarity between clients and therapists. Nonetheless, it is true that one obstacle to effective REBT with religious clients occurs when the therapist and client "get on too well" (Ellis & Dryden, 1997, p. 58). For many reasons, excessively positive transference and countertransference rooted in perceptions of religious similarity may pose serious obstacles to therapeutic progress (Ellis, 1985; Kehoe & Gutheil, 1984; Spero, 1981). Although helpful in creating an initial working alliance, shared religious faith may serve to distract both the therapist and client from the main tasks of psychotherapy. A shared and collusive focus on prayer, doctrinal discussions, theological debates, and so on, may contribute to the clients' philosophy of low frustration tolerance by allowing them to consistently avoid the task of self-confrontation and change.

Kehoe and Gutheil (1984) described a case in which both the therapist and client were members of the clergy. Rather than promote change, the client, with his therapist's assistance, became highly resistant to treatment. These authors noted three important signals that excess religious similarity may be contributing to resistance: (a) Clients may offer "catechistic responses" or highly rote, ritualized, and impersonal responses to questions about themselves and their experience; (b) Clients may become "confessional" in their stance, framing their experience as indicative of failure and avoiding full disclosure to the therapist for fear that it will demonstrate their culpability or spiritual badness; and (c) Clients may begin to "deindividuate" in therapy and speak from the perspective of dogma, doctrine, and so on, rather than from their own experience. One sign that deindividuation has occurred is when clients avoid speaking in the first-person singular and speak instead in general terms ("we know that God hates sin").

If the client has gone to great lengths to seek out a therapist of the same faith, then that therapist would do well to ask why the client did so and consider whether the client is hoping the therapist will play along with spiritualized defenses. The therapist should guard against such collusion and actively confront potential diversions from the hard work of undisturbing oneself. When therapists challenge the client's religiously based defenses, they should be prepared for reactions ranging from anger to fear (Narramore, 1994).

Other Contextual Factors

Golden (1983) noted several environmental or contextual features of therapy that may also contribute to slow progress or failure in psychotherapy.

Certain of these obstacles have particular relevance to the treatment of religious clients. Relatives, friends, or associates may deliberately or inadvertently sabotage a client's progress in treatment. Common examples include pastors, parents, or friends from church encouraging the client to simply "turn over to God" all their problems and concerns. They may quote Scriptures, pray vigorously with the client, and suggest all manner of spiritual solutions to the person's primary disturbances. Unfortunately, such "interventions" may serve to heighten the client's shame or guilt about the problem and may leave them feeling more inadequate in their faith and spiritual maturity than might originally have been the case. Members of the client's church may additionally take strong exception to "secular" solutions to any problem and may enjoin the client to discontinue therapy, particularly if they discover the professional does not share the client's religious beliefs. Although most pastors are quite aware of their limitations with respect to counseling, there are exceptions. Some religious leaders may become particularly punitive toward any parishioner who seeks assistance beyond the boundary of the church. In more extreme cases, the client may actually be required to choose between continuing in treatment or remaining in good standing with family, friends, and church members.

When others sabotage (intentionally or not) the work of REBT with religious clients, the therapist may use these opportunities to show the client more about how REBT can alleviate disturbing responses to difficult events. When threatened by his spouse with separation if he continues therapy, the client can be shown that although such a choice by his wife would certainly be unpleasant, very sad, and unfortunate, it would not necessarily be catastrophic or life ending. He may continue to become less disturbed by events that previously led to profound depression and may reasonably decide that the behavioral constraints promoted by his religious group (and his spouse) are somewhat rigid and incongruent with his own understanding of the Bible.

When the severely anxious client reports to the therapist in her third session that "my friends laid hands on me last night and prayed for me, so I don't think I'll need any more therapy," the wise REBT therapist is quick to point out that such prayer may in fact have "cured" her anxiety and she may indeed not require further treatment. At the same time, the therapist may suggest that God sometimes works through therapy instead of prayer alone and it would be perfectly acceptable for her to return should she have further problems with anxiety.

Finally, when the therapist receives an angry call from a pastor, stating that his parishioner simply needs to become active in a "Men's

Accountability Group" through the church, the therapist might actively support this additional dimension to treatment and collaborate with the pastor and his client (with appropriate release of confidentiality) to add such a support group to the man's weekly involvements. Through such collaboration, the therapist hopes to elicit greater support from the client's religious network while creating a further opportunity for REBT in vivo assignments. For example, the client may then be asked to disclose to his men's group his ongoing problem with domestic violence.

A SUMMARY OF METHODS FOR OVERCOMING CLIENT RESISTANCE

The most common causes and indicators of resistance to REBT with religious clients have been discussed, and several strategies for dealing elegantly with such obstacles have been offered. Next, a summary of the primary methods for overcoming resistance in therapy with religious clients is presented.

Unconditionally Accept the Client

If the therapist fails to effectively communicate unconditional regard for and acceptance of the client, it is unlikely that much that is truly "therapeutic" will occur in the treatment relationship. REBT therapists work vigorously and consistently to show resistant clients unconditional acceptance even with all of their behavioral and emotional problems. Before moving to confront resistant client behaviors, it is critical to have first established a therapeutic alliance rooted in respect of clients and their religious convictions, regardless of how nutty these may appear to the therapist.

Demonstrate Respect for the Client's Religiousness

Many conservatively religious clients may be highly fearful of and resistant toward psychotherapy. They maintain socially reinforced concerns about the dangers inherent in secular intervention. In working with such clients, the REBT therapist is challenged to establish credibility through maintenance of a flexible, collaborative, and respectful stance toward the client's ideology, scriptural interpretations, and faith-based behavior. Confrontation of essential religious beliefs will likely heighten clients' resistance and is probably clinically inappropriate (McMinn & Lebold, 1989). Research suggests that clients who highly value their religion are more likely to evaluate a therapist positively whom they perceive as generally proreligious or at least supportive of the client's religion (McCullough & Worthington, 1995).

Demonstrate Expertise

I (AE) have taught for years that REBT therapists had better know more than their clients about being healthy! Although excellent therapists are highly collaborative in their approach to clients, they are also not "equals" with those they treat and will do well to begin teaching clients what they know early in therapy. Often, it is desirable that the therapist help the client successfully overcome a minor (or preliminary) problem with the techniques of REBT before the client will be willing to entrust the therapist with a more vexing disturbance. Successful REBT therapists are quick to get to work and communicate a good deal of confidence to clients that they will most likely be able to help them substantially with their problems.

Translate REBT Into the Religious Language of the Client

One of the surest ways to reduce, or even eliminate, client resistances based on theologic or faith-based concerns, is to carefully translate the essential tenets and techniques of REBT into the client's own faith language (W. B. Johnson & Ridley, 1992b; Propst, 1982). Therapeutic expectations can be made more powerful and religiously based fears reduced when the therapist takes the time to translate the treatment's active ingredients into "safe" or "familiar" framework of a religious worldview. Conceptualizing REBT with strongly religious clients as a cross-cultural process may be helpful here (W. B. Johnson, Ridley, & Nielsen, 2000). So, instead of telling clients it is important for them to dispute irrational beliefs, the therapist may suggest that clients will feel better when they begin challenging the Biblical truthfulness or accuracy of some of the things they believe (W. B. Johnson, 1993). The therapist may further show clients that being disturbed is not God's intent and that they will most likely become better prepared to serve God and do God's will when less disturbed.

Relentlessly Dispute Disturbance Causing Beliefs

Although therapists will ideally be consistently and forcefully encouraging and supportive of clients (Ellis & Dryden, 1997), they are also well advised not to relent when it comes to disputing the client's salient irrational beliefs—particularly those that undergird resistance. The secret often lies in the therapist's ability both to translate the disputation into the client's religious language, and to carefully create "theologic" or "therapeutic" dissonance. For example, when the resistant client says "The Bible is all I need to change," therapists do not discount their faith, but may work to dispute the accuracy of this claim via creation of doubt and dissonance (e.g., "Yes, God certainly wants us to read the Bible, but I'm not sure the Bible says it is intended as a self-help book or that it says it has answers to every problem we might have") (Lovinger, 1979; Narramore, 1994). Narramore (1994) offered another nice example of this approach with a client who insisted that she "should not need anyone but God." To this claim, he responded, "Yes, our relationship with God is absolutely crucial, but you know, when God saw that Adam was alone, he didn't tell Adam 'What's the matter with you Adam? You have me. That should be enough.' He created Eve. God apparently made us so that we need each other" (p. 253).

As another example, consider the following exchange between an angry male client presenting for marital therapy and an REBT therapist:

Client: She seems to have no respect for my leadership in the home.

Therapist: Help me understand what you mean by "no respect."

Client: She insists on working outside the home even though I made it clear that was unacceptable to me.

Therapist: And when she does that you feel _____?

Client: Upset, . . . very angry.

Therapist: And what do you tell yourself about your wife working outside the home in spite of your wishes that gets you so angry?

Client: That she shouldn't do it, that the Bible is clear that women should obey their husbands. Like Ephesians 5:22 "Wives, be subject to your husbands, as to the Lord."

Therapist: So, demanding that your wife not do what she is doing gets you very angry. Has your anger helped you or your marriage in any way?

Client: (long pause) . . . No.

Therapist: The scripture you mentioned is certainly important and suggests that in healthy marriages, wives are committed to their husbands and at times make sacrifices for them.

Client: That's right.

Therapist: I wonder though, what are your thoughts about the verses before and after the one you mentioned.

Client: Like what?

Therapist: Like Ephesians 5:21, "Be subject to one another out of reverence for Christ," and Ephesians 5:25, "Husbands love your wives, as Christ loved the church and gave himself up for her." It seems to me that Paul was telling husbands *and* wives to serve one another, love one another and give up some things for one another.

Client: [*long pause*] Yes.

In both examples, the clients' problem beliefs are disputed from within their own faith surround. Resistance subsides as clients come to understand that the therapist is neither interested in theological debates, nor hostile toward faith. Rather, the therapist consistently presents the client with alternative ways of interpreting reality via dissonance-producing challenges to fixed and distorted interpretations of Scripture. Although the therapist in the second example clearly had command of biblical content, this is not necessary in most cases.

Unangrily Reveal Client Resistances

Although interested in conveying unconditional acceptance and establishing a sense of trust with religious clients, REBT therapists are also unlikely to allow obvious resistances to treatment to go unconfronted. Therapists had better show clients that their refusal to work on their problems will generally lead to bad consequences and needless suffering (pragmatic disputation). Skilled REBT therapists resist temptations to become angry or inpatient with resistant clients and understand that their clients, like all fallible human beings, were born "highly disturbable" and prone to irrational beliefs, including some of a religious nature.

Use Referencing

It may be helpful with some religious clients to encourage them to develop a list of the disadvantages of their current behavioral and emotional problems. For example, how is their pronounced passivity (although congruent with their idiosyncratic interpretation of Scripture) getting them what they want or what God may want for them? By referring to this list many times a day and adding to it regularly, clients may become more dissatisfied with the status quo and lessen their resistant stance in therapy.

Proselytize

As sharing one's faith is often a hallmark of religious belief and practice, recommending that religious clients seek opportunities to convince others of the value of REBT may be quite congruent with their behavior pattern and faith commitments. Resistant clients who can become evangelical in vigorously teaching others the principles of REBT are more likely to change their own beliefs and cognitions about REBT, and ideally will begin applying the techniques more actively to their own disturbance.

Vigorously Confront Low Frustration Tolerance

Having established a workable alliance centered on respect for clients and their religious faith, unconditional acceptance, and therapeutic collaboration, the efficient REBT therapist is also careful to maintain a markedly vigorous and powerful style in disputing the clients' irrational beliefs and confronting their poor frustration tolerance (Ellis, 1985; Ellis & Dryden, 1997). Clients need to see clearly that they have nothing to lose and everything to gain from enduring the hard work associated with real change. As was noted in chapter 6, the degree to which a client is convinced of alternative rational beliefs will become evident in changed behavior. Both the impact of low frustration tolerance (LFT) and remedies for LFT become evident with the assignment of homework. Assign homework! Religiously congruent examples of saints who have suffered greatly and become better able to serve God are invoked and clients are challenged to convince the therapist that they hold more rational and helpful beliefs firmly instead of weakly or lightly.

Remain Flexible

It is highly desirable that the REBT therapist remain flexible and willing to experiment with a wide range of therapeutic techniques in a persistent effort to help deeply religious clients. After all, the therapist may need to tread carefully but boldly into the unfamiliar territory of theistic belief and religious behavior without appearing disrespectful or challenging of the client's fundamental faith commitment. So, therapists may experiment with many of the unique interventions covered in this book and may be willing to develop their own variations depending on the unique client's presentation.

III

Special Issues and Applications

8

Guilt and REBT

Guilt is, of course, a common theme in psychotherapy. It frequently creates confusion and presents complex problems for psychotherapists and clients, especially religious clients and the psychotherapists attempting to treat them. For example, religious clients may view guilt as both a positive and a negative phenomenon—an experience given them by God for their benefit. REBT provides a unique model and methods for clarifying the separable elements in a client's guilt experience. Rational emotive examination of guilt may provide religious clients with *religiously* acceptable relief from the self-defeating aspects of their guilt and, furthermore, may actually help clients behave in ways they find *religiously* more acceptable.

The theory and techniques of REBT offer at least four helpful insights about treating the distress that religious clients experience from guilt: First, whereas guilt clearly creates an unpleasant emotional experience, it is not a single, circumscribed, easily defined emotion. Rational emotive theory holds that there are few, if any, really simple emotions. Even if a simple, or pure, emotion seems to exist, as in the case of a client struck by a seizure, it would be a fleeting, temporary phenomenon that would quickly give way to complex thoughts about the seizure followed by several consequent emotions. Like most emotional experiences, therefore, guilt usually includes complex cognitive, emotional, and behavioral components. Furthermore, it will likely include helpful, as well as self-defeating, cognitive, emotional, and behavioral components.

Second, clients and therapists are easily confused by the co-occurrence of helpful and self-defeating emotions. For example, strong frustration is usually a helpful, if unpleasant, emotion, because it motivates individuals to solve a problem. On the other hand, anger is both unpleasant and self-defeating, because anger usually leads to some loss of control. Therapists often encourage clients to get angry in hopes of motivating and activating them, although this may lead to poorly controlled, emotional outbursts. Strong frustration would also motivate and activate a client, but in a controlled, well-modulated manner. Clients and therapists are also likely to be confused by the difference between the helpful, rational emotional elements of guilt and the self-defeating, irrational emotional components of guilt. A psychotherapist who encourages all clients to give up all guilt could lead religious clients to experience ambivalence about, conflict over, or even resistance to therapy.

Third, irrational guilt will, ironically, quite often interfere with clients' religiosity, and rational guilt will likely contribute to appropriate, desired religiosity (as defined by clients' own theologies). Shame and remorse, for example, may both occur during a guilt experience. Shame is likely to dissuade a client from attempting to apologize or make restitution to one he or she has wronged, whereas remorse is likely to encourage these reparative, repentant acts.

Fourth, rational emotive analysis of a client's guilt experience (e.g., an A-B-C analysis of guilt) will usually differentiate the helpful, but unpleasant, emotions associated with rational or good guilt from the self-defeating emotions associated with irrational or bad guilt. Once unpleasant, but helpful, emotions are unraveled from irrational, self-defeating emotions, religious clients are usually better able to drop their self-defeating bad guilt and, prompted by helpful good guilt, get on with accomplishing their goals, including their own religious goals.

DEFINING GUILT

Though it is common during psychotherapy to hear a client say, "I feel guilty," such statements illustrate tricks played on us by our use of language (as clarified in General Semantics; Hayakawa, 1940/1990; cf. Korzybski, 1933;). Ask people how they felt after committing a faux pas and most will say something like, "I felt so stupid," or "I felt like a fool." Such statements confuse *B* in the A-B-C model, *B*eliefs about the self, with *C*, the emotional *C*onsequence of the belief. The statement, "I *feel* stupid," reveals that one *believes* one has acted stupidly or foolishly, that one has also labeled one's *self* stupid or a fool, and *then* one feels an emotion that is a consequence of that belief, probably embarrassment or shame.

Consider that whereas it is common for people to say, "I feel guilty," the statement is at odds with classic definitions of guilt. Most dictionaries define *guilt* as an event, rather than as emotion; as a state of being, or as a legal, moral, or ethical fact:

Guilt, noun; from Middle English *gilt* [and] Anglo Saxon *gylt*, a fault or offense. 1) the act or state of having done a wrong or committed an offense; culpability, legal or ethical. 2) conduct that involves guilt; wrongdoing; crime; sin. (from *Webster's Unabridged Dictionary of the English Language*, McKechnie, 1979, p. 809).

Neither do definitions of *guilty* describe an emotion:

Guilty, adjective; 1) having guilt; deserving blame or punishment; culpable. 2) having one's guilt proved; legally judged an offender. 3) showing or conscious of guilt; as, a *guilty* look. 4) of or involving guilt or a sense of guilt; as, a *guilty* conscience. (McKechnie, 1979, p. 809)

The popularization of psychology may actually have changed the way individuals use language so that they now use the word *guilt* to define an emotion. However, what is that emotion? Is it really separate from other more easily defined and more clearly understood emotions? Is it actually a single, circumscribed emotion? Therapists do clients no favor by allowing them to lump together the complex emotions they experience during a guilt experience under the single title of guilt.

Rational emotive behavior theory holds that because emotions are inextricably linked with beliefs, a client's emotional experiences are best understood and defined in the context of the client's beliefs. Emotional experiences have their ultimate meaning in the context provided by the client, especially the context and meaning provided by the client's beliefs, most especially the context provided by the client's core, evaluative beliefs. Whether the client's descriptions of or labels for emotional experiences fit particular technical definitions for emotion is less important than the actual interrelation between beliefs, behaviors, and emotions that the client has constructed and that the client is presenting to the therapist in the session at hand. Rational emotive behavior theory holds that, during the session, the client's current beliefs are integral to defining the emotional experience of guilt with which the therapist will work during the session.

HELPFUL VERSUS
SELF-DEFEATING GUILT

The theory of REBT does not assume that all unpleasant emotions are necessarily targets for change. Indeed, unpleasant emotions are unhealthy only if they are self-defeating. Whether emotions are self-defeating really becomes clear in light of the client's goals. Many decidedly unpleasant emotions are healthy and helpful when viewed in this light, including concern, irritation, frustration, annoyance, disappointment, and some kinds of fear. This is also true of many unpleasant emotions associated with the experience of guilt. Although these emotions may be quite unpleasant, some may be helpful to the individual experiencing the guilt (including sadness, regret, and remorse) and to society, and others may be self-defeating.

REBT does not offer clients relief from guilt through encouraging them to ignore or trivialize their misbehavior, and it does not fit the theory of REBT to simply encourage religious clients to disavow their religious beliefs about right and wrong. Rather, REBT suggests that some of the unpleasant emotions associated with misbehavior (and, subsequently, with guilt) may helpfully prevent future misbehavior, whereas other emotions are likely to be self-defeating, preventing clients from accomplishing their goals and either inefficiently preventing future misbehavior or even leading to more misbehavior in the future. Clients who feel guilty will very frequently experience both an unpleasant but helpful emotion, and an unpleasant *and* self-defeating emotion as part of their guilt experience. Differentiating between these emotions and their causes is key to helping clients.

THE A-B-CS OF GUILT:
RELIGIOUS ACTIVATING EVENTS

A religious client's guilt will usually arise through violation—perhaps only perceived—of rules linked with religious beliefs. Although clients need not be religiously committed to experience guilt about misbehavior, adherence to a religious belief system likely yields increased guilt proneness (Meek, Albright, & McMinn, 1995; Richards, 1991; Richards & Potts, 1995; Rickner & Tan, 1994). Because organized religious belief systems usually include rules for living, the violation of which induce guilt, religious belief systems may restrict behaviors that are unrestricted outside the religious belief system. Because devoutly religious clients are likely to organize their lives around religious doctrines and rules, greater belief in or devotion to religious tradition may also yield greater opportunities for experiencing guilt.

Sabbath observance and religious dietary rules are just two examples of religious rules that have both an overall organizing effect and, perhaps, an increased potential for inducing guilt. Some religious traditions have strict rules about activity on the Sabbath. In areas where a particular religious tradition is predominant, businesses may close in accordance with Sabbath observance. For example, the Israeli state airline, El Al, does not fly from Friday night through Saturday night, the times of the Jewish Sabbath. Most people select their diet based on their appetites and health concerns, but some have other considerations: Jews and Moslems consider pork unclean; Adventists and Hindus may experience guilt for eating meat; an observant Hindu may experience especially severe guilt for eating beef and consider eating beef from a cow a greater sacrilege than eating beef from a bull (Ward, 1997).

Because different religions proscribe different behaviors, clients' adherence to religious rules may introduce considerable complexity for psychotherapists attempting to understand their religious clients' guilt. Clients from different religious backgrounds may, because of their religious beliefs, view the same behaviors quite differently. Clients from different religious backgrounds may view the same behavior as unremarkable or as sinful. Those who view a behavior as sinful are likely to experience guilt if they catch themselves in such behavior.

When facing the prospect of psychotherapy with a "nonbeliever," religious individuals may feel suspicious because they believe (often correctly) that psychotherapists who do not share their religious convictions may misunderstand, ignore, ridicule, or otherwise challenge their religious beliefs and the rules associated with these beliefs (Bergin, Payne, & Richards, 1996; Worthington, 1986). If a therapist questions whether a particular behavior is really all that wrong, a religious client, rather than experiencing relief from guilt, may simply resist the therapist. Indeed, the client may experience even greater guilt for considering a therapist's suggestion that a sinful behavior is inconsequential.

Beliefs, Not Activating Events

Rational emotive behavior theory and technique offers a clear path through the complexity and confusion posed by the complexity of Activating events that may lead to guilt for religious clients. The preferred, rational emotive behavioral goal of the session is almost always helping clients understand and change their Beliefs. The upset that brings clients to psychotherapy usually has its roots in irrational, absolutistic, evaluative Beliefs. According to REBT theory, the most efficient way to reduce that upset is to replace these absolute evaluations with rational, preferential evaluations.

Clients will often come from environments that seem foreign or odd to their therapists, including religious backgrounds. Environments and perceptions about these environments are all Activating events. However odd or foreign they may seem, they are less the source of self-defeating emotions and behaviors than how clients evaluate their world. It is the evaluative Beliefs that drive emotions more than Activating events and clients' perceptions of these events. Religiously defined Activating events, however idiosyncratic they may seem, may also be more sacred to the religious client, creating a riskier setting for the therapist attempting to deal with guilt. Whether unscientific or illogical or impractical, if it is a religious truth for the client, it is likely to seem true to the client. During REBT, it is still just another Activating event, however.

A religious therapist working with a client from the same religious background is certainly not guaranteed smooth agreement about religious truths. Even when the therapist and client share religious traditions, they may disagree strongly about what is truth; they may disagree about what constitutes correct doctrine, for example. Even when working with a shared religious background, it still probably works better to seek the elegant solution of helping the client understand and challenge absolutistic, and therefore irrational, evaluative Beliefs. Getting sidetracked with Activating events (e.g., whether this or that idea is correct doctrine) is risky, as can be seen in my (SLN) first and only session with Martha.

Martha's Guilt (Demanding and Anger at the Self). Though Martha, a 21-year-old university student, and I (SLN) came from the same religious background (the Church of Jesus Christ of Latter-day Saints, or the Mormon church), we viewed the religious rules implicated in Martha's guilt quite differently. Martha quickly and correctly detected this disagreement and resisted. Martha's irrational demands, not her idiosyncratic view of Mormon doctrine, were the primary source of her self-defeating distress, although I missed this until too late. Her irrational evaluative Beliefs, not her views of religious doctrine (views I considered to be idiosyncratic) were the best targets for REBT disputation.

Martha indicated on her intake questionnaire that she wanted help controlling her weight, and her binging and purging. She indicated on the intake questionnaire that she had been binging and purging for about 3 years. Martha reported that at 5'2", she weighed 135 pounds, and stated that she had the goal of losing at least 20 pounds. Following is part of our discussion about her eating patterns:

SLN: Help me understand what you mean when you say you overeat.

Martha: I just eat too much.

SLN: Do you eat until you feel stuffed or uncomfortably full so that it's easier for you to vomit?

Martha: I used to do that, but not for 6 or 7 months now. No. But I still overeat.

SLN: So you don't make yourself vomit anymore?

Martha: Oh, I still make myself vomit. But I can do it without stuffing myself.

SLN: So, do you stick a finger down your throat?

Martha: Sometimes, but usually I can do it if I just think about vomiting in the right way–disgusting!

SLN: When's the last time you made yourself vomit?

Martha: Two nights ago.

SLN: What happened?

Martha: Well, I had some cereal in the morning, and a tuna sand-wich–but without mayonnaise–and a salad at lunch; and pasta with tomato sauce and a salad at dinner.

SLN: Did you eat several salads or lots of spaghetti or something?

Martha: No, not really.

SLN: I guess I don't understand what you mean by overeating, then.

Martha: Well, I ate a candy bar last night.

SLN: A candy bar. Was it a big candy bar?

Martha: No, it was just a regular Snickers® bar.

SLN: And you felt really full after you ate the candy bar?

Martha: Well . . . really . . . I guess I felt guilty.

SLN: About the candy bar? So you made yourself throw up because you felt guilty about eating the candy bar?

Martha: Yeah.

SLN: What are you telling yourself about eating that candy bar?

Martha: It was wrong.

SLN: Help me understand why it's wrong for you to eat a candy bar.

Martha: It's against the Word of Wisdom.

The Word of Wisdom is LDS Scripture consisting of advice about diet, which Latter-day Saints believe was given to their first prophet Joseph Smith by God in 1840 (Doctrine and Covenants 89). The Word of Wisdom advises against use of alcohol, tobacco, coffee, and tea, and encourages sparing consumption of meat in a diet consisting mainly of grain products, fruits, and vegetables. Latter-day Saints believe that both better physical health and improved spiritual acuity will come through obedience to the Word of Wisdom.

The Word of Wisdom says nothing whatever about sweets, overeat-ing, or gluttony, although some interpret it this way. More importantly, it appears that Martha interpreted it in this way and it thus provided her with a jumping off point for her guilt. Martha had idiosyncratically extended and embellished this religious rule so that, in her mind, it condemned being overweight and, presumably, other kinds of self-inflicted poor health. I began to examine and challenge this idea. We shared the same religious background, but Martha saw this as an attack on her religious beliefs. I was challenging her Activating event, here:

SLN: The Word of Wisdom forbids Snickers® bars?

Martha: No, but it does say to be healthy.

SLN: So it's a sin for you to eat Snickers® bars?

Martha: Yeah.

SLN: Me, too? You see, I like candy (I pointed out the half-full candy jar in the office).

Martha: No. But I think the Word of Wisdom means you should be healthy—we should be healthy.

SLN: So you feel guilty because you're eating something that's unhealthy for you?

Martha: Right.

SLN: So, according to the Word of Wisdom you *have to* abstain from chocolate?

Martha: I don't have to abstain from chocolate, but I do have to get control of my eating and my weight. It's a sin to be overweight.

SLN: I guess I missed that part of the Word of Wisdom–the part that says it's a sin to be overweight. Could you show me in the Scriptures?

Martha: I'm not sure it says that, but that's what it means! That's what keeps me from blowing up like a balloon, too.

Because I was quite familiar with the Word of Wisdom, I knew that its 21 verses say nothing about sweets or about being overweight. Furthermore, it makes promises about, but does not require good health, nor does it condemn ill health, even self-inflicted ill health as occurs with gluttony. I thought that refreshing Martha's memory by reading the actual words of the Scripture might challenge her exaggerated idea. However, Martha believed, correctly, that I intended to challenge her interpretation of Scripture. Her interpretation of Scripture was her Activating event. She also correctly anticipated that I was about to challenge whether she was really guilty of *sin* at all. Her belief that she had sinned by eating a candy bar, a notion that few other Mormons would indorse, was also an *Activating* event. I thought that if Martha were shown that the Word of Wisdom does not really support the notion that overweight and overeating are sins, then she could begin to view the situation differently.

Martha said, ". . . that's what it means!" with considerable vehemence. She added, "That's what keeps me from blowing up like a balloon, too!" It was quite evident from the expression on her face and from the tone of her voice that, at best, she was irritated; more probably, she was angry at me for challenging her interpretation of Scripture. We might speculate that my questions seemed like an attack on Scripture. Martha also stated that she believed that her guilt usefully helped her control her weight, so perhaps she did not want to lose an effective weight control mechanism.

Martha did not return for the next session, so there was no chance to follow up. In retrospect, it seems clear that the most upsetting element in Martha's thinking–the active ingredient in her upset–was her evaluative demand, "I *have to* get control of my eating and my weight." I (SLN) was giving more attention to her views of the doctrine and her view that she was breaking a commandment. These were both part of the *Activating* event. Her demand that she must adhere to this interpretation of the Word of Wisdom was the evaluative *Belief* that created her guilt.

Given that Martha was making strong demands of herself, demands that she could not meet, it is likely that the emotions she experienced when she said she felt guilty occured as a cycle of anger at herself, followed by shame. Keeping the distinction between doctrine and her evaluative *Beliefs* straight could have saved wasted time, perhaps, prevented Martha's resistance, and brought her back to another session.

B's, Not A's. Martha's response highlights the importance of detecting and separating irrational *evaluative* Beliefs (demands, catastrophizing, frustration intolerance, and self-rating) from inferential beliefs, including unrealistic, unempirical perceptions of the world, whether a real, physical world or in the client's religious world of theological ideas and belief. Inferential beliefs describe the world and include thoughts answering questions like, "What? Where? Why? When? and How?" These inferences clarify for people how the world is, how others are, and why this is so–and, for example, what their religion's doctrines say about their world and experience. Martha was upset by several beliefs, including her belief that Scripture dictates she control her weight when she was having great difficulty controlling her weight. It might be argued that almost all religious guilt arises from similar sets of beliefs, such as the belief that Scripture forbids adultery. This is not incorrect, for clearly the belief that Scripture dictated a certain eating pattern contributed to Martha's upset.

Rational emotive behavior theory holds, however, that evaluative beliefs are quite separate from and go well beyond inferences. Evaluative beliefs can most fully explain the emotion, whereas inferences only set the stage. Whatever inferences individuals form about their world, evaluations give their inferences emotional importance. Inferential beliefs answer questions like "What is going on here?" Evaluative beliefs answer the question, "So what?" An evaluative belief explains and clarifies desirable or undesirable, valuable versus less valuable. Rational evaluative beliefs remain at the level of preference, and irrational evaluative beliefs move to the absolute levels of demanding and evaluating people as a whole.

REBT holds, then, that Martha was upset in two ways, one rational and potentially self-helping, the other irrational and likely self-defeating. First, she was sad, irritated, and concerned about her eating and her weight. Why? Because she wanted to eat less and wanted to weigh less. She mixed this personal desire with what was probably a lifelong desire to obey Scripture–as *she* interpreted it, to be sure. Second, Martha was self-defeatingly depressed, anxious, and angry at herself because she insisted that she "should" eat less, because she demanded that she "must" control her weight, and because it was completely unacceptable that she disobeyed this Scripture in this particular way.

Martha's interpretation of the Scripture was somewhat idiosyncratic. It is likely that most practicing Latter-day Saints would have disagreed with Martha's interpretation that eating candy or being overweight was sinful behavior. Unfortunately, however, her therapist set off on an unhelpful, inelegant, side trip of challenging her inferences about doctrine. Indeed, it may be that my (SLN's) knowledge of Latter-day Saint Scripture made it more likely that I would challenge Martha's inferences. This may explain why one outcome study found that nonreligious cognitive-behaviorists had better outcomes with religious clients than religious cognitive-behavioral therapists (Propst et al., 1992). Religious therapists may have been uncomfortable with doctrinal slippage. Someone ignorant of the Word of Wisdom might have viewed Martha's description of overeating as sin as an unusual idea that, nonetheless, could be healthy in an unusual culture. Accepting Martha's view of eating candy bars as an unusual religious truth, the nonreligious therapist could then, more elegantly, have moved on to treating her guilt by challenging the notion that she must not fall short of obeying this particular commandment.

It could have been as simple as this kind of question, "I understand that you consider it a sin to eat too much, especially candy bars. But what does it do for you to say that you *must never* sin in this way? Especially when you are having real trouble with eating? How does it make you feel to demand that you must have more self-control? What if you only wanted to get better control and lose weight, but refused to demand that you change your habits *right now*? How would you feel then?"

What REBT calls the elegant solution is likely to point to a clear way through the complexities of true doctrine. Look for the shoulds, musts, oughts, have tos, got tos, need tos, the awfuls, and look for the human rating. Once these evaluative demands are detected, then the therapeutic picture will become clearer. Consider how, in the following case of Rachel's guilt, the potentially confusing picture of guilt without any obvious sin became clear when the evaluative belief was detected:

Rachel's Guilt (Self-Rating and Shame).   Clients need not transgress in order to feel guilt. Rachel's case illustrates such free floating guilt. Rachel was a 20-year-old honor student at the university. She came to therapy seeking treatment for depression. Rachel was attending the university on a "full ride" academic scholarship that paid for her tuition, fees, and books. Part of her depression was linked with the following "guilty feeling: "

SLN: Tell me what you mean when you say you feel guilty.

Rachel: Well, I feel guilty when I'm around my roommate Leah.

SLN: Have you done something to her?

Rachel: No . . . I don't know.

SLN: Tell me when you feel guilty.

Rachel: We're taking a Chinese class together–Mandarin. She's a Chinese major and it's my minor. She's having lots of trouble with it. She works hard at it, but I don't have to. I'm getting A's and she's getting C's and she feels badly about her grades. I try not to let her know how I'm doing, but sometimes she asks. And even if I don't tell her, she can tell from conversation exercises in class that I know Chinese much better than her. She seems upset with *me* sometimes!

SLN: So you feel guilty because it's hard for her and easy for you.

Rachel: I guess so. I try to help her, but she just gets so frustrated sometimes that I don't want to be around her.

SLN: Let's try a little experiment. Tell me again how you feel about this–how you feel about easily getting A's while Leah gets C's with great difficulty, even after she works very hard, and even though she's *majoring* in Chinese while you're just *minoring* in Chinese. Tell me how this feels, but use some other word besides guilty. When you see how hard it is for her and how easy it is for you, you feel . . . what? But don't use the words guilt or guilty.

Rachel: Don't say, I feel guilty? But I feel *guilty!* I don't know what else I feel.

SLN: Sure you know. You just haven't figured out how to put it into words yet. Tell me how you feel, but use some other word besides guilty, maybe some word that's a synonym for how you feel. Try saying it in Mandarin if you like, then translate it into English. You feel . . . what?

Rachel: I feel . . . unworthy? Yeah, that's it, when I'm around Leah, I feel unworthy.

Note how helpful this simple search for a synonym was. Rachel was showing how her beliefs were activated by her roommate's difficulties in school, and in the process providing a highly descriptive insight into the A-B-Cs of her guilt experience. First she called her feeling guilt, then she called it unworthiness. Of course, unworthiness is not an emotion! Rather, unworthiness it is an evaluative belief about one's essential status. Rachel was also revealing the immediacy, automatic quality, and vividness of her beliefs about herself. Her statement revealed a tacit link between her evaluative beliefs about herself and the emotions that arose as a consequence of these beliefs. This is the B-C connection, the connection between the *B*elief and the *C*onsequent emotion discussed in chapter 4. So closely related were Rachel's beliefs and emotions in this situation that they flowed automatically and seamlessly into one another in her mind. She confused what she believed about the situation and about herself with what she felt. She felt guilty, meaning she believed that she was unworthy of her good performance and easy grades when her roommate Leah's performance was poor despite hard work. We continued:

SLN: But you see, "unworthy" and "guilty" are not emotions, they're ideas. At some level you're *telling* yourself that you are unworthy. You're telling yourself that somehow you're unworthy of, don't deserve, and are, therefore, guilty of getting good grades! What makes a person worthy or unworthy? Deserving or undeserving?

Rachel: I don't know.

SLN: Perhaps not, but you do believe that you aren't worthy of good grades. You get good grades but you are not . . . what? Good enough?

Rachel: Good enough? Yeah, I guess that's right.

SLN: So, you see, you feel what you feel because you believe that you're not a good enough person to deserve your good grades.

Rachel: It just doesn't seem fair that Leah gets worse grades than me.

SLN: Because?

Rachel: She works harder at it than I do. I'm no better than her!

SLN: Well, we can certainly agree there. You are *no better* than Leah, but you're probably a good deal *smarter* than she is. Or, at least, you have a better ear for Chinese than Leah. Based on your scholarship you probably have much better grades and test scores than Leah, too, in all academic realms. I'll bet that you do better in almost every class you take than she does.

Rachel: I don't know. I don't *want* to know. And I don't want her to know how I'm doing, either.

SLN: Right! She might feel even worse if she knew, so don't let her know if you don't want to. But, you're doing very, very well in school, so she might notice, and if she notices she might feel upset about it. But notice, what you call guilt is really an emotion that arises from believing that you're not good enough. So how do people feel when they say to themselves that they are not good enough? That they are unworthy?

Rachel: Embarrassed? Ashamed?

SLN: Sure. You believe that you're not good enough to deserve the good grades you get, and then you feel ashamed when you see Leah get worse grades. It seems to me that both you and Leah are confusing smarts and grades with something else about you. Right? What?

Rachel: I don't know. How good we are?

SLN: Yes! Like many other students *and* professors. And probably you and Leah are also telling yourselves that if Leah works quite hard at Chinese, because she's a *good* person she . . . what?

Rachel: She ought to get better grades?

SLN: Yes, and since you're not a better person than Leah and since you don't work all that hard to get nearly perfect grades in Chinese, you somehow don't deserve and shouldn't get such good grades.

So, Rachel's guilt experience was comprised mostly of shame, arising from her self-rating. In an ironically humble way, she actually bought into the intellectual fascism that exists at most universities, an idea that seems to dictate that smarter people are more valuable people. Because she did not believe that she was more valuable than Leah, but because she had a vague notion that good performance in class may show something like that–indeed her roommate Leah may have believed this—she was, therefore, not accepting that she was, simply put, more intelligent and efficient at Chinese than Leah. Rachel was able to leave this guilt behind after just one session. This is what seemed to wrap it up for her later in the session:

SLN: Of course, there are some ways you could *not* deserve your good grades. If you cheated you would not deserve good grades. Did you cheat?

Rachel: Of course not!

SLN: Or if you bribed the teacher or if the teacher favored you because you were his daughter or lover or something. Is that what happened?

Rachel: No! Of course not! And it would have to be *her* daughter or lover –my Chinese professor's a woman.

SLN: Sorry. Or, perhaps you embezzled brains when God was handing them out? You know, maybe something got mixed up in the pre-existence.

Rachel: Uh, I don't think so [*laughing*]. I think God is capable of working out such things correctly.

SLN: But, of course, even if you had cheated on your Chinese tests—which you didn't—would that make you unworthy of good grades in other classes? Would cheating change you in some immutable way?

Rachel: I don't know.

SLN: Could *anything* change a person's essence? If someone cheats or shoplifts or curses or misbehaves in any way, do they, themselves, become creatures of lesser substance or content? Are they, thereafter, festering, fermenting, maggoty, runny, infectious, stinking piles of manure?

Rachel: [*Laughing*] No.

SLN: Oh? What if you cheated, shoplifted, cursed or in some other way misbehaved?

Rachel: No, I wouldn't be manure.

After discussing her "guilt," we went on to discuss Rachel's concerns about socializing. Not surprisingly, she also believed that she wasn't good enough, "cool" enough, really, for many other students—too bookish, she said. After trying socializing homework assignments, including forcing herself to flirt with boys she found attractive, all the while reminding herself that a human being's substance or essence cannot change, Rachel felt much better. She reminded herself before, during, and after each bout of flirting that she and the young man whose attention she was trying to capture were utterly equal in every essential human way, although they obviously differed in practical ways such as intelligence, height, socially defined attractiveness, and so forth. She also reminded herself that, based on her experience, she was likely more intelligent than most other students, less intelligent than just a very few, but not an essentially more or less adequate human being. She came to three more sessions spaced over 2 months and then decided she needed no further visits.

Rachel's guilt was nearly "free floating" in that she could not tie her feelings to a particular sin. Of course, many clients, especially many religious clients—experience guilt because they are overtly and consciously telling themselves something about their behavior. For this reason, REBTers can actually welcome client reports of guilt. Once clients report guilt, they are also likely to produce the self-talk most closely associated with the guilt, giving a potentially quick and clear window into their irrational beliefs. Thereafter, it is quite possible that their guilt will be alleviated by cognitive-behavioral techniques, especially techniques that speak to the core, evaluative beliefs that are likely to energize the guilt. Finally, addressing the core elements will often be enough to relieve the guilt and correct the behaviors about which the client is experiencing guilt, as Dan's case illustrates.

Dan's Guilt (Depression and Discouragement). Dan, a devoutly religious, 30-year-old, mechanical engineer, came to therapy saying that he was "filled with guilt" about masturbating. He masturbated once or twice a week. This had been going on for about 15 years. Over the years, Dan had frequent discussions with ecclesiastical leaders about his masturbation. After discovering masturbation on his own as a teenager, he had masturbated frequently until told this was religiously forbidden. Some leaders had advocated punitive steps to help him stop, and others recommended some supportive steps. He had managed to stop for several long periods, including a period of about a year at the beginning of a proselyting mission for the Church of Jesus Christ of Latter-day Saints. He was required to refrain from masturbating for 3 months prior to beginning his mission. He was able to do so and did not masturbate again for another 10 months after beginning his missionary service. But, Dan explained, that he had served in Holland, where he was continually confronted with nudity in advertising. He felt tempted to look and, he said, he felt "ashamed and horrified" that he was "turned on" by what he saw. Eventually, he began masturbating again. He contacted his ecclesiastical leader, the president of his mission, whom he found quite understanding, forgiving, and supportive. After talking with his mission leader, he had masturbated infrequently, perhaps four or five more times during the next 14 months of his mission. After he returned home, he had sometimes masturbated as often as once or twice a day.

Dan was single, but very much wanted to marry. He explained that he would not let himself date the same woman more than once or twice, feeling that he was "unworthy" of the kind of partner he would want. We had the following conversation during our first session:

SLN: So, right now you're masturbating a little more than once a week. Tell me about the last time you masturbated.

Dan: Well, it was Sunday. I thought it was Monday morning, but it was really Sunday night, still. You know, the time changed to daylight savings. I had already set the clock forward in my office, so I thought it was Monday morning, but it was still really Sunday. I thought I had gotten through Sunday, and then, when I noticed it was after midnight, I felt this let down and started cruising the net and then I masturbated. Then when I went to bed I saw that it was actually still Sunday!

SLN: It sounds like that part's quite upsetting to you.

Dan: Sure. I've always managed not to mess up on the Sabbath.

SLN: So what are you telling yourself about masturbating on Sunday?

Dan: Don't you get how wrong that was! I should *never* have done that. I should, at least, have been able to keep track of the Sabbath. I feel so horrible for having done that.

SLN: I think we need to concentrate on what you're telling yourself about the Sabbath.

Dan: We're supposed to keep the Sabbath day holy.

SLN: Right, I understand that part. But I don't understand what you're telling yourself about not having done what you're supposed to do. What are you telling yourself about masturbating on the Sabbath day?

Dan: I just feel like it's a horrible thing for me to do. It's inexcusable, especially after all these years.

SLN: After all these years of masturbating it's inexcusable because . . . ?

Dan: After all these years of working at stopping I should be able to stop. I feel like I'm a lost cause.

Dan was very explicit in describing his thinking and feelings, so that assessment of his irrational beliefs was quite easy. He "felt"—believed really—that he was "a lost cause." Disputing could begin with his self-rating. He also said that he *should* be able to stop after all these years and that his behavior was inexcusable, so disputing could begin with his demanding. He said that it was a horrible thing for him to masturbate on Sunday, so this horriblizing about his behavior could also be disputed. I decided to begin by disputing his self-rating:

SLN: When you say you feel that you're a lost cause, I'm guessing that you're feeling bad about yourself. You're telling yourself something about you. Something like, I masturbated again, this time on a Sunday, therefore I am . . . What?

Dan: I'm . . . such a worthless sinner!

SLN: So, because you sinned in this particular way, masturbating on the Sabbath, that makes you worthless. But you see, if you think *anything* could make you worthless, no matter what it might be—spitting on the sidewalk, or whatever—you will be giving yourself at least one *extra* problem. So here you have three problems, instead of just two.

Dan: What do you mean?

SLN: In the present case you did two things which you very much did not want to do. You wanted to stop masturbating, but masturbated again. You also wanted to keep the Sabbath day holy, but masturbated late on a Sunday night. So, you did these two things you didn't want to do and feel disappointed. But the extra problem comes from you telling yourself not just that you wish you hadn't misbehaved, but *also* that you are worthless for having misbehaved. You have the extra problem of feeling depressed and discouraged because you think of yourself as worthless. How will *anyone* feel if he tells himself—and *believes*, as *you* believe—that he is worthless?

Dan: I guess he'll feel worthless.

SLN: Right, but you see, worthless is an idea. But how does that belief cause one to feel? What would that feeling be for you? What do you feel when you tell yourself—*and believe*—that you are worthless?

Dan: I feel pretty lousy. I feel discouraged. Sometimes I feel despair.

SLN: And those are self-defeating emotions. Do those emotions encourage you? Does calling yourself worthless and feeling despair motivate you to go to Church? Do you believe that you *can* stop masturbating?

Dan: No.

SLN: In fact, I would guess that the more worthless you think you are, the more depressed you feel, the more likely you are to masturbate. Right?

Dan: Yes, that's seems about right.

Dan's clear description of his self-rating made it easy to begin to dispute this irrational belief. This first challenge was a functional or pragmatic disputation. I was challenging Dan to examine the practical effects of his irrational belief. I attempted to lead him to see that this belief's function in his life was to upset him in such a way that it actually interfered with him overcoming his masturbation problem—pretty ironic! Thereafter, I attempted to develop a disputation based on the authoritative evidence against human rating available from the religious Scriptures in which he believed.

SLN: You seem pretty religious. Do you read your Scriptures?

Dan: I try to.

SLN: Where is it written in Scripture that *anyone* is worthless?

Dan: I'm not sure. It does talk about Hell.

SLN: Sure, people suffer when they misbehave or make mistakes. But it sounds to me like you're expert at punishing yourself. I'm not sure God would need to punish you any more than you already have punished yourself. Why would He need to send you to Hell when you put yourself there over and over again? But you are adding an extra burden to the suffering by believing that sin makes you worthless. Whatever punishment you receive, how will you feel if you also say, "And I'm worthless?"

Dan: I don't know.

SLN: Well, since you mentioned Hell, imagine identical twin brothers who commit some grievous sin. Let's say they committed adultery with identical twin sisters and died from heart attacks just afterward. So, they wake up to find themselves in Hell for the same sin. Now, they are identical in every way and their sins are identical; their punishments are identical. Would either brother be happy to be in Hell?

Dan: No, of course not.

SLN: So, they are both unhappy. But one believes, "I sure blew it! Hell is sure hot! I really wish I hadn't screwed up!" His brother believes, "I sure blew it! Hell is sure hot! I really wish I hadn't screwed up! Being in Hell surely proves what a worthless pile of crap I am!" Which brother is the most unhappy.

Dan: They'll both be unhappy.

SLN: Indeed, they will probably both be unhappy. But who is most likely to feel depressed?

Dan: I guess the second one.

SLN: And which one thinks most like you?

Dan: The second one.

SLN: Could you work to think differently? What would it be like if you began to tell yourself, "I am not bad because I do things I don't want to do?"

Dan: I don't know. I don't think I could believe that. It wouldn't be right.

SLN: Look, do you remember King Benjamin in the Book of Mormon? Do you remember what he's famous for?

Dan: Sure. Just before he died he commanded his people to come to the temple. He climbed a tower and gave a sermon on service and keeping the commandments to his people.

SLN: The people listening—is it possible that some of them masturbated? Maybe the ancients never touched their penises, except to urinate, that is. Maybe they hadn't discovered masturbation—too busy watching hieroglyphics, perhaps.

Dan: No, probably some of them masturbated.

SLN: Is it possible that they masturbated as often as you?

Dan: Perhaps.

SLN: At the beginning of his speech King Benjamin said this, would you read the underlined part?

Dan: "I have not commanded you to come up hither to trifle with the words which I shall speak, but that you should hearken unto me, and open your ears that ye may hear, and your hearts that ye may understand" (Mosiah 2: 9; Book of Mormon).

SLN: So, was he just joking around with them?

Dan: No, he sounds serious.

SLN: And among the other things he said was this. Would you read this second underlined part?

Dan: "And I, even I whom ye call your king, am no better than ye, yourselves, are . . . " (Mosiah 2: 26).

SLN: What do you think he meant?

Dan: I sounds pretty clear. It seems that he believes in equality.

SLN: But what about the men in the audience that masturbated? Including the men who chronically masturbated, for years and years? Don't you think he can have believed he was no better than the listeners *except* for the ones who masturbated on the Sabbath?

Dan: I see what you mean. Probably not.

SLN: Well, perhaps he was lying or just saying what he thought they wanted to hear. Perhaps he was deluded. If I remember correctly, he was quite old at the time he said this, so it may be that dementia was setting in. What do you think? Was it pathology speaking or was he speaking with authority from God?

Dan: I believe he was speaking with authority from God.

SLN: Okay. If you believe that, then what could you begin telling yourself about masturbating?

Dan: That I'm not a bad person for masturbating?

SLN: What if you said it less tentatively? What if you said it as if you *believed* it? What if you really *did* believe that you were neither a better nor a worse person for any reason, only better *off* or worse *off*?

Dan: I would feel a lot better.

SLN: Can you tell a difference between better and better off, worse and worse off?

Dan: Sure. Better and worse seem like it's me; better off and worse off sounds like my circumstances.

SLN: What about sin? Worse? Or worse *off*?

Dan: Worse off.

Dan left our session with the assignment to talk forcefully to himself, reminding himself that what King Benjamin had said would apply to him, while working to accept that sexual thoughts were an understandable part of his cognitive and emotional nature, although they were troublesome given his marital status and his desire to better control his sexual behavior.

Dan came to four more sessions. We added a response-cost system to his disputations. He gave me an envelope containing five $20 bills and agreed that we would flush a $20 bill down the toilet if he masturbated except at a specific, prearranged time. He would receive the entire $100 back if he did not masturbate for 4 months.

He reported in subsequent weeks that he had little trouble resisting the urge to masturbate. He also found that he was more comfortable with a new woman he had asked out, so he kept asking her out. Dan came back after 4 months for the $100, which he spent on a very nice date. He then came back a little more than 9 months later and reported that he had masturbated just once during the entire 9 months. He had stopped dating the first woman, but had been dating a different woman for about 6 months.

Dan reported that self-acceptance was really the key to his newfound control over masturbation. He said that he still noticed and got turned on by some thoughts, but did not really feel guilty about it and did not feel very tempted to masturbate. After the one time he had masturbated, Dan decided that it was not really very important that he had masturbated again—just once in more than 8 months.

Self-defeating emotions associated with guilt are the focus of attention during REBT, not the verity of rules that clients believe they have broken, including the verity of clients' religious rules—even if the REBT therapist disbelieves or disagrees with the religious rules! Whether the client's behavior constitutes misbehavior or sin in the therapist's view is important, but not the major point. REBTers need neither agree with nor attempt to change the client's conception of what constitutes religious "truth" or religious error to the client in order to help the client deal with self-defeating distress arising because of guilt. REBTers need only return to the preferred goal of understanding clients' core irrational beliefs (self-rating, demanding, or catastrophizing), demonstrating the self-defeating effects of these beliefs, and helping the client dispute these irrational beliefs.

When clients say they feel guilty, they are often referring to a self-defeating emotion. If so, then these emotions are an appropriate focus for

REBT. If when clients say they feel guilt they are referring to unpleasant but healthy and helpful emotions, then these emotions are probably not an appropriate target for REBT. How then can these self-defeating emotions be defined? Self-defeating emotions are those emotions that interfere with clients accomplishing their goals, including their religious goals.

THE A-B-CS OF GUILT

Because of its focus on core beliefs, REBT offers a unique opportunity for helping the client understand feelings associated with guilt, including a productive approach to dealing with the self-defeating distress that may arise because of guilt. Whatever the client's guilt, REBT holds that the self-defeating emotions and behaviors that arise because of guilt will be linked with irrational beliefs (IBs), including human rating, demanding, and awfulizing. My (SLN's) attempt to "correct" Martha's view of the Word of Wisdom was an unfortunate diversion from this preferred REBT goal of detecting and challenging her core IBs. By suggesting that we check Scripture, I was attempting to challenge the A, the activating event. As is often the case, this diversion was less efficient than more direct investigation and challenging of the irrational beliefs underlying her distress. Furthermore, because Martha interpreted this as challenging a religious truth, she was quick to resist therapy.

It is likely that most Latter-day Saints would agree that Martha was exaggerating and embellishing the Word of Wisdom, because the Word of Wisdom says nothing whatever about how much a person should weigh. However, rather than focusing on what the Word of Wisdom actually did and did not prohibit (this would be a kind of doctrinal dispute best settled ecclesiastically), the preferred REBT approach for dealing with such religious problems would be to point out and dispute irrational demands like Martha's: "I don't think I have to abstain, but I do *have to* get control of my eating and my weight." This was the likely core of her self-defeating emotions and behaviors.

By assessing which beliefs contribute to self-defeating emotions, REBT and the A-B-C model can help simplify the complexities of dealing with guilt. Martha's description quickly clarified what it meant for her to experience guilt. What she called guilty feelings were really feelings of shame and self-directed anger. She was angry at herself (her first guilty feeling) because she believed she had to get control of her weight, although she had not. She felt ashamed (her second guilty feeling) because she believed that she was weak for not controlling her weight and for falling back on vomiting to control her weight.

According to this kind of rational emotive behavioral analysis of guilt experiences, when individuals come to the conclusion that they are guilty of some misbehavior, the guilt event (our conclusion) activates beliefs about what it means to be guilty of such misbehavior. As a consequence of these beliefs about what it means to be guilty of particular misbehaviors, people experience emotions consistent with their beliefs. Guilty feelings are the feelings which clients create for themselves when they believe they are guilty of—that is, culpable for—some misbehavior.

A wide range of feelings might be involved, some healthy, some self-defeating. Helpful emotions might arise when individuals think that one is culpable for misbehavior include sadness, regret, and remorse. These guilt-related emotions are helpful and healthy in that they are likely to motivate one to avoid future misbehavior and, where appropriate and possible, to correct problems arising from misbehavior. Rachel felt sad about Leah's problems with Chinese and sad that Leah seemed upset with her. She was also concerned about how their friendship might suffer—all quite helpful, if unpleasant. Self-defeating emotions might arise in association with a sense of guilt and include embarrassment, shame, and depression. These emotions are self-defeating because they decrease motivation and generally lead people to avoid the behaviors that will solve problems. Rachel was ashamed of good grades and felt guilty for getting As—not helpful!

Shame and embarrassment are likely to prevent acknowledgment of wrong-doing or attempts to repair or make restitution for damage caused by one's misbehavior, because restitution may require confession or some other acknowledgment. Depression is self-defeating because it leads to general de-motivation for all behavior. Dan reported that he found it difficult to visit with his Bishop (the pastor of his LDS congregation) and related that he was more likely to masturbate when he felt depressed. Avoidance of ecclesiastical leaders and increased misbehavior (as defined by a person's own religious rule system) show the effects of bad guilt. Freed from self-defeating aspects of the guilt experience, clients can move on to accomplish their goals, including their religious goals.

9

Forgiveness and REBT

Forgiveness is likely to be highly valued as a human/spiritual process among most religious clients—particularly those with Jewish and Christian backgrounds. Forgiveness is often seen as producing important intrapersonal, interpersonal and spiritual outcomes which religious clients may view as central to healthy living and obedience to God. Should REBT therapists encourage their clients to forgive those who have wronged them? Should therapists facilitate the forgiveness process as part of psychotherapy? Our answer is simply *it depends*. Whether a therapist is wise to incorporate forgiveness into the REBT treatment process hinges on the particular client, his or her specific religious beliefs and the nature of the client's disturbance about the offender and the offense. In this short chapter, we will describe the nature of forgiveness, Biblical and theological support for forgiveness as a matter of faith, and an REBT perspective on when and how to support forgiveness of others as a therapeutic intervention.

DEFINING FORGIVENESS

Webster's dictionary defines forgiveness this way: (1) to give up resentment against or the desire to punish; to stop being angry with; to pardon; (2) to give up all claim to punish or exact penalty for (Webster's, 1979). In Judeo-Christian traditions, forgiveness is encouraged as a way to reconcile and heal both bitterness and negative memories associated with interpersonal hurts (McCullough & Worthington, 1994). Frankl (1969) clearly viewed forgiveness as a method of modifying one's attitude about situations (especially perceived wrongs) that one cannot effectively change. Gassin and Enright (1995) described forgiveness as "foreswearing of negative affect and judgement by an injured party directed at someone who has inflicted a significant, deep and unjust hurt" (pp. 38-39).

Forgiveness does not require any action on the part of another, meaning the party viewed as having offended is not required to apologize, change in any manner or even accept forgiveness. In other words, forgiveness is unilateral and (ideally) without condition. Most religious clients will understand forgiveness as a moral-religious obligation in cases in which they have been wronged. In our experience, the healthiest religious clients will also see forgiveness as a process intended by God as a method for helping them reduce their own emotional disturbance. Scriptures suggest that forgiving others leads both to desirable spiritual outcomes such as restoration of a right relationship with God and greater ability to imitate God in relationships with others, and helpful emotional outcomes such as decreased bitterness (hostile rumination) regarding an offender. Thus beyond a Biblical mandate, many clients will understand that freely choosing to forswear vengeance and give up rage is likely to help them live with more equanimity and less upset than those who do not forgive. The problem for many clients is not the idea of forgiveness but the process. Moving from rage to mere annoyance or disappointment may seem nearly impossible.

BIBLICAL/THEOLOGICAL UNDERPINNINGS OF FORGIVENESS

All faiths with roots in the Judeo-Christian tradition are likely to embrace the concept and practice of forgiveness (Rokeach, 1973). Both Old Testament and New Testament scriptures are filled with examples and directives concerning the obligation to forgive (Meek & McMinn, 1997).

In Jewish (Old Testament) scriptures, forgiveness is required to restore men and women to God and to one another (Gladson, 1992). Because all people are viewed as fundamentally sinful and as having transgressed God's laws, human beings are by nature in need of divine forgiveness. For Jewish and Christian clients, Old Testament conceptions of forgiveness focus on the concealment or hiding of offenses from God's eyes (e.g. "Happy are those whose . . . sin is covered" Psalms 32:1). Sin could also be distanced from the person (Psalm 86:5), cleansed, blotted out or eliminated (Isaiah 43:25). However conceived, the Jewish person would find peace in having secured God's forgiveness for sin through sacrifice, ritual or prayer. Such divine grace offered a model for human to human forgiveness. So, in one Biblical account, Joseph's brothers, who had grievously wronged Joseph by selling him into slavery, are suffering a famine and must rely on Joseph's graceful forgiveness for survival. Joseph provides a model for restoring human community by choosing to forgive his brothers without condition.

Similarly, New Testament Christian scriptures are replete with exhortations to forgive one another as a way of life and a way of modeling God's forgiveness to one another (e.g., "Bear with each other and forgive whatever grievances you may have against one another. Forgive as the Lord forgives you" [Colossians 3:13], "Be kind to one another, tender-hearted, forgiving one another as God in Christ has forgiven you" [Ephesians 4:32]). Simultaneously, the Bible warns Christians of the effects of refusing to forgive (e.g., "Whatever we judge in another we are doomed to become or to reap in our own lives," Romans 2:1). The death of Jesus on the cross is viewed as the ultimate act of forgiveness in that the blood of Jesus is said to have been "poured out" for the forgiveness of human sin (Matt 26:28). Christian clients will generally understand that their need for forgiveness is rooted in the essential depravity or sinfulness inherent in humanity (Meek & McMinn, 1997). They will often view forgiveness as essential for their relationship with God, the well being of the wrong doer and even the health of the larger religious community.

In sum, most Jewish, Catholic and Protestant clients will highly value the practice of forgiving other people (Rokeach, 1973). Forgiveness is seen as a divine mandate and the very heart of the Christian faith hinges on acceptance of God's forgiveness via the sacrifice of Christ. Rather than view forgiveness as a burden, many religious clients will see it as an opportunity to model Christ, thereby following his example and possibly winning others to faith in the process. Still, the REBT therapist is likely to encounter clients for whom forgiveness has become a troubling burden and a prime source of self-downing. Scriptures such as Ephesians 4:26 "Don't let the sun go down on your wrath," may be used by clients (and even worse, by some therapists) to rate themselves when anger cannot easily or rapidly be altered.

Religious clients will often be concerned about the implications of not forgiving. Biblical scriptures warn of the negative effects of withholding forgiveness and nurturing wrath or anger. Resentment, blaming and chronic negative affect regarding another person or an event often serve as signals for the Judeo-Christian client that forgiveness is needed in order to reduce bitterness and anger, "vengeful thoughts and actions form the mire that keep a person stuck. Therefore, forgiveness is the essence of successful living, with the self and with others" (Jones-Haldeman, 1992, p. 146). Benson (1992) noted that the alternatives to forgiveness are quite destructive and many religious men and women will readily relate to the old Chinese proverb which states "the one who pursues revenge should dig two graves" (p. 76). This sentiment may hold both pragmatic and significant spiritual import for religious clients.

SHOULD REBT THERAPISTS INTRODUCE OR ENCOURAGE FORGIVENESS?

Although Christian and Jewish clients may be highly inclined to view forgiveness as an essential part of their religious commitment, it is important for the REBT therapist to keep in mind that religious clients will vary widely with regard to the personal and clinical salience of forgiveness (Johnson & Nielsen, 1998). In fact, apart from its religious meaning, forgiveness may not be viewed as particularly relevant to many therapy clients (Tjeltveit, 1986). It is also true that research support for forgiveness as a therapeutic intervention is quite sparse (McCullough & Worthington, 1994), and that the supposed benefits of forgiving others (e.g., decreased depression and anger and increased well-being, self-efficacy and relationship adjustment) have simply not been convincingly supported in outcome studies.

Of primary concern are those situations in which a therapist introduces forgiveness as a therapeutic process with a client who does not share the therapist's commitment regarding the relevance of forgiveness to the clinical problem at hand. Some religiously oriented therapists may introduce forgiveness as a focus of treatment and communicate an "unhealthy urgency to forgiveness" (Meek & McMinn, 1997, p. 57).

Clients may then feel forced to forgive those at whom they are angry in order to please the therapist. This will be particularly troubling to those religious clients already prone to self-downing or other secondary disturbances about their anger. Ironically, Jesus never *demanded* that anyone he encountered forgive. Rather, we can only forgive others when we ourselves have changed first, typically by recognizing our role in creating emotional disturbance and deciding to relinquish the role of angry victim (Jones-Haldeman, 1992).

Although introducing forgiveness or insisting that clients forgive both raise significant ethical concerns in therapy, the REBT therapist may encounter religious clients who themselves introduce forgiveness of others as a therapy goal and who assign significant personal/spiritual meaning to forgiveness. Gassin and Enright (1995) described several potentially therapeutic meanings of forgiveness for Christian clients. These include: (a) *educative*—forgiveness is an opportunity to learn about oneself and God, (b) *vehicle of blessing*—God will bless those who suffer and forgive, (c) *emulative*—forgiveness is a chance to emulate Christ who suffered for injustices, and (d) *development*—the bad situation and wrong done is a catalyst for spiritual development.

Should the REBT therapist address forgiveness in psychotherapy? We think the answer is yes if the client is religious and understands forgiving as spiritually significant within his or her faith context. With clients who value forgiveness, REBT offers a particularly elegant approach to enhancing the probability that forgiveness will occur. By focusing treatment on the client's own disturbance *about* the offense and the offender, the therapist assists the religious client with creating the necessary and sufficient conditions for forgiveness to occur.

AN REBT APPROACH TO FORGIVENESS

In contrast to traditional conceptions of how to best facilitate forgiveness, REBT therapists are inclined to view the choice to forgive as one of several positive outcomes of elegant psychotherapy targeting the client's irrational beliefs about the offender and the offense. Thus REBT therapists are considerably less interested in whether the client eventually decides to formally forgive another person and more interested in whether the client makes a significant philosophical (and often spiritual) shift from demanding and human rating to accepting and refusal to rate another. When this shift occurs, the anger and depression which have kept the client "stuck" emotionally are likely to dissipate. And when clients are no longer rageful or depressed, they are typically more inclined to forgive. Thus REBT uses cognitive disputations to achieve *affective preparation* for eventual forgiveness.

When a religious client presents with anger at another person or group, and has a stated interest in forgiving and overcoming his or her anger, it is quite likely that the REBT therapist will find the source of the client's disturbance in three specific forms of irrational belief. First, many clients will engage in *Human Rating* of those who have offended them. So, the parents of a child who has been sexually molested may believe strongly that the offender is subhuman and deserves to be condemned to eternity in hell. They may even pray that the molester experiences a painful death and suffers for eternity. Most of us can well understand this irrational rating of the essential nonhumanness of a sex offender, murderer, or other overt criminal. However, clients may engage in equally irrational human rating and experience equally intense rage following comparatively minor offenses or slights by others. These reactions will hinge largely on the client's irrational tendencies, personality characteristics and the unique context of the offense. In any case, rating the worth of offenders will likely keep clients experiencing dysfunctional emotional consequences (anger) and subsequently inhibit their ability to forgive the offender. Effective REBT in this case will hinge on disputation of the belief that human beings are *ratable*. For example, Fisher (1985) taught Borderline clients to forgive their parents by seeing them as fallible, but not evil.

A second and equally rancorous irrational belief which often inhibits forgiveness is a *demand* about the offending event itself such as "he should not have done that to me," and "it is awful that God has allowed me to be unjustly wronged in this manner." When clients engage in demands that events must or should not have occurred (even though they obviously have), that such events are catastrophic and completely awful (equal to or more than 100% bad), or that they are unable to tolerate or bear the reality of the offense (I-can't-stand-it-itis), they arrange the cognitive conditions for anger, anxiety and depression. The REBT therapist can quickly help the client accept the reality that the hated event *did* occur and that although it is quite bad and unpleasant, it is bearable.

Finally, some religious clients may develop *secondary symptom distress* about not forgiving. In such cases, the clients are likely to see their upset and anger as only partially controllable and they may engage in multiple attempts to forgive their offender or "turn their anger over to God" only to find themselves angry once again. These clients are subsequently likely to begin self-downing or negatively assessing their own value as a result of their perceived *failure* to forgive. This secondary disturbance is likely to result in anxiety or depression and may stem from the client's assessment that he or she has failed to abide by a religious conviction that forgiveness is required, and further, that the ability to easily forgive is a sign of spiritual maturity or obedience.

In sum, making demands about the offense or event, evaluating the offender(s) as less than fully human, and negatively rating one's self when forgiveness does not readily occur are all ways in which religious (and often nonreligious) clients effectively keep themselves mired in anger and depression. To increase the probability that clients will become prepared to forgive by becoming less affectively disturbed, the REBT approach will directly dispute these three irrational tendencies. In the section that follows, we will provide brief examples of several disputational approaches which may be applied to each of these irrational beliefs.

DISPUTING FORGIVENESS-INHIBITING IRRATIONAL BELIEFS

For the client struggling with forgiveness-inhibiting affect, each of the primary approaches to disputation may be appropriate and useful. *Logical* disputes may include the following:

How does it follow that because you didn't want something to happen, then it cannot occur?

Does it strike you as overgeneralizing to say that because she did this, she is evil?

I'm not sure I'm familiar with the biblical scripture that says you are worthless when you have trouble forgiving.

Where is it written that bad things *shouldn't* happen to you?

Does it make sense that he should be condemned for doing this to you, while you are free to be fallible in your own way without being condemned?

Why *must* you forgive right away?

Similarly, the therapist may utilize *Reality-Testing* Disputes to address anger or depression which inhibit forgiveness. Here the REBT therapist pushes clients to carefully assess whether their beliefs are consistent with empirical reality *or* religious scripture. In most cases, religious clients will engage in global human rating and rigid demanding that can neither be supported by empirical evidence or the essential tenets and scriptures of their own faith. Some examples of reality-testing disputes include the following:

Show me proof that you cannot tolerate what has happened.

How exactly would it be catastrophic if you were human and unable to forgive?

Show me the scriptures which encourage you to hate those who wrong you.

Is it possible that you could be happy and go on *in spite* of what he did to you?

If God allowed this to happen, why can't *you* accept it?

How is it *terrible* that you feel anger and aren't ready to forgive?

Pragmatic disputes are likely to be quite useful for disputing forgiveness-inhibition. It is unlikely that ongoing rage at an offender or self-downing about one's anger will make the client more adaptive or happy. Even devout religious clients who are most prone to self-denial will typically understand that their beliefs are dysfunctional in the sense of working at odds with their best interests (overcoming anger and other negative consequences). Simply stated, clients are asked to consider how being angry at one who has wronged them is helping them achieve their goal of forgiveness:

As long as you believe that this wrong *must* not have occurred, how will you feel?

Help me understand exactly how your rage at _____ is helping you?

When you tell yourself you are no good for not forgiving, does that help you forgive?

So how has your rage been helping you serve the Lord?

Do you suppose that when you feel depressed about not forgiving, God is better able to help you forgive?

Is this rage you feel worth it?

A *didactic* disputational strategy may also prove useful with religious clients. The REBT therapist might emphasize the connection between the specific forgiveness-inhibiting irrational beliefs discussed above and the client's negative emotional consequences (primarily anger). It is important to help clients understand the link between anger and difficulty forgiving. This educative intervention might occur early in treatment as the therapist teaches the A-B-C model of REBT. Didactic intervention also allows the REBT therapist familiar with the client's faith to provide a faith-based rationale for overcoming anger and moving on to forgiveness while simultaneously correcting disturbance-supporting views of scripture. For example, the Christian client who believes God demands instant forgiveness might be told "actually, nowhere in the New Testament does Jesus '*demand*' that anyone he encounters forgive. Instead, Jesus invites us to forgive—knowing it will ultimately be good for us to do it. Also, forgiveness in the Bible seems to allow Christians to participate in drawing others to Christ. So in 1st Peter (2:2) and other places, we find people being drawn to Jesus by the mercy they receive from Christians. I'm not sure why you are demanding that you forgive when Jesus never demanded this of you. In fact, isn't it true that he died on the cross for you precisely because humans fail to do the things they are supposed to?"

Vicarious Modeling is another form of intervention which might be especially useful with religious clients struggling with forgiveness. Several authors have discussed the importance of modeling forgiveness for clients (McCullough & Worthington, 1994; Meek & McMinn, 1997). REBT therapists may increase the chance of clients forgiving themselves and others by intentionally modeling unconditional acceptance of clients. When a therapist utterly and consistently refuses to rate a client for behavior inside or outside the therapy session, the therapist helps to create a forgiveness-facilitating environment. In addition to providing unconditional regard for clients, therapists can explicitly model forgiveness in at least two important ways. First, they may model self-forgiveness by openly admitting failures to clients and sharing how they have refused to self-down in spite of them ("you know, when I got confused with my scheduling and missed several client appointments, I became very angry with myself and then had to really slow things down and stop telling myself I was an idiot for simply being human. I know God doesn't think I'm an idiot and if He ignores my mistakes, why shouldn't I? So, I ended up just annoyed and motivated to do a better job with schedules!").

Second, the REBT therapist may model forgiveness of others. In this case, it is important to show the client how a negative emotional reaction (C) was generated by specific irrational beliefs (IBs) and how disputation of these beliefs led to a different and more functional consequence. Finally, the therapist should attempt to make clear just how reduced anger or upset helped prepare him or her to forgive. Again, coping models are highly preferable to mastery models. Finally, the therapist may invoke examples of others in the client's life who have also suffered various wrongs without becoming chronically enraged and unable to forgive. Here the therapist wants the client to ask, "how is it that he or she suffered as I did and yet did not become bitter and hostile?"

Finally, the REBT therapist may help some religious clients overcome forgiveness-inhibiting emotional reactions via *negative rational emotive imagery*. Here clients close their eyes and imagine themselves in the situation in which they were "wronged" (A) and try to experience their usual anger, rage or depression (C). Then, they are asked what internal statements seem to be related to their upset. Clients are then asked to change their feelings from anger or depression to a more constructive negative emotion. As always when using imagery in REBT, it essential to help clients understand *how* they were able to change their emotions (e.g., by altering their statements about the situation, the offender and possibly themselves).

10

REBT with Specific
Religious Groups

This final chapter summarizes the distinctive beliefs and practices of the dominant religious groups in the United States today. Several examples of religiously oriented IBs for each religious group are offered as a means of highlighting the way clients with specific religious worldviews may express irrational philosophies. Protestantism, Catholicism, Judaism, Islam, Buddhism, and Hinduism are discussed. Although REBTers may encounter clients from other religious faiths, this will probably be rare. Further, familiarity with the major religious traditions discussed in this chapter may provide the REBT therapist with a solid foundation from which to treat clients from small or unfamiliar religious communities.

PROTESTANT CLIENTS

Attempting to describe the most common beliefs and concerns of Protestant clients is a perilous task. At any time in the United States, there are nearly 2,000 separate Christian denominations, most of which would be characterized as Protestant in one form or another (Lovinger, 1984, 1990). In 1992, the Gallup Organization estimated that 56% of Americans describe themselves as Protestant (Hoge, 1996). "Mainline" Protestant churches include Lutheran, Presbyterian, Reformed, Episcopal, and Methodist denominations, and although other groups may easily be included, the use of the term Protestant here is most consistent with these broad denominations.

Sola Gratia, or justification "by faith alone," is generally considered the battle cry of the Protestant reformation. In rejecting the Roman Catholic Church's authority and control over teaching and justification, the early reformers insisted on the full authority of the Bible as God's inspired word and God's divine grace as the sole method for addressing human sin. At the heart of Protestant doctrine is the firm belief that all human religious efforts to attain salvation are futile. Rather, salvation comes only through accepting God's grace, even though people are not deserving of it. Therefore, it is God who takes the initiative to save people, and through the death of Jesus Christ on the cross, grace has been personally offered to every man and woman who then may respond by accepting grace on faith (Brown, 1965). Although wisdom, dedication, and good behavior are certainly valued attributes among devout Protestants, there is rather frequent risk that the Protestant client (and sometimes a larger church) will neglect the "grace freely given" distinctive of Protestantism and focus excessively on good works or right behavior. This is most likely to be the case when a client presents with demands regarding self or awfulizing regarding some behavior or personal quality.

Variations in doctrine among Protestant denominations are not necessarily marked and differences in belief and behavior between Protestant clients of different denominational affiliation may be substantial or nonexistent. Yet, each denomination may reasonably be characterized by some historically unique doctrine and/or ritual (Lovinger, 1984). For example, Calvinist churches may place considerable emphasis on hard work and prosperity may be viewed as a sign of God's favor. Baptist churches vary considerably but are often characterized by intense devotion, acceptance of the Bible as sole authority, and substantial importance placed on faith and repentance for sin as requirements for salvation. Methodist denominations often stress grace as freely given for salvation and justification. Yet "saved" sinners are expected to continue to seek perfection or freedom from deliberate sin. Quaker (Friends) churches adhere to very little formal dogma and emphasize direct personal contact with God in the form of quiet meditation and spiritual seeking. Finally, Pentecostal or Holiness churches are likely to view the Bible as full and final authority in all matters and view the original biblical text as inerrant. They may additionally emphasize the sinful nature of human beings and the necessity of hard work required for achieving sanctification.

In addition to their unique denominational background, it is common for Protestant clients to vary along at least two additional dimensions with respect to faith issues. The first is the liberalism-fundamentalism dimension. If Protestant clients are liberal, or "modern," in theology and faith, then they may be broad thinking with respect to sources of truth and inclined to embrace science as a means of modernizing or informing the meaning attributed to older doctrines. Although liberalism may be healthy and suggest greater amenability to REBT and other forms of therapy, highly liberal clients may struggle with ambivalence with respect to religious beliefs and may experience punishment or disapproval from more conservative peers or group members (Lovinger, 1990). Clients tending toward the fundamentalist end of this dimension are likely to be firm and confident in religious belief and adhere to an inerrant view of the Scriptures. Problematically, they may be less flexible than more liberal Protestant clients and may be particularly reactive to interventions or disputations that challenge fundamental interpretations of Scripture or idiosyncratic religious belief.

The second dimension of interest to the REBT therapist working with Protestant clients is the ecumenicalist-exclusivist dimension (Lovinger, 1984). Clients from ecumenical churches or those holding more ecumenical beliefs are likely to be more flexible concerning whether a person may obtain salvation (become "saved") outside of their specific denomination. Clients with exclusivist beliefs (common of strongly conservative or fundamentalist denominations) are less inclined to believe salvation is possible outside their narrow denominational beliefs and rituals. Exclusivist clients are likely to be more easily threatened by Socratic or other REBT disputations that question limitations placed on God's ability and willingness to save whoever He chooses.

Protestant clients are likely to present with irrational beliefs that vary widely in style and content. Yet, Protestantism by nature is likely to increase the probability of certain forms of demanding, awfulizing, self-rating, and intolerance. When Protestant clients make demands about themselves, others, or the world around them, the demands may have to do with adhering to biblical teachings for right belief and behavior. Depending on their denomination, clients may hear regularly that Jesus alone stands between them and an eternity of suffering in hell. Perceived failure to live by the teachings of Jesus or doubts about assurance of salvation may plague some Protestant clients. Demanding irrational beliefs may take many forms and include the following:

I must be perfect as Christ Jesus was perfect.

I have to show God that I am deserving of grace by never having sinful thoughts or behavior.

Living the way God wants me to live must not be so hard.

Other people ought to believe what I do or they must suffer in hell.

If I obey God's laws, pray and ask to be forgiven for my sin, I must go to heaven.

Awfulizing as a derivative of demandingness may also be common among Protestant clients and center again around catastrophic thinking about oneself, others, or the world outside. Christian clients in general tend to catastrophize behavior that they view as counter to biblical requirements. "Sinful" behavior, whether this involves a lustful thought or multiple episodes of adultery, will often generate awfulizing, particularly among more fundamentalist clients. The flow of thinking may go something like this: "I have sinned before God, which I absolutely should not have done. My sin is awful and terrible and I may not be forgiven for it. I am certainly in danger of going to hell, and that possibility is catastrophic!" Likewise, the behavior of others or conditions in the world may be awfulized. Here are some examples:

It is terrible that others ridicule us for our religious beliefs and practices.

Society is becoming less God-fearing by the second. It is awful that so many people seem to ignore God's requirements for righteousness.

I am a complete failure as a Christian because I can't seem to stop coveting things others have.

It is terrible when my children don't go to church.

If Protestant clients are notorious for an irrational tendency, it may be that of rating human worth. Generalized evaluations or denigrations of people (themselves and others) may be encouraged by decontextualized scriptures or doctrinal beliefs. Scriptures exhorting one to "be ye perfect" may become the focus of clients who less frequently hear or are less inclined to focus on Scriptures that remind them that all human beings are "fallen," "sinful," and like "filthy rags." For clients with a vulnerability to negative self-evaluation or automatic negative thoughts regarding self, sermons emphasizing fire, brimstone, and complete purity or "righteousness" in thought and behavior may be especially troubling. Many Protestant clients from denominations with a more fundamentalist emphasis are prone to perfectionistic self-demands that can rarely be achieved and subsequently lead to all varieties of self-downing. Most typically, however, the client may equate behavioral or cognitive imperfection with failure in the most substantial or meaningful terms. Examples of human worth ratings common to Protestant clients include the following:

God could never really love someone who has sinned as grievously as I.

Because I seem to fail so completely to abide by biblical principles and commandments, it proves that I am evil and despised by God.

Because my life is miserable and difficult, God is withholding His blessings. I am completely undeserving.

I deserve to suffer eternally for the awful thing I have done.

Those who persecute me for my faith are evil to the core and deserve to suffer

The final category of irrational belief is low frustration tolerance. Protestant clients are likely to be as skilled as others at convincing themselves they cannot stand life's discomforts and inconveniences. Certain activating events may be particularly likely to lead to disturbance secondary to intolerance among Protestant clients. These may include changes in the structure or content of church services, inability to work or be "productive" in some way (i.e., frustration of the "Protestant ethic"), and confrontation with Protestant doctrine or practice that contradicts that of the church. One might make the case that the multitude of small Protestant denominational groups may in itself be a testament of sorts to the tendency for descendants of the Protestant Reformation to engage in low frustration tolerance. Specifically, Protestants may at times be quite intolerant of diverging beliefs regarding issues such as the necessity of baptism in order to receive salvation or requirements for qualifications to pastor. Church splitting and demonimational fragmentation are often indicative of poor frustration tolerance within churches over time. Examples of client statements suggesting low frustration tolerance include:

I can't stand not knowing if I'll go to heaven.

If members of this church believe women can be a pastor, I can't tolerate staying.

I can't stand giving up drinking and smoking as the church requires.

I will not stand for my spouse not honoring me in exactly the way the Bible commands.

The rigidity and dogmatism among other church members is too much for me to bear.

CATHOLIC CLIENTS

The Roman Catholic Church is the largest single Christian church and currently comprises roughly 20% of the U.S. population. Linked directly to the earliest Christian gatherings following the life and death of Jesus Christ, the Catholic Church acknowledges the primacy and authority of the Pope on all matters of faith and practice. As Christ's representative on earth (the "Vicar of Christ"), the Pope stands as the head of a hierarchy of bishops and priests. When speaking with full authority (ex cathedra) and defining matters of faith or morals, the Pope's utterances are regarded as infallible and binding on all Catholics. At the center of the faith stand Holy Communion (mass) and six other sacraments including baptism, confirmation, penance (or reconciliation), ordination, marriage, and the anointing of the sick (extreme unction). The church is highly sacramental and ceremonial in corporate worship, liturgy and individual religious practice.

In approximately 1054, eastern Catholic churches (Greek, Russian, Syrian, and Armenian) split from the western Catholic churches largely as a rejection of the claim of the Bishop of Rome (Pope) to supreme authority. The resulting Eastern Orthodox Church also disagreed with a statement in the Nicene Creed added by the western church in which the Spirit is said to proceed from the Son, as well as from the Father. In the Eastern Orthodox Catholic Church, authority belongs not to any individual, but to the Ecumenical Council, whose function is to interpret the "holy tradition." Eastern Orthodox churches tend to be less centralized and more variable in worship style and liturgy than Roman Catholic churches. Clinically, Eastern Orthodox persons are likely to be more accepting of pleasure and satisfaction and somewhat less rigid regarding the minutia of religious practice (Lovinger, 1990). However, for the purposes of this discussion, no distinction will be made between Roman Catholic and Eastern Orthodox clients.

Although Catholics are likely to express the full range of human disturbance common of all clients, shame and guilt may be two of the most common presenting problems among practicing Catholics or clients with a Catholic upbringing. Guilt may proceed from perceived failures or shortcomings religiously. These may include wrong behavior toward others, neglect of significant religious practice requirements (e.g., attendance at mass), or violation of church teaching regarding sexual practices. Shame, often the result of self-imposed or other humiliation or embarrassment, has more to do with self-rating secondary to perceived religious failings. Shame is often relevant when Catholic clients present with significant inhibitions around things such as bodily pleasure or satisfaction over accomplishment (Lovinger, 1990).

The humorous introduction sometimes given by Catholic clients when the topic of religion emerges in psychotherapy, "I'm a recovering Catholic," conveys a good deal about the demanding beliefs often associated with this faith. Catholic education in different generations and locals has been notorious, even legendary, for inculcating demands for perfect behavior. Many Catholic clients will have well rehearsed demanding beliefs regarding correct thinking and behaving, avoidance of sin, confession of sin, penance, and fear or shame related to full experience of pleasure. Demanding irrational beliefs may include:

My life ought to be free of sin.

I must confess each and every sin I commit

I absolutely should have attended mass this week.

Catholic clients might additionally be prone to awfulize situations and events that cause doubt with respect to faith or lead them to the conclusion that they have committed grievous sins. For example, in the Catholic Church, divorce will typically mean that the client is not able to fully participate in the Church's sacraments (e.g., communion). In response, an irrational belief might be, "It is terrible and awful that the church will no longer let me practice as a full member and I can imagine nothing worse than my spouse leaving me and causing me this pain." Other awfulizing beliefs might include:

It is terrible that I have sinned in this way.

It is awful that I didn't tell the priest "everything" in confession.

It is terrible that I had a sexual relationship before becoming married.

If members of the church discovered what I had done, it would be catastrophic.

Ratings of human worth may be one of the most troubling categories of irrational thinking among Catholic clients. Shame, guilt, and confusion experienced in the context of the church while growing up, may lead to automatic negative evaluations of self as an adult. In light of the church's emphasis on rules governing morality and personal conduct, and in light of the historic focus on confession and penance, it is not difficult to understand how Catholic clients could become prone to self-downing. Indeed, self-rating appears to be somewhat institutionalized in different Catholic communities. Examples of human worth ratings may include:

The fact that I must continue to go to confession for the same sin proves that I am worthless.

The adulterer is surely more sinful and less worthy than I, who have only contemplated adultery.

Because I have failed so miserably to live according the Church's dictates, I have no business attending mass or otherwise affiliating with the Church.

Irrational thinking among Catholic clients may additionally be characterized by low frustration-tolerance (LFT). Catholic clients may be particularly intolerant of perceived errors or shortcomings on their own part. If educated and/or socialized in a shame-based milieu, avoidance of shame may be achieved by perfectionistic strivings and stern self-punitive reactions to apparent personal shortcomings. Catholic clients may also be quite concerned about issues concerning the afterlife status of loved ones. What was a departed relative's status with respect to the essential sacraments? Where does this person's soul currently reside? Clients may demonstrate extreme LFT on this issue and insist that "knowing" the answer to these questions is essential for their own rest and well-being. Other examples of a philosophy of LFT among Catholic clients may include:

I can't stand it if my spouse does not attend mass with me.

It is intolerable that I have failed to live in accordance with the Church's teachings.

I can't stand the thought that I might go to hell (at least for awhile).

JEWISH CLIENTS

Formalized as a religion in the late 6th century B.C., Judaism is the oldest of the world's three great monotheistic religions and is the parent of both Christianity and Islam. Jews believe in only one God, the transcendent and eternal creator and ruler of the world. God sees and knows everything and has chosen the Jewish people to serve as a light and example to the human race. Judaism has no formal creed, but the "Law," or *Torah* (the first five books in the Bible), is viewed as God's distinctive method of revealing Himself to his people. At the heart of the Jewish faith is the existence of a covenant between God and his people. Unlike a contract, the covenant is not mutually negotiated but offered unilaterally by God to his chosen people.

The *Shema* contains three passages from the Law that are read every morning and evening by the devout Jew. It begins this way: "Here, O Israel, the Lord our God, the Lord is one and you shall love the Lord your God with all your heart and with all your soul, and with all your might. And these words which I command you shall be upon your heart." Indeed, pious Jews seek to love God with their entire being and that love is expressed in practical obedience to the Law of God in everyday life.

The Law contains 613 commandments covering every area of daily life from civil law to personal hygiene and diet. Although many Jews no longer rigidly adhere to all the laws of the Torah, Orthodox Jews observe them to the finest detail. Most Jews belong to a synagogue, although most do not attend weekly. Religious leaders, Rabbis, have studied Jewish Law and serve to instruct congregations in the faith and make decisions concerning Jewish legal questions. In Jewish life, there are several critical rites and rituals. Being born of a Jewish mother is an important part of identity, as is the bar mitzvah for Jewish boys at age 13 (signaling maturity and expectation that one will fulfill all duties of an adult Jew). Devout Jewish men pray three times per day at home or in the synagogue, and devout Jewish housewives are expected to safeguard the religious purity of the home by, among other things, preparing Kosher meals. The Sabbath, beginning Friday at sundown and extending through Saturday, is a critical and respected time of renewal and rest.

Orthodox Judaism is characterized by a "Torah-true" approach to life in that every aspect of life is to be governed by the Law. Orthodox Jews engage in daily study of the Torah and conform their life obediently to its propositions and rituals, including the strict rules of Sabbath observance, dietary laws, and prayer three times per day. *Reformed* Judaism began in the Enlightenment of the 15th century and was substantially influenced by science and the cultural mood of change and growth. Reformed Jews are, on scientific grounds, unlikely to view the Torah as factual and binding. They are likely to have abandoned dietary laws and often adhere to modernized or liberal versions of ritual and worship. Between Orthodox and Reformed Judaism are Conservative Judaism and other more moderate branches.

Jewish clients are likely to come from strong (although sometimes enmeshed) families and rejection of family values may lead to anxiety and conflict. Difficulties with independence and autonomy from family and guilt related to independence are common among Jewish clients (Lovinger, 1990). For example, selection of a non-Jewish partner is likely to lead to substantial conflict with parents and parents may engage in parental blackmail (using their own sacrifices to make demands children). Jewish families, and therefore Jewish clients, often value hard work, educational accomplishment, careful observance of ritual and ethical practices, and concern for the needy. Most importantly, religion for the Jew is seldom separate from life, rather it saturates all elements of it. Thus, for many Jewish clients, therapeutic issues will necessarily be religious issues.

Demanding irrational beliefs among Jewish clients may take many forms but the following are some possibilities:

My children must honor God's Law as I have always done

The Rabbi ought to know exactly what God commands in this situation.

I must never, under any circumstances, violate Kosher dietary requirements.

I have to love God with all my heart at all times and in all situations.

Anyone who has watched a Woody Allen movie will likely have seen a wonderfully neurotic Jewish character (usually played by Allen himself). Allen's character is typically a master at awfulizing and catastrophizing. In one short Allen movie, he is plagued throughout by the larger than life image of his Jewish mother's face looming above him, critically evaluating him at every turn. Allen's response is extreme anxiety and if he were to verbalize his belief, it might go something like, "It is terrible and awful when my Jewish mother does not approve of me." Other examples of awfulizing include:

It is worse than 100% bad when I violate God's laws.

When Jewish people are persecuted, it is utterly awful.

It is catastrophic that my son has married a Christian woman.

Jewish clients may also be predisposed to some unique manifestations of human worth ratings. These might focus on damnation directed at self for violation of the personal covenant with God via failure to adhere to God's Law or damnation directed at others for perceived anti-Semitism in one form or another, for example:

If my Jewish parents have rejected me, I am certainly damned and unlovable.

States or individuals who harm God's chosen people certainly deserve God's eternal wrath.

My failure to know and fully adhere to the Torah is clear evidence of my worthlessness.

Finally, low frustration tolerance is just as likely to strike the Jewish client as any other. LFT may take many forms. The REBT therapist should be well prepared to dispute such irrational beliefs. Very often, this may merely require pointing out the lengthy history of persecution directed at Jewish people from the 6th century B.C. forward. If the clients' ancestors survived captivity in Egypt and extreme persecution in concentration camps, how is it that they cannot stand their current trials and discomforts? LFT beliefs may include:

I can't stand it if I am slighted or ridiculed as a result of my Jewish faith.

Adhering to God's commandments is too hard.

I cannot stand the rigidity of my more orthodox Jewish family members.

My spouse's rejection of her God-given duties is intolerable.

ISLAMIC CLIENTS

Islam is the fastest growing religion in the United States. The origin of Islam dates to Mecca around the year 610 when the prophet Muhammad came to understand he was receiving messages from God and that he was to convey these to others. Muhammad sincerely believed these revelations to be God's own direct composition. Due to persecution, Muhammad emigrated to Medina where the religion of Islam took shape and grew radically. By 630, Muhammad and Islam overtook Mecca and the Islamic faith has been a powerful religious and political force since that time. *Muslim* refers to one who lives life according to God's will. *Islam* literally means submission to God. Work, religion, and politics are inextricably intertwined for the Islamic person.

Muhammad taught that God (*Allah*) was One and that he was both merciful and all-powerful, controlling the course of all life events. The Islamic Confession of Faith is a pillar of Islam culture and worship: "I bear witness that there is no god but God: I bear witness that Muhammad is the Apostle of God." Muslim's hold that on the last day, God will judge persons according to their acts and assign them to heaven or hell. The main ritual forms of the Islamic faith were modeled after Muhammad's own example. They include worship (or prayer), almsgiving, fasting, and the pilgrimage to Mecca. Corporate worship and prayer are considered critical for devout Muslims. There are five prayer times daily, each preceded by obligatory ritual washing, dawn, midday, midafternoon, sunset, and night. Prayer serves to remind Muslims in a regular and disciplined manner of their status before God as whorshipful servants.

The *Koran* is the sacred book of the Islamic faith. It is seen as a perfect revelation from God, a faithful reproduction of an original engraved on a tablet in heaven that has existed from all eternity. Many Muslims memorize the entire Koran in Arabic (it is nearly as long as the Christian New Testament). Muslims quote the short first chapter of the Koran repeatedly in Arabic during each of the five daily prayers. Copies of the Koran are highly venerated and touched or read by Muslims only after ceremonial cleansing. During the month of Ramadan, Muslims fast during daylight hours. This is a time for intense worship, prayer and reaffirmation, and reconciliation in relationships. It is a time for inward existential reflection and renewal. The end of Ramadan marks the beginning of Muhammad's ministry. At some point in life, each Muslim is strongly encouraged to make a Hajj, or pilgrimage, to Mecca and the holy places surrounding Mecca.

Islam understands itself fundamentally as being "natural religion," in that every created thing exists in dependence on God, in obedience to His creative and sustaining power, and with the purpose of expressing adoration to God. This should then lead to a conscious commitment to a life of thankful and praise-giving obedience to God. Although some Muslim clients will have assimilated an American identity and become adaptable in thought and practice, others may be more strict in their religious belief and practice and may be deeply committed to the worldwide Islam movement that strives for a global Islamic order (Lovinger, 1996). For less traditional Muslim clients, the view that "everything is God's will" may have been replaced by a view that humans are capable of rationality and responsible behavior. Rational emotive behavioral assessment with Muslim clients will require some evaluation of the extent to which they are is highly traditional or less traditional in views about predisposition and the potential of human beings for changing wrong thinking and thereby producing different outcomes.

Demanding beliefs among Muslim clients may have to do with perfect submission to the will of God, political expansion of Islamic faith, or fastidious adherence to prayer, worship, fasting, and so on. Examples might include:

Others must understand, honor or convert to Islam.

I must understand Allah's perfect will for my life.

I ought to make a pilgrimage to Mecca.

I should be more careful to fully participate in Ramadan as my faith requires.

Awfulizing or catastrophizing beliefs among Muslims may take unique forms as well:

It is terrible that I have not memorized the Koran and that others see this.

It is catastrophic that I have done many bad things and that Allah may assign me to hell.

The fact that Allah allows infidels to dishonor Islam is horrible.

Human worth ratings among Islamic clients may be quite similar to those of Jewish or Christian clients. Perceived failures in one's own attempts to adhere to God's demands via the Law (Koran) or denigration of others for similar failings or slights to the Islamic faith may lead to severe devaluations of human worth:

When I fail to adhere to Muhammad's example, I must hate myself.

If bad things happen to me, it proves that I am worthless in Allah's eyes.

Those who deny the Apostleship of Muhammad or the Oneness of God should suffer.

Finally, irrational beliefs rooted in low frustration tolerance may take unique form:

I can't stand fasting all day.

It is overwhelming that so many Muslims are growing "weak" in faith.

It is intolerable that Allah does not reward my devout worship.

I cannot bear the way some members of my faith treat women.

BUDDHIST CLIENTS

Siddharta Guatama, who would one day become *Buddha*, was born in 560 B.C. on the border between India and Nepal. Buddha was an ordinary man of high class in Indian culture. Following many journeys and ranging life experiences, Buddha is said to have immersed himself in contemplation under a fig tree. He experienced "enlightenment" and achieved the highest level of spiritual development and understanding possible for human beings. Enlightenment is somewhat equivalent to salvation in other faith traditions and indicates a special religious knowledge that goes far beyond the limits of reason and the intellect. Enlightened knowledge results in freedom from selfishness, greed, and ignorance. Knowledge of this kind cannot come from any outside influence (e.g., study, holy writing, revelation from God, etc.), but only via hard contemplative work.

Buddha's teaching (*dharma*) was memorized by his followers and only much later committed to writing. Buddhism does not center around veneration of one person or god. Buddha himself was not a god or a god-sent mediator. He emphasized that he could not act as a savior or mediator for others. His teaching is viewed by followers as timeless and not linked to history, or subject to change. Buddhists hold that divinity exists in every person and that every person is a *Bodhisattva,* or one who bears within him- or herself the immortal essence. Buddhists are encouraged to strive to reach Buddha's spiritual level and thereby become Buddhas themselves. Although Buddhists hold to the existence of some God, God's existence is seen as beyond understanding and even outside the grasp of God himself. Tangible manifestations of the divine in each human being are much more salient to the Buddhist.

Dharma, or the "sense of law," holds that moral and physical laws rule the universe. These laws are unalterable, pervasive, and eternal. *Karma* is a law holding that one's actions or works determine one's rebirth (good or bad conditions). This is the moral order of the world from which none can escape. Another law, "the fatal law," holds that every part of the universe, not only human beings, is subject to change and decay. Buddha also described Four Nobel Truths, including:

1. The universal human experience of suffering (the effects of past karma).
2. The cause of suffering is the craving or grasping for wrong things or for the right things in the wrong way. When human beings overvalue the wrong things they suffer. Nothing in the material world can or should be depended upon completely.
3. Suffering can cease through achievement of enlightenment
4. The way to salvation (enlightenment) is the Nobel Eightfold Path, which includes right knowledge, right attitude, right speech, right action, right living, right effort, right mindfulness, and right composure.

The devout Buddhist client will highly value the contemplative life, opportunity for solitude, and simplicity. In addition to self-reflection and intentional contemplation, service to others is also highly valued. Buddha once said, "One act of pure love in saving life is greater than spending the whole of one's time in religious offerings to the Gods." Buddhist clients are considerably less focused on organized religious activity and more keenly honoring of self-discipline, personal growth, and moral maturity. The nature and form of irrational thinking among Buddhist clients has not previously been explored and the examples of irrational beliefs that follow are more speculative than those described for the foregoing religious groups. A Buddhist client may present with demands regarding self or the laws of the universe. Examples might include:

I must become enlightened.

I have to be more self-disciplined.

I ought to be spending more time serving others.

I should have better karma

Awfulizing beliefs among Buddhist clients might also be reflective of primary religious concerns. Buddhist clients, by virtue of their contemplative and reflective practices, may be less inclined than other clients to catastrophize regarding things of this world. Recognizing the immutable laws of karma and reincarnation, any event (or number of events) in this life may not be viewed as carrying the same life and death significance for the Buddhists as may be true for clients of other faith traditions. Still, REBT holds that all human beings are predisposed to self-disturbance and irrationality. Even the most contemplative and apparently serene Buddhist man or woman may at times struggle with awfulizing irrationalities. Examples might include:

It is awful that I have struggled so long and yet feel no more enlightened than when I began.

It is catastrophic that my karma has led me to such a miserable life.

Not even the Buddha could endure such a terrible situation.

Similarly, Buddhist clients may be prone to human worth ratings:

Because I am unable to hold to right living, right action, etc., it proves I am a failure.

My poor position in life is evidence of bad karma and thus my own badness.

Finally, Buddhist clients may at times engage in thinking based on a philosophy of LFT. Again, the contemplative nature of Buddhism and ideas about karma, reincarnation, and the requirement for hard contemplative work may help devout Buddhists to be less prone to discomfort intolerance. Buddha himself learned to accept intense boredom, discomfort, and (we imagine) the agonizing work of intentional, long-term reflective work. The fact that hard work in this life is seen as critical to development and movement toward enlightenment may serve to enhance temporary frustration tolerance. Nonetheless, LFT may take the following forms with Buddhist clients:

I can't stand working so hard at self-reflection.

Self-denial is unbearably uncomfortable.

It is intolerable that I have so much bad karma to overcome.

HINDU CLIENTS

Although its roots date back 5,000 years, Hinduism was not formally considered a religion until approximately 1200 A.D. Hinduism may best be considered a culture and a way of life versus a formal creed-based religion. In fact, Hinduism has often been referred to as a federation of cults or a collage of ideas and spiritual aspirations. *Hindu* is the Persian word for Indian and Hinduism emphasizes a way of living rather than a way of thought. Most Hindus believe in God in some form, although many do not. Individual Hindus may reverence one god, many, or none. One Hindu saying goes "God is one though many," although most Hindus acknowledge the presence of *Brahma* (God), which is considered a world soul, a cosmic and absolute consciousness. Hindus generally identify fully with God and most Hindu religious practices are directed toward the realization of the individual's oneness with God. Worship, if it exists, is generally individual versus corporate.

Nature is seen as alive and sacred and Hindu worshipers often seek solitude in natural surroundings to discover meaning. Rivers in particular are seen as the source of support and spiritual life. The sacred river Ganges is itself the symbol of life without end. As is true for Buddhists, Hindus hold strongly to the principle of Karma, the belief that work or action and consequences of action within one existence flow into the next existence and influence character. Karma is an immutable law and cannot be altered. Related to karma is the notion of *Samsara,* or the flow of life from birth to death and then on to rebirth, and so on. This is the principle of reincarnation, or transmigration. Every human being is locked into a cycle of recurring life. The soul is forever on a round of births and rebirths. Karma and Samsara together help the Hindu understand apparent inequities economically, physically, and otherwise. Certainly these are seen as changing from existence to existence. Hindus hope that through good work and action, they will eventually win release (*Moksha*) from this chain or cycle. This stands in contrast to the Buddhist belief that hard contemplative work, resulting in enlightenment, is the key to release from the cycle of reincarnation.

Most practicing Hindus are vegetarian and honor all living things. Sacred scriptures in the Hindu faith include the *Vedas* and the *Upanishads.* The Vedas are four books containing hymns, prayers, revelations, and general spiritual wisdom. The Upanishads are a series of 108 poems dealing with the search for meaning in life and the universe. More so than the other religious traditions discussed in this chapter, Hindus are likely to be widely varied with respect to specific beliefs and religious practices. Because the majority of Hindus outside of India and nearby Asian countries are likely to be acculturated to some extent away from Hindu belief and practice, it is important to carefully assess the extent to which Hindu clients hold personally salient religious beliefs. Like Buddhist clients, Hindus may be inclined toward contemplative and solitary prayer and worship versus corporate religious expressions. They may be concerned with right thought and good deeds, but less concerned about offending a more personal or individual God. Heaven and Hell are unlikely to be immediate concerns as acceptance of reincarnation and the everlasting nature of the soul and life cycle are common. Use of Hindu wisdom literature in therapy may be useful in facilitating change.

Demanding irrational beliefs among Hindu clients may be similar to those among Buddhist clients:

I should spend more time in prayer and reading wisdom literature.

I ought to have better karma.

Others should respect my belief in reincarnation.

Awfulizing may also take many forms:

It is unthinkable that my children do not adhere to my Hindu beliefs and practices.

The killing of animals for food is terrible.

It is awful that I have been unable to win freedom from the cycle of rebirth.

Hindu clients may be prone to irrational thinking of the self-downing variety. Negative rating of the self may be particularly notable around issues of karma and adherence to practice of prayer, study, and worship. Some examples of human worth ratings include:

My physical disability is proof of my terrible karma and low value.

Were I a better person, I would certainly be more devout in my worship and study time.

My ex-spouse is evil and deserves bad karma and an eternity of rebirths.

Finally, Low frustration tolerance may be evident in the presenting concerns of Hindu clients. This form of irrationality may include generic LFT or difficulty with tolerance rooted more directly in Hindu belief:

I can't stand my lousy karma.

The idea of more lives and rebirths is intolerable.

The fact that others seem less devout in their Hindu practice, yet richer or happier than I is utterly unacceptable.

References

Alford, B. A., & Beck, A. T. (1997). *The integrative power of cognitive therapy.* New York: Guilford.

Allport, G. W., & Ross, J. M. (1967). Personal religious orientation and prejudice. *Journal of Personality and Social Psychology, 5,* 432–443.

American Psychological Association (1992). Ethical principles of psychologists and code of conduct. *American Psychologist, 47,* 1597–1611.

American Psychological Association (1993). Guidelines for providers of psychological services to ethnic, linguistic, and culturally diverse populations. *American Psychologist, 48,* 45–48

Backus, W. (1985). *Telling the truth to troubled people.* Minneapolis, MN: Bethany House.

Bandura, A. (1997). *Self-efficacy: The exercise of control.* Englewood Cliffs, NJ: Prentice-Hall.

Barrett, D. B., & Johnson, T. M. (1998). Religion: World religious statistics. In D. Calhoun (Ed.), *Britannica book of the year, 1998* (p. 314). Chicago, IL: Encyclopedia Britannica.

Bartlett, F. C. (1932). *Remembering: A study in experimental and social psychology.* Cambridge, England: Cambridge University Press.

Bartley, W. W., III. (1984). *The retreat to commitment* (rev. ed.) Peru, IL: Open Court.

Batson, C. D., Schoenrade, P., & Ventis, W. L. (1993). *Religion and the individual: A social-psychological perspective.* New York: Oxford University Press.

Beal, D., Kopec, A. M., & DiGiuseppe, R. (1996). Disputing client's irrational beliefs. *Journal of Rational-Emotive and Cognitive-Behavior Therapy, 14,* 215–229.

Beaman, A. (1978). Rational-emotive therapy and Christian contrition. *Rational Living, 13,* 17–18.

Beck, A. T. (1976). *Cognitive therapy and the emotional disorders.* New York: International Universities Press.

Beck, A. T. & Beck, R. W. (1972). Screening depressed patients in family practice. A rapid technique. *Postgraduate Medicince, 52,* 81–85.

Beck, A. T., & Emery, G. (1985). *Anxiety disorders and phobias: A cognitive perspective.* New York: Basic Books.

Beck, A. T., Rial, W. Y., & Rickels, K. (1974). Short Form of Depression Inventory: Cross validation. *Psychological Reports, 34,* 1184–1186.

Beit-Hallahmi, B. (1980). *Psychoanalysis and religion: A bibliography.* Norwood, PA: Norwood Editions.

Beit-Hallahmi, B. (1989). *Prolegomena to the psychological study of religion.* Lewisburg, PA: Bucknell University Press.

Benson, C. K. (1992). Forgiveness and the psychotherapeutic process. *Journal of Psychology and Christianity, 11,* 76–81.

Bergin, A. E. (1980). Psychotherapy and religious values. *Journal of Consulting and Clinical Psychology, 48,* 75–105.

Bergin, A. E. (1983). Religiosity and mental health: A critical reevaluation and meta-analysis. *Professional Psychology: Research and Practice, 14,* 170–184.

Bergin, A. E. (1991). Values and religious issues in psychotherapy and mental health. *American Psychologist, 46,* 394–403.

Bergin, A. E., & Jensen, J. P. (1990). Religiosity of psychotherapists: A national survey, *Psychotherapy, 27,* 3–7.

Bergin, A. E., Masters, K. S., & Richards, P. S. (1987). Religiousness and mental health reconsidered: A study of an intrinsically religious sample. *Journal of Counseling Psychology, 34,* 197–204.

Bergin, A. E., Payne, I. R., & Richards, P. S. (1996). Values in psychotherapy. In E. Shafranske (Ed.), *Religion and the clinical practice of psychology* (pp. 297–325). Washington, DC: American Psychological Association.

Bergin, A. E., Stinchfield, R. D., Gaskin, T. A., Masters, K. S., & Sullivan, C. E. (1988). Religious life-styles and mental health: An exploratory study. *Journal of Counseling Psychology, 35,* 91–98.

Bernard, M. E. (1993). *Staying rational in an irrational world.* New York: Carol Publishing.

Beutler, L. E. (1972). Value and attitude change in psychotherapy: A case for dyadic assessment. *Psychotherapy, 9,* 262–267.

Brown, R. M. (1965). *The spirit of Protestantism.* New York: Oxford University Press.

Bufford, R. K., Paloutzian, R. F., & Ellison, C. W. (1991). Norms for the spiritual well-being scale. *Journal of Psychology and Theology, 19,* 56–70.

Cândea, V. (1987). Icons. In M. Eliade (Ed.), *The encyclopedia of religion* (Vol. 7, pp. 67–70). New York: Macmillan.

Carter, D. M. (1986). An integrated approach to pastoral therapy. *Journal of Psychology and Theology, 14,* 146–154.

Chapman, M. (1993). Everyday reasoning and the revision of belief. In J. M. Puckett, & H. W. Reese (Eds.), *Mechanisms of everyday cognition* (pp. 95–113). Hillsdale, NJ: Lawrence Erlbaum Associates.

Clark, T. W. (1992). Relativism and the limits of rationality. *The Humanist, 52,* 25–32, 42.

Derrida, J. (1976). *Of grammatology.* Baltimore, MD: Johns Hopkins University.

Diener, E. Emmons, R. A., Larsen, R. J., & Griffin, S. (1985). The satisfaction with life scale. *Journal of Personality Assessment, 49,* 71–75.

DiGiuseppe, R. A. (1991). A rational-emotive model of assessment. In M. E. Bernard (Ed.), *Using rational-emotive therapy effectively: A practitioner's guide* (pp. 151–172). New York: Plenum.

DiGiuseppe, R. A., Exner, T., Leaf, R., & Robin, M. (1988). *The development of a measure of rational/irrational beliefs.* Poster session presented at the World Congress on Behavior, Edinburgh, Scotland.

DiGiuseppe, R. A., Robin, M. W., & Dryden, W. (1990). On the compatibility of rational-emotive therapy and Judeo-Christian philosophy: A focus on clinical strategies. *Journal of Cognitive Psychotherapy: An International Quarterly, 4,* 355–368.

Donahue, M. J. (1985). Intrinsic and extrinsic religiousness: Review and meta-analysis. *Journal of Personality and Social Psychology, 48,* 400–419.

Dougherty, S. G., & Worthington, E. L. (1982). Preferences of conservative and moderate Christians for four Christian counselor's treatment plans. *Journal of Psychology and Theology, 10,* 346–354.

Dryden, W. (1990). *Creativity in rational-emotive therapy.* Loughton, England: Gale Centre Publications.

Dryden, W. (1995). *Brief rational emotive behaviour therapy.* London: Wiley.

Dryden, W., DiGiuseppe, R., & Neenan, M. (2000). *A primer on rational-emotive therapy* (2nd ed.) Champaign, IL: Research Press.

DuPuy, H. (1984). A measure of psychological well-being. In N. K. Werger, M. E. Mattson, C. D. Furberg, & J. Elinson (Eds.). Assessment of Quality of life (pp. 353–356). New York: Lecajq Publishing.

Elkin, I. (1994). The NIMH treatment of depression collaborative research program: Where we began and where we are. In A. E. Bergin & S. L. Garfield (Eds.), *Handbook of psychotherapy and behavior change* (pp. 114–139). New York: Wiley.

Ellingson, T. (1987). Music: Music and religion. In M. Eliade (Ed.), *The encyclopedia of religion* (Vol. 10, pp. 163–172). New York: Macmillan.

Ellis, A. (1975). *How to live with a neurotic: At home and at work (rev. ed.).* Hollywood, CA: Wilshire Books (Original work published 1957).

Ellis, A. (1958). Rational psychotherapy. *Journal of General Psychology, 59,* 35–49.

Ellis, A. (1962). *Reason and emotion in psychotherapy.* Secaucus, NJ: Citadel.

Ellis, A. (1969). A weekend of rational encounter. *Rational Living, 4,* 1–8.

Ellis, A. (1971). *The case against religion: A psychotherapist's view.* New York: Institute for Rational Living.

Ellis, A. (1972). *Psychotherapy and the value of a human being.* New York: Institute for Rational-Emotive Therapy. Reprinted in Ellis, A. & Dryden W. (1990). *The essential Albert Ellis.* New York: Springer.

Ellis, A. (1973a). *Humanistic psychotherapy: The rational-emotive approach.* New York: McGraw-Hill.

Ellis, A. (1973b). My philosophy of psychotherapy. *Journal of Contemporary Psychotherapy. 6,* 13–18.

Ellis, A. (1977a). *Anger—How to live with and without it.* Secaucus, NJ: Citadel Press.

Ellis, A. (1977b). Fun as psychotherapy. *Rational Living, 12,* 2–6.

Ellis, A. (1979). The issue of force and energy in behavioral change. *Journal of Contemporary Psychotherapy, 10,* 83–97.

Ellis, A. (1980). Psychotherapy and atheistic values: A response to A. E. Bergin's "Psychotherapy and religious values." *Journal of Consulting and Clinical Psychology, 48,* 635–639.

Ellis, A. (1981). The use of rational humorous songs in psychotherapy. *Voices, 16,* 29–36.

Ellis, A. (1983a). *An impolite interview with Albert Ellis* (rev. ed.). New York: Institute for Rational-Emotive Therapy.

Ellis, A. (1983b). How to deal with your most difficult client–you. *Journal of Rational-Emotive Therapy, 1,* 3–8.

Ellis, A. (1983c) *The case against religiosity.* New York: Institute for Rational-Emotive Therapy.

Ellis, A. (1985). *Overcoming resistance: Rational-emotive therapy with difficult clients.* New York: Springer.

Ellis, A. (1986). Do some religious beliefs help create emotional disturbance? *Psychotherapy in Private Practice, 4,* 101–106.

Ellis, A. (1987a). The impossibility of achieving consistently good mental health. *American Psychologist, 42,* 364–375.

Ellis, A. (1987b). The use of rational humorous songs in psychotherapy. In J. W. F. Fry & W. A. Salamed (Eds.), *Handbook of humor and psychotherapy* (pp. 265–287). Sarasota, FL: Professional Resource Exchange.

Ellis, A. (1988). *How to stubbornly refuse to make yourself miserable about anything—yes, anything!* Secaucus, NJ: Lyle Stuart.

Ellis, A. (1991). Using RET effectively: Reflections and interview. In M. E. Bernard (Ed.), *Using rational-emotive therapy effectively* (pp. 1–33). New York: Plenum.

Ellis, A. (1992). My current views on rational-emotive therapy (RET) and religiousness. *Journal of Rational-Emotive and Cognitive-Behavior Therapy, 10,* 37–40.

Ellis, A. (1994a). My response to "Don't throw the therapeutic baby out with the holy water": Helpful and hurtful elements of religion. *Journal of Psychology and Christianity, 13,* 323–326.

Ellis, A. (1994b). *Reason and emotion in psychotherapy* (rev. and updated). New York: Birch Lane Press.

Ellis, A. (1996a). A social constructionist position for mental health counseling: A response to Jeffrey T. Guterman. *Journal of Mental Health Counseling, 18,* 16–28.

Ellis, A. (1996b). *Better, deeper and more enduring brief therapy: The Rational Emotive Behavior Therapy approach.* New York: Brunner/Mazel.

Ellis, A. (1996c). Postmodernity or reality? A response to Allen E. Ivey, Don C. Locke, and Sandra Rigazio-DiGilio. *Counseling Today, 39*(2), 26–27.

Ellis, A. (1997). Response to Jeffrey T. Guterman's response to my critique of "A social constructionist position for mental health counseling." *Journal of Mental Health Counseling, 19,* 57–63.

Ellis, A. (1998). *How to control your anxiety before it controls you.* New York: Citadel.

Ellis, A. (1999). *How to make yourself happy and remarkably less disturbed.* San Luis Obispo, CA: Impact Publishers.

Ellis, A. (2000a). Can rational-emotive behavior therapy (REBT) be effectively used with people who have devout beliefs in God and religion? *Professional Psychology: Research and Practice, 31,* 29–33.

Ellis, A. (2000b). *Self-help therapy that really works.* Atascadero, CA: Impact Publishers.

Ellis, A., & Becker, I. (1982). *A guide to personal happiness*. North Hollywood, CA: Wilshire.

Ellis, A., & Dryden, W. (1997). *The practice of rational emotive behavior therapy* (rev. ed.). New York: Springer.

Ellis, A., & Harper, R. A. (1997). *A guide to rational living* (New and updated ed.). North Hollywood, CA: Melvin Powers.

Ellis, A., Gordon, J., Neenan, M., & Palmer, S. (1997). *Stress counseling: A rational emotive behavioural therapy approach*. London: Cassell.

Ellis, A., & MacLaren, C. (1998). *Rational emotive behavior therapy: A therapist's guide*. Atascadero, CA: Impact Publishers.

Feyerband, P. (1975). *Against method*. New York: Humanities Press.

Fisher, S. E. (1985). Identity of two: The phenomenology of shame in borderline development and treatment. *Psychotherapy, 22,* 101–109.

Frankl, V. (1969). *Man's search for meaning: An introduction to logotherapy*. New York: Washington Square Press.

Freud, S. (1912). The dynamics of transference. In J. Strackey (Ed.), *Standard edition of the complete works of Sigmund Freud* (Vol. 12 pp. 97–108). London: Hogarth.

Fuchs, S., & Ward, S. (1994). What is deconstruction and where and when does it take place? *American Sociological Review, 59,* 481–500.

Gallup, G. C., J. (1989). *The people's religion: American faith in the 90's*. New York: Macmillan.

Gartner, J., Larson, D. B., & Allen, G. D. (1991). Religious commitment and mental health: A review of the empirical literature. *Journal of Psychology and Theology, 19,* 6–25.

Gass, S. C. (1984). Orthodox Christian values related to psychotherapy and mental health. *Journal of Psychology and Theology, 12,* 230–237.

Gassin, E. A., & Enright, R. D. (1995). The will to meaning in the process of forgiveness. *Journal of Psychology and Christianity, 14,* 38–49.

Genia, V. (1994). Secular psychotherapists and religious clients: Professional considerations and recommendations. *Journal of Counseling and Development, 72,* 395–398.

Gergen, K. J. (1991). *The saturated self*. New York: Basic Books.

Gergen, K. J. (1995). Postmodernism as humanism. *Humanistic Psychologist, 23,* 71–82.

Giglio, J. (1993). The impact of patients' and therapists' religious values on psychotherapy. *Hospital and Community Psychiatry, 44,* 768–771.

Ginter, E. J. (1989). If you meet Moses/Jesus/Mohammed/Buddha (or associate editors of theory) on the road, kill them! *Journal of Mental Health Counseling, 11,* 335–344.

Gladson, J. A. (1992). Higher than the heavens: Forgiveness and the old testament. *Journal of Psychology and Christianity, 11*, 125–135.

Glasser, W. (2000). *Reality therapy in action.* New York: Harper Collins.

Goldberg, D. P. (1972). The detection of psychiatric illness by questionnaire: A technique for the identification and assessment of non-psychotic psychiatric illness. Oxford: Oxford University Press.

Golden, W. L. (1983). Resistance in cognitive behavior therapy. *British Journal of Cognitive Psychotherapy, 1*, 33–42.

Goleman, D. (1995). *Emotional intelligence.* New York: Bantam.

Gorsuch, R. L. (1988). Psychology and religion. *Annual Review of Psychology, 39*, 201–221.

Gove, P. B. (1981). *Webster's third new international dictionary of the English language (unabridged eds.).* Springfield, MA: G. & C. Merriam Co.

Grau, A. F. (1977). Religion as rational. In J. L. Wolfe & E. Brand (Eds.), *Twenty years of rational therapy* (pp. 131–135). New York: Institute for Rational Living.

Greenberg, D., & Witztum, E. (1991). Problems in the treatment of religious patients. *American Journal of Psychotherapy, 35*, 554–565.

Greenberg, L. S., Rice, L. N., & Elliott, R. (1993). *Facilitating emotional change.* New York: Harper Perennial.

Guralnik, D. G. (1982). *Webster's new world dictionary of the American language. 2nd college ed.* New York: Simon and Schuster.

Guidano, V. F. (1991). *The self in process.* New York: Guilford.

Guterman, J. T. (1994). A social constructionist position for mental health counseling. *Journal of Mental Health Counseling, 16*, 226–244.

Guterman, J. T. (1996a). Doing mental health counseling: A social constructionist revision. *Journal of Mental Health Counseling, 18*, 228–252.

Guterman, J. T. (1996b). Reconstructing social constructionism: A response to Albert Ellis. *Journal of Mental Health Counseling, 18*, 29–40.

Guterman, J. T. (1996c). Tales of mental health counseling. *Journal of Mental Health Counseling, 18*, 300–306.

Hauck, P. A. (1972). *Reason in pastoral counseling.* Philadelphia: Westminster.

Hauck, P. A. (1991). *Overcoming the rating game.* Louisville, KY: Westminster.

Haughness, N. (1993). Postmodern anti-foundationalism examined. *Humanist, 53*, 19–20.

Hawkins, I. L., & Bullock, S. L. (1995). Informed consent and religious values: A neglected area of diversity. *Psychotherapy, 32*, 293–300.

Hayakawa, S. I. (1940/1990). *Language in action (5th ed.).* New York: Harcourt Brace.

Hayek, F. A. (1978). *New studies in philosophy, politics, economics, and the history of ideas.* Chicago: University of Chicago Press.

Hayes, S., Nelson, R., & Jarrett, R. (1987). The treatment utility of assessment: A functional approach to evaluating assessment quality. *American Psychologist, 42,* 963–974.

Heidegger, M. (1962). *Being and time.* New York: Harper & Row.

Held, B. S. (1995). The real meaning of constructivism. *Journal of Constructivist Psychology, 8,* 305–315.

Hoge, D. R. (1996). Religion in America: The demographics of belief and affiliation. In E. Shafranske (Ed.), *Religion and the clinical practice of psychology* (pp. 21–42). Washington, DC: American Psychological Association.

Hollon, S. D., & Beck, A. T. (1994). Cognitive and cognitive-behavioral therapies. In A. E. Bergin & S. L. Garfield (Eds.), *Handbook of psychotherapy and behavior change* (pp. 428–466). New York: Wiley.

Hood, R. W., Spilka, B., Hunsberger, B., & Gorsuch, R. (1996). *The psychology of religion* (2nd ed.). New York: Guilford.

Hoshmand, L. T., & Polkinghorne, D. E. (1992). Redefining the science-practice relationship and professional training. *American Psychologist, 47,* 55–66.

Hunsberger, B., Alisat, S., Pancer, S. M., & Pratt, M. (1996). Religious fundamentalism and religious doubts: Content, consciousness and complexity of thinking. *International Journal of the Psychology of Religion, 6,* 39–49.

Ivey, A. E., & Goncalves, D. (1988). Developmental therapy: Integrating developmental process into the clinical practice. *Journal of Counseling and Development, 66,* 406–413.

Ivey, A. E., & Rigazio-DiGilio, S. A. (1991). Toward a developmental practice of mental health counseling: Strategies for training practice, and political unity. *Journal of Mental Health Counseling, 13,* 21–26.

Johnson, S. A. (2000). *Incorporating religion into rational emotive behavior therapy with the Christian client.* New York: Institute for Rational-Emotive Behavior Therapy.

Johnson, W. B. (1992). Rational-emotive therapy and religiousness: A review. *Journal of Rational-Emotive and Cognitive Behavior Therapy, 10,* 21–35.

Johnson, W. B. (1993). Christian rational-emotive therapy: A treatment protocol. *Journal of Psychology and Christianity, 12,* 254–261.

Johnson, W. B. (in press). To dispute or not to dispute: Ethical REBT with Religious Clients. *Cognitive and Behavioral Practice.*

Johnson, W. B., DeVries, R., Ridley, C. R., Pettorini, D., & Peterson, D. (1994). The comparative efficacy of Christian and secular rational-emotive therapy with Christian clients. *Journal of Psychology and Theology, 22,* 130–140.

Johnson, W. B., & Johnson, W. L. (1997). Counseling conservatively religious fathers: Salient treatment issues. *Journal of Psychology and Christianity, 16,* 36–50.

Johnson, W. B., & Nielsen, S. L. (1998). Rational-emotive assessment with religious clients. *Journal of Rational-Emotive and Cognitive-Behavior Therapy, 16,* 101– 123.

Johnson, W. B., & Ridley, C. R. (1992a). Brief Christian and non-Christian rational-emotive therapy with depressed Christian clients: An exploratory study. *Counseling and Values, 36,* 220–229.

Johnson, W. B., & Ridley, C. R. (1992b). Sources of gain in Christian counseling and psychotherapy. *The Counseling Psychologist, 20,* 159–175.

Johnson, W. B., Ridley, C. R., & Nielsen, S. L. (2000). Religiously sensitive rational emotive behavior therapy: Elegant solutions and ethical risks. *Professional Psychology: Research and Practice, 31,* 14–20.

Jones, S. L. (1989). Rational-emotive therapy in Christian perspective. *Journal of Psychology and Theology, 17,* 110–120.

Jones-Haldeman, M. (1992). Implications from selected literary devices for a new testament theology of grace and forgiveness. *Journal of Psychology and Christianity, 11,* 136–146.

Kehoe, N., & Gutheil, T. G. (1984). Shared religious belief as resistance in psychotherapy. *American Journal of Psychotherapy, 38,* 579–585.

Kelley, T., & Strupp, H. (1992). Patient and therapist values in psychotherapy: Perceived changes, assimilation, similarity, and outcome. *Journal of Consulting and Clinical Psychology, 60,* 34–40.

Kelly, G. (1955). *The psychology of personal constructs (2 vols).* New York: Norton.

Kirkpatrick, L. A. (1997). A longitudinal study of changes in religious belief and behavior as a function of individual differences in adult attachment style. *Journal for the Scientific Study of Religion, 36,* 207–217.

Kopec, A. M., Beal, D., & DiGiuseppe, R. (1994). Training in RET: Disputational strategies. *Journal of Rational-Emotive and Cognitive-Behavior Therapy, 12,* 47–60.

Korzybski, A. (1933/1990). *Science and sanity: An introduction to non-Aristotelian systems and general semantics.* Concord, CA: International Society of General Semantics.

Kwee, M.G.T., & Ellis, A. (1997). Can multimodal and rational emotive behavior therapy be reconciled? *Journal of Rational-Emotive and Cognitive-Behavior Therapy, 15,* 95–132.

Lannert, J. L. (1991). Resistance and countertransference issues with spiritual and religious clients. *Journal of Humanistic Psychology, 31,* 68–76.

Larson, D. B., & Larson, S. (1994). *The forgotten factor in physical and mental health: What does the research show?* Rockville, MD: National Institute for Healthcare Research.

Lasure, L. C., & Mikulas, W. L. (1996). Biblical behavior modification. *Behavior Research and Therapy, 34,* 563–566.

Latourette, K. S. (1975). *A history of Christianity: Beginnings to 1500.* New York: Harper & Row.

Lawrence, C. (1987). Rational-emotive therapy and the religious client. *Journal of Rational-Emotive and Cognitive-Behavior Therapy, 5,* 13–21.

Lawrence, C., & Huber, C. H. (1982). Strange bedfellows? Rational-emotive therapy and pastoral counseling. *Personnel and Guidance Journal, 61,* 210–212.

Lazarus, A. A. (1968). Learning theory and the treatment of depression. *Behavior Research and Therapy, 6,* 83–89.

Lazarus, A. A. (1989). *The practice of multimodal therapy.* Baltimore: Johns Hopkins University Press.

Lazarus, R. S. (1999). The cognition-emotion debate: A bit of history. In T. Dalgleish & M. J. Power (Eds.), *Handbook of cognition and emotion* (pp. 3–19). New York: John Wiley.

Lewis, K. N., & Lewis, D. A. (1985). Impact of religious affiliation on therapists' judgments of patients. *Journal of Consulting and Clinical Psychology, 53,* 926–932.

Linehan, M. (1993). *Cognitive-behavioral treatment of borderline personality disorder.* New York: Guilford.

Lovinger, R. (1984). *Working with religious issues in therapy.* Northvale, NJ: Jason Aronson.

Lovinger, R. (1990). *Religion and counseling: The psychological impact of religious belief.* Northvale, NJ: Aronson.

Lovinger, R. J. (1979). Therapeutic strategies with "religious" resistances. *Psychotherapy: Theory, Research and Practice, 16,* 419–427.

Lovinger, R. J. (1996). Considering the religious dimension in assessment and treatment. In E. P. Shafranske (Ed.), *Religion and the clinical practice of psychology* (pp. 327–363). Washington, DC: American Psychological Association.

Lyons, L. C., & Woods, P. J. (1991). The efficacy of rational-emotive therapy: A quantitative review of the outcome research. *Clinical Psychology Review, 11,* 357–369.

Mahoney, M. (1974). *Cognition and behavior modification.* Cambridge, MA: Ballinger.

Mahoney, M. (1991). *Human change processes.* New York: Basic Books.

Mahoney, M. J. (1995). *Cognitive and constructive psychotherapies: Theory, research and practice.* (2nd ed.). New York: Springer.

Maultsby, M. C. (1975). *Help yourself to happiness: Through rational self-counseling.* New York: Institute for Rational-Emotive Therapy.

McClendon, J.W.W., & James, M. (1975). *Understanding religious convictions.* Notre Dame, IN: University of Notre Dame Press.

Maultsby, M. C., Jr. (1984). *Rational behavior therapy.* Englewood Cliffs, NJ: Prentice-Hall.

Maultsby, M. C., & Ellis, A. (1974). *Techniques for using rational-emotive imagery (REI).* New York: Institute for Rational Living.

McCullough, M. E., & Worthington, E. L. (1994). Encouraging clients to forgive people who have hurt them: Review, critique, and research prospectus. *Journal of Psychology and Theology, 22,* 3–20.

McCullough, M. E., & Worthington, E. L. (1995). College student's perceptions of a psychotherapist's treatment of religious issues: Partial replication and extension. *Journal of Counseling and Development, 73,* 626–634.

McKechnie, J. L. (Ed.). (1979). *Webster's new twentieth century dictionary of the English language unabridged* (2nd ed.). New York: Simon & Schuster.

McMinn, M. R., & Lebold, C. J. (1989). Collaborative efforts in cognitive therapy with religious clients. *Journal of Psychology and Theology, 17,* 101–109.

Meehl, P. E. (1959). Some technical and axiological problems in the therapeutic handling of religious and valuational material. *Journal of Counseling Psychology, 6,* 255–259.

Meek, K. R., Albright, J. S., & McMinn, M. R. (1995). Religious orientation, guilt, confession, and forgiveness. *Journal of Psychology and Theology, 23,* 190–197.

Meek, K. R., & McMinn, M. R. (1997). Forgiveness: More than a therapeutic technique. *Journal of Psychology and Christianity, 16,* 51–61.

Meichenbaum, D. (1977). *Cognitive-behaviour modification: An integrative approach.* New York: Plenum.

Meissner, W. W. (1996). The pathology of beliefs and the beliefs of pathology. In E. P. Shafranske (Ed.), *Religion and the clinical practice of psychology* (pp. 241–267). Washington, DC: American Psychological Association.

Menninger, K. (1961). *Theory of psychoanalytic technique.* New York: Basic Books.

Miller, W. R. (1988). Including client's spiritual perspectives in cognitive-behavior therapy. In W. R. Miller & J. E. Marten (Eds.), *Behavior therapy and religion: Integrating spiritual and behavioral approaches to change* (pp. 43–56). Newbury Park, CA: Sage.

Millon, T. (1987). Manual for the MCMI-II. Minneapolis, MN: National Computer Systems.

Mills, D. (1994). *Overcoming self-esteem*. New York: Institute for Rational-Emotive Therapy.

Moran, G. (1987). Religious education. In M. Eliade (Ed.), *The encyclopedia of religion* (Vol. 12, pp. 318–323). New York: Macmillan.

Narramore, B. (1994). Dealing with religious resistances in psychotherapy. *Journal of Psychology and Theology, 22,* 249–258.

Neimeyer, G. J. (1993). The challenge of change: Reflections on constructive psychotherapy. *Journal of Cognitive Psychotherapy, 7,* 183–194.

Neimeyer, R. A. (1993). Constructivism and the cognitive psychotherapies: Some conceptual and strategic contrasts. *Journal of Cognitive Psychotherapy, 7,* 159–171.

Neimeyer, R. A., & Mahoney, M .J. (1995). *Constructivism in psychotherapy.* Washington, DC: American Psychological Association.

Nielsen, S. L. (1994). Rational-emotive therapy and religion: Don't throw the therapeutic baby out with the holy water! *Journal of Psychology and Christianity,* 13, 312–322.

Nielsen, S. L., Johnson, W. B., & Ridley, C. R. (2000). Religiously sensitive rational emotive behavior therapy: Theory, techniques and brief excerpts from a case. *Professional Psychology: Research and Practice, 31,* 21–28.

Overholser, J. C. (1995). Elements of the Socratic method: IV. Disavowal of knowledge. *Psychotherapy, 32,* 283–292.

Overholser, J. C. (1999). Elements of the Socratic method: VI. Promoting virtue in everyday life. *Psychotherapy, 36,* 137–145.

Palmer, S. J., & Keller, R. R. (1990). *Religions of the world: A Latter-day Saint view.* Provo, UT: Brigham Young University.

Pargament, K. I. (1997). *The psychology of religion and coping.* New York: Guilford.

Pargament, K. I., & Park, C. L. (1995). Merely a defense? The variety of religious means and ends. *Journal of Social Issues, 51,* 13–32.

Peck, M. S. (1978). *The road less traveled.* New York: Simon & Schuster.

Popper, K. R. (1985). *Popper selections.* (D. M. Miller, ed.). Princeton, NJ: Princeton University Press.

Powell, J. (1976). *Fully human, fully alive.* Valencia, CA: Tabor.

Propst, R. L. (1980). The comparative efficacy of religious and nonreligious imagery for the treatment of mild depression in religious individuals. *Cognitive Therapy and Research, 4,* 167–178.

Propst, R. L. (1982). Cognitive therapy via personal belief structures. In L. Abt & I. Stuart (Eds.), *The newer therapies: A source book* (pp. 81–94). New York: Von Nostrand Reinhold.

Propst, R. L. (1996). Cognitive-behavioral therapy and the religious person. In E. P. Shafranske (Ed.), *Religion and the clinical practice of psychology* (pp. 391–408). Washington, DC: American Psychological Association.

Propst, R. L., Ostrom, R., Watkins, R., Dean, T., & Mashburn, D. (1992). Comparative efficacy of religious and non-religious cognitive-behavioral therapy for the treatment of clinical depression in religious individuals. *Journal of Consulting and Clinical Psychology, 60,* 94–103.

Pruyser, P. (1971). Assessment of the patient's religious attitudes in the psychiatric case study. *Bulletin of the Menninger Clinic, 35,* 272–291.

Pruyser, P. (1977). The seamy side of current religious beliefs. *Bulletin of the Menninger Clinic, 41,* 329–348.

Raimy, V. (1975). *Misunderstandings of the self.* San Francisco: Jossey Bass.

Ragan, C., Malony, H. N., & Beit-Hallahmi, B. (1980). Psychologists and religion: Profession factors associated with personal belief. *Review of Religious Research, 21,* 208–217.

Raskin, J. D. (1995). On ethics in personal construct theory. *Humanistic Psychologist, 23,* 97–114.

Rayburn, C. A. (1985). Some ethical considerations in psychotherapy with religious women. *Psychotherapy, 22,* 803–812.

Richards, P. S. (1991). Religious devoutness in college students: Relations with emotional adjustment and psychological separation from parents. *Journal of Counseling Psychology, 38,* 189–196.

Richards, P. S., & Bergin, A. E. (1997). *A spiritual strategy for counseling and psychotherapy.* Washington, DC: American Psychological Association.

Richards, P. S., & Potts, R. W. (1995). Using spiritual interventions in psychotherapy: Practices, successes, failures, and ethical concerns of Mormon psychotherapists. *Professional Psychology: Research and Practice, 26,* 163–170.

Rickner, R. G., & Tan, S. Y. (1994). Psychopathology, guilt, perfectionism, and family of origin functioning among Protestant clergy. *Journal of Psychology and Theology, 22,* 29–38.

Robb, H. B. (1988). *How to stop driving yourself crazy with help from the Bible.* New York: Institute for Rational-Emotive Therapy.

Robb, H. B. (1993). Using RET to reduce psychological dysfunction associated with supernatural belief systems. *Journal of Cognitive Psychotherapy: An International Quarterly, 7,* 281–289.

Rogers, C. R. (1961). *On becoming a person.* Boston: Houghton-Mifflin.

Rokeach, M. (1960). *The open and closed mind: Investigations into the nature of belief systems and personality systems.* New York: Basic Books.

Rokeach, M. (1973). *The nature of human values.* New York: The Free Press.

Rowan, A. B. (1996). The relevance of religious issues in behavioral assessment. *The Behavior Therapist, 19,* 55–57.

Sampson, E. E. (1989). The challenge of social change in psychology. Globalization and psychology's theory of the person. *American Psychologist, 44,* 914–921.

Shafranske, E. P. (1996). Religious beliefs, affiliations, and practices of clinical psychologists. In E. P. Shafranske (Ed.), *Religion and the clinical practice of psychology* (pp. 149–162). Washington, DC: American Psychological Association.

Shafranske, E. P., & Malony, H. N. (1990). Clinical psychologist's religious and spiritual orientations and their practice of psychotherapy. *Psychotherapy, 27,* 72–78.

Shafranske, E. P., & Malony, H. N. (1996). Religion and the clinical practice of psychology: A case for inclusion. In E. P. Shafranske (Ed.), *Religion and the clinical practice of psychology* (pp. 561–586). Washington, DC: American Psychological Association.

Shelton, J. L., & Levey, A. (1981). *Behavioral assignments and treatment compliance.* Champaign, IL: Research Press.

Silverman, M. S., McCarthy, M., & McGovern, T. (1992). A review of outcome studies of rational-emotive therapy from 1982–1989. *Journal of Rational-Emotive and Cognitive-Behavior Therapy, 10,* 111–186.

Simms, E. (1994). Phenomenology of child development and the postmodern self: Contriving the dialogue with Johnson. *The Humanistic Psychologist, 22,* 228–235.

Speight, R. M. (1987). Creeds. In M. Eliade (Ed.), *The encyclopedia of religion* (Vol. 4, pp. 138–140). New York: Macmillan.

Spero, M. H. (1981). Contertransference in religious therapists of religious patients. *American Journal of Psychotherapy, 35,* 565–575.

Spero, M. H. (1985). *Psychotherapy of the religious patient.* Springfield, IL: Thomas.

Stern, E. M. (Ed.). (1985). *Psychotherapy and the religiously committed patient.* New York: Haworth.

Stoop, D. (1982). *Self-talk: Key to personal growth.* Old Tappan, NJ: Revell.

Tan, S. Y. (1996). Religion in clinical practice: Implicit and explicit integration. In E. P. Shafranske (Ed.). *Religion and the clinical practice of psychology* (pp. 365–387). Washington, DC: American Psychological Association.

Thurman, C. (1989). *The lies we believe.* Nashville, TN: Thomas Nelson.

Tillich, P. (1953). *The courage to be.* New York: Oxford University Press.

Tjeltveit, A. (1986). The ethics of values conversion in psychotherapy: Appropriate and inappropriate counselor influence on client values. *Clinical Psychology Review, 6,* 515–537.

van Eemeren, F. H., Grootendorst, R., & Kruiger, T. (1984). *The study of argumentation.* New York: Irvington.

Vernon, A. (1989a). *Thinking, feeling, behaving: An emotional education curriculum for adolescents grades 7–12.* Champaign, IL: Research Press.

Vernon, A. (1989b). *Thinking, feeling, behaving: An emotional education curriculum for children.* Champaign, IL: Research Press.

Walen, S., DiGiuseppe, R., & Dryden, W. (1992). *A practitioner's guide to rational-emotive therapy.* New York: Oxford University Press.

Ward, G. C. (1997). India: Fifty years of independence. *National Geographic, 191,* 2–57.

Warnock, S.D.M. (1989). Rational-emotive therapy and the Christian client. *Journal of Rational-Emotive and Cognitive-Behavior Therapy, 7,* 263–274.

Watt, W. M. (1987). Creeds: Islamic creeds. In M. Iliade (Ed.), *The encyclopedia of religion* (Vol. 4, pp. 150–153). New York: Macmillan.

Webster's new twentieth century dictionary (1979). *(2nd ed.).* New York: Simon & Schuster.

Weishar, M. (1993). *Aaron T. Beck.* London: Sage.

Wessler, R. A., & Wessler, R. L. (1980). *The principles and practice of rational-emotive therapy.* San Francisco, CA; Jossey-Bass.

Whitehead, A. N. (1957). *Religion in the making: Lowell lectures, 1926.* New York: Macmillan.

Wilson, G. T. (1995). Behavior therapy. In R. J. Corsini & D. Wedding (Eds.), *Current Psychotherapies (5th ed.* pp. 197–228). Itasca, IL: Peacock.

Wolpe, J. (1958). *Psychotherapy by reciprocal inhibition.* Stanford, CA: Stanford University Press.

Wolpe, J. (1990). *The practice of behavior therapy (4th ed.).* New York: Pergamon.

Worthington, E. L. (1986). Religious counseling: A review of published empirical research. *Journal of Counseling and Development, 64,* 421–431.

Worthington, E. L. (1988). Understanding the values of religious clients: A model and its application to counseling. *Journal of Counseling Psychology, 35,* 166–174.

Worthington, E. L., & Gascoyne, S. R. (1985). Preferences of Christians and non-Christians for five Christian counselor's treatment plans: A partial replication and extension. *Journal of Psychology and Theology, 13,* 29–41.

Wulff, D. M. (1991). *Psychology of religion: Classic and contemporary views.* New York: John Wiley.

Yates, A. (1975). *Theory and practice of behavior therapy.* New York: Wiley.

Young, H. (1984). Practicing RET with Bible-Belt Christians. *British Journal of Cognitive Psychotherapy, 2,* 60–76.

Zuesse, E. M. (1987). Ritual. In M. Eliade (Ed.), *The encyclopedia of religion* (Vol. 12, pp. 405–422). New York: Macmillan.

Author Index

A
Albright, J.S., 205, 267
Alford, B.A., 47
Alisat, S., 55, 264
Allen, G.D., 6, 262
Allport, G.W., 67

B
Backus, W., 4
Bandura, A., 47, 54, 157–58, 255
Barrett, D.B., 5, 255
Bartlett, F.C., 12, 255
Bartley, W.W., III, 42, 255
Batson, C.D., 55, 256
Beal, D., 104, 265
Beaman, A., 4, 256
Beck, Aaron T., 43, 46–47, 64–65, 98, 150–51, 154, 156–57, 258, 264, 271

Beck, R.W., 43, 46–47, 64–65, 98, 150–51, 154, 156–57, 258
Beit-Hallahmi, B., 4, 6, 28, 256, 258, 269
Benson, C.K., 230, 258
Bergin, Allen E., xi, 6–7, 113, 181, 206, 256, 258, 264, 269
Bernard, M.E., 51, 256, 258
Beutler, L.E., 6, 259
Brown, R.M., 238, 259
Bufford, R.K., 68, 259
Bullock, S.L., 7, 263

C
Cândea, V., 27, 259
Carter, D.M., 4, 259
Chapman, M., 103, 259
Clark, T.W., 42, 259

Subject Index